POLITICAL ECONOMY IN PARLIAMENT
1819–1823

POLITICAL ECONOMY IN PARLIAMENT 1819-1823

BARRY GORDON
University of Newcastle
New South Wales

BARNES & NOBLE
BOOKS
10 East 53d St., New York 10022
(a division of Harper & Row Publishers, Inc.)

First published 1976 by
THE MACMILLAN PRESS LTD
London and Basingstoke

Published in the U.S.A. 1977 by
HARPER & ROW PUBLISHERS, INC.
BARNES & NOBLE IMPORT DIVISION

Printed in Great Britain

Library of Congress Cataloging in Publication Data

Gordon, Barry J
Political economy in Parliament, 1819-1823.

Includes bibliographical references and index.
1. Great Britain—Economic conditions—19th
century.   2. Great Britain—Economic policy.
3. Economics—History—Great Britain.   4. Great
Britain. Parliament.   I. Title.
HC255.G64   1977   330.9'41'074   76-28823
ISBN 0-06-492493-9

For Moira

Contents

Acknowledgements

Throughout the preparation of this book I have benefited greatly from the support and advice of several of my colleagues at the University of Newcastle. These include, my wife, to whom the work is dedicated; Mr and Mrs W. J. Sheehan, Department of Economics; Dr John Fisher, Department of Economics; and Professor Gregory McMinn, Department of History. Mr Edward Flowers, Miss Joan Murray and the staff of the Auchmuty Library were generous in their assistance. Mr Barry Jory and Mr William Keegan undertook some of the bibliographic research associated with the project.

B.G.

University of Newcastle
New South Wales
February 1976

The bitter argument between economists and human beings has ended in the conversion of the economists. But it was not by the fierce denunciation of moralists, nor by the mute visible suffering of degraded men, that this conversion was effected. What the passionate protests of *Past and Present* and the grave official revelations of government reports could not do, the chill breath of intellectual criticism has done. Assailed for two generations, as an insult to the simple natural piety of human affections, the Political Economy of Ricardo is at last rejected as an intellectual imposture. The obstinate, blind repulsion of the labourer is approved by the professor.

Arnold Toynbee
Ricardo and the Old Political Economy (1879)

Lord Keynes speaks of the tradition of the Classical Economists as being 'marked by a love of truth and a most noble lucidity, by a prosaic sanity free from sentiment or metaphysic, and by an immense disinterestedness and public spirit'. I myself share this view; I find it hard to understand how anyone who has given serious attention to the actual works of these men however much he may disagree with them, can question their integrity and their transparent devotion to the general good.

Lionel Robbins
The Theory of Economic Policy in English Classical Political Economy (1952)

1 Introduction: Politicians and Principles

Gone is that gold, the marvel of mankind,
And pirates barter all that's left behind.
No more the hirelings, purchased near and far,
Crowd to the ranks of mercenary war.
The idle merchant on the useless quay
Droops o'er the bales no bark may bear away;
Or, back returning, sees rejected stores
Rot piecemeal on his own encumber'd shores:
The starved mechanic breaks his rusting loom,
And desperate mans him 'gainst the coming doom.
Then in the senate of your sinking state
Show me the man whose counsels may have weight.

Lord Byron
The Curse of Minerva (1811)

This is a study of the interaction of economic doctrine, political practice and the train of events during difficult days for the British economy. The period was also a crucial one in the development of economic thought.

If one phrase could capture the reality of the times it would be 'silent revolution'. That phrase was on the lips of a number of the more perceptive contemporary observers and has occurred to a few modern historians. In truth, much of the original stuff of the later nineteenth and early twentieth centuries was fashioned at this juncture although, at first glance, the years concerned might be discounted as portion of a limbo extending from near the end of the turbulence of the immediate post-Napoleonic period to the first reform of parliament.[1]

British society, wracked by tensions, was still struggling to find a new equilibrium after over twenty years of involvement in war. An unpopular, and sometimes reactionary, government was managing to cling to power with the aid of an ineffectual, almost diffident, opposition. At the same time, that government was beginning to effect a change in the nature of statutory social reform. One consequence of this was an alteration in the significance of the civil service organs of central government.[2] A related trend was associated with the emergence of a new and powerful economic orthodoxy which had begun to take shape around the writings of a retired, Benthamite stock-jobber and loan contractor, David Ricardo (1772—1823). He and his disciples, notably James Mill and J. R. McCulloch, had started a secular version of an intellectual holy war to reform the conduct of public policy in the light of the truths of their recently formulated creed. Ricardo entered the Commons in 1819.

DAVID RICARDO

Ricardo was a man of extraordinary logical ability.[3] To that ability was allied a substantially correct vision of the growth potential developed by the national economy during the Napoleonic period. He had also begun to anticipate the manner in which an independent and professionalised civil service might aid in the realisation of that potential.[4] He entertained no special pessimism concerning the future of the British economy, provided the nation had good government and wise laws such as he believed he was advocating.

Ricardo was also very much his own man. He was not a spokesman for the interests of the 'middle class', although since they glossed over many of the fundamental divergencies of interest within that so-called 'class', it is possible that some of his followers would have wished to see him in that role.[5] Again, he was not the representative voice in parliament for the businessmen of his day. Historians in search of such a voice would be better advised to look to Alexander Baring than to Ricardo. It should also be noted that Ricardo retained a remarkable degree of consistency between his parliamentary statements and published works. The old charges of inconsistency do not hold up.[6]

Against these attributes must be set a certain parochialism which led Ricardo to generalise too readily on the basis of a limited range of commercial experience. As Professor Fetter has remarked, Ricardo usually assumed that there was 'a stockbroker in every man'.[7] A related and more fundamental defect was the absence of a philosophical or historical perspective which was adequate to match his powers as an economic analyst.[8] In the words of one of his parliamentary contemporaries, Ricardo was 'a man who might calculate well and read deeply, but who had not studied mankind'.[9]

If Ricardo had had access to the range of social statistics available to the modern economist there would have been some counter for the consequences of these defects. His consistent preference was to reason in terms of that which was measurable, so much so that he tended to discount the significance of factors he could not submit to quantitative testing. Given adequate statistics, the scope of his theorising would have been broader and his generalisations would have been more cautiously applied. In their absence, however, he argued 'without duly taking into account in practice the condition of things . . . as if a mechanician were to construct an engine without taking into consideration the resistance of the air in which it was to work, or the strength and the weight and the friction of the parts of which it was to be made'.[10]

THE CRITICS OF RICARDO

In parliamentary debate support for Ricardo came mainly from aristocrats (who were nearly all large landowners) and from lawyers, many of whom also had extensive property interests. Reasoned opposition was offered by businessmen and bankers. These spoke against Ricardo on behalf of the entrepreneur in both manufacturing and agriculture.

Chief among Ricardo's opponents was the man who above anyone else commanded the respect of the House on commercial affairs, the man whom Benjamin Disraeli later described as 'the greatest merchant England perhaps ever had', Alexander Baring.[11] Although Ricardo and Baring were able to agree on some issues — repeal of the usury laws and full repayment of creditors in respect of the national debt — they were otherwise at odds on matters of economic policy. Most notable were Baring's criticisms of Ricardo as a guide to sound monetary practice. Another to probe Ricardo's deficiencies as an economist, in both theory and its applications, was the London banker Mathias Attwood. In particular, Attwood saw through the fantasies which Ricardo had helped construct concerning the progress of production in agriculture and the social impact of the poor law system. These critics were at times ably supported by progressive agriculturalists (John Curwen and John Bennett), members sympathetic to the needs of wage earners (the nabob Peter Moore, the Renfrewshire reformer John Maxwell, the brewery executive Thomas Fowell Buxton) and by a variety of other businessmen including William Heygate (Lord Mayor of London), Hudson Gurney (of the Norwich banking family) and Edward Ellice (the 'bear' of the Canadian fur trade).

Commercial men in the Commons were among the pioneers of an anti-Ricardian movement in economic thought which was to lead to the overthrow of the dominance of political economy by Ricardo's system. This work, aided by the crises and depressions of 1825–6 and 1829–30, eventually resulted in what one historian of ideas has quite rightly called 'the outstanding period of creative debate in the history of classical economics', the years from 1830 to 1840.[12] A major object of the present study is to articulate the dimensions of anti-Ricardian thinking within parliament and to note the parallels in the monograph and periodical literature of 1819—23.

PROMINENT POLITICIANS AND RICARDO

The views of Ricardo on such matters as the currency, taxation and the future of British agriculture were of great assistance to Lord Liverpool's tory administration in combat against its critics. The radical Ricardo served the conservatives well in this respect. However the government did not reciprocate in that they took any major policy initiatives during his period in parliament that were directly attributable to his advocacy.

Over the five years that Ricardo was in parliament, the tories were reluctant to implement any of the policies that he regarded as important. Admittedly they restored a gold standard and began moves toward freer trade, but even these steps were not undertaken in the manner Ricardo favoured. Thus his bullion plan was sidetracked by a combination of governmental and Bank of England action. The freeing of trade proceeded more in accord with calculations concerning effective central civil service regulation of economic activity than imperatives derived from *laissez-faire*.[13] One of the main protagonists in the campaign, William Huskisson, was frequently a critic of Ricardo on the floor of the Commons. Further, Ricardo's corn law proposals were rejected, the usury laws still stood, and the poor laws remained unrepealed. The sinking fund was retained, as was a massive public debt and high levels of taxation.

Among leading members of the tory party there was considerable sympathy for some aspects of Ricardo's analysis of the state of the economy. Thus Castlereagh and Liverpool accepted the thesis that the problems of English agriculture stemmed from the 'over-cultivation' of land. Huskisson and Peel were in fundamental agreement with Ricardo on the basis of a sound currency system. Peel also subscribed to Ricardo's Malthusianism and to his peculiar reading of the dimensions of contemporary social conflict. All of those in the administration were very ready to agree with Ricardo that the continuing wartime legacy of high taxation did not create special disadvantages for agriculturalists relative to other producers.

On the opposition benches Henry Brougham could agree with Ricardo concerning population theory but found little else in common. The Marquis of Lansdowne, who was the effective whig leader in the Lords for most of the period, was an ardent free trader. Further, he supported the general tenor of Ricardo's monetary pronouncements, but otherwise Lansdowne stressed problems and suggested policies which were not Ricardian. In general, Ricardo was a great disappointment to leading whigs. He quite failed to discomfit the tories in the manner and at the times they had hoped.

THE TRUE PRINCIPLES OF POLITICAL ECONOMY

By the early 1820s economic controversy in Britain had taken on many of the dimensions that are still with us today. As Asa Briggs observes: 'There was a highly technical discussion between "political economists", a noisy and emotional conflict between economic interests, a zig-zag argument among politicians, many of whom changed their minds, and eventually a war of highly-organized political associations, employing new resources of propaganda and the old language of crusades.'[14] On each of these levels the new political economy associated with David Ricardo was a powerful force in the debate. For many of the influential participants at and around the mid-point of this decade, political economy *was* Ricardianism.

The particular set of theories and policies which was so identified lacked much of the range of subtleties and qualifications to be found at times in the 'highly technical discussion' conducted by the more capable devotees of the new social science. Contemporary Ricardianism, for all save a small band of *aficionados*, had a rigid doctrinal character. It is more plainly represented by James Mill's *Elements of Political Economy* (1821, revised 1823 and 1826, reissued 1844) or the first edition of J. R. McCulloch's *Principles of Political Economy* (1825) than by Ricardo's own *Principles of Political Economy and Taxation* (1817, revised 1819 and 1821). Its flavour is better conveyed by the earlier items in the series of articles which McCulloch wrote for the *Edinburgh Review* between 1818 and 1837 than by the pamphlets and papers which Ricardo published from 1809 to 1823.

This is not to say that Ricardo was not a Ricardian. He could sometimes be as doctrinaire as his disciples, a fact attested by a variety of passages in his writings and by various of his parliamentary utterances. However, as in the case of most outstanding intellects, the man's thought transcended at least some of the limitations of the creed with which contemporaries and near-contemporaries identified him.

The sketch of Ricardianism which follows in this chapter does not do justice to Ricardo the economist.[15] Rather, as a necessary background to the analysis of parliamentary debate, it seeks to outline those ideas which could be associated with Ricardo and his followers by a member of parliament who was making a conscientious attempt to inform himself concerning current opinion amongst the speculators on political economy. It is a sketch of 'public' rather than 'private' or 'professional' Ricardianism, since most supporters and opponents (unlike the modern historian of economic analysis) were obliged to judge Ricardo's political interventions on that basis.

FREEDOM OF TRADE

Belief in the efficacy of a *laissez-faire* policy with respect to the production and distribution of the national product was a fundamental tenet of the Ricardian creed. Within an economy, acts of exchange of goods for money, labour, or other goods should be undertaken in a legal framework which allowed the participants the maximum possible freedom to establish the ratios of exchange by their own volition. Protection of local industry from external competition should be progressively abandoned. Protectionist measures reduced economic welfare by distorting the pattern of economic activity compared with its optimal distribution as given by the geographic disposition of resources.[16] In addition tariffs and similar restrictions prevented the owners of capital from bestowing the full benefits of their potential for stimulation of employment and consumption.

The advocacy of freedom of trade was related to a campaign for the establishment of individual liberties in a variety of spheres. Thus Ricardo was most sympathetic to the cause of Catholic emancipation.[17] McCulloch was active on the issue of the rights of workers to combine in trade unions, treating the matter as a direct application of the principle of *laissez-faire*.[18] Above all, the question of economic liberty came to be closely associated with that of reform of parliamentary representation.[19]

Economic liberty was also allied to the quest for retrenchment in government expenditures. 'For the Benthamites,' Arthur Taylor has observed, 'even the best government was a necessary evil.'[20] Taxation was a source of price inflation, diminution of incentive, and retardation of economic growth.[21] Government expenditure did not effect any increase in demand throughout the economy. Rather, it tended to transfer demand from productive to unproductive venues. Thus Ricardo wrote to McCulloch that he could not 'say one word in defence of' the theory that increased governmental expenditure in times of war could be the cause of increased national output.[22]

MALTHUSIAN POPULATION DOCTRINE

Also fundamental in Ricardianism was adherence to the population-resources analysis associated with the name of T. R. Malthus. Apart from checks provided by war, famine and 'moral restraint', the inevitable tendency in any society was for population increase to press hard against the means of subsistence. James Mill, for example, declared, 'That population, therefore, has such a tendency to increase as would enable it to double itself in a small number of years, is a proposition resting on the strongest evidence, which nothing worth the name of evidence has been brought to controvert.'[23]

In addition, Mill went on, as 'capital has a less tendency than Population to increase rapidly' and as 'human happiness cannot be secured by taking forcible methods to make capital increase as fast as population', it was clear that 'the grand practical problem is, To find the means of limiting the number of births'.[24]

Those who espoused this doctrine usually displayed also a fervent belief in the promotion of a system of universal secular education as crucial in the alleviation of the social condition of the masses. More than any other measure, this promised an eventual extrication of society from the population-resources problem. The zeal for such a system was sufficient to permit staunch advocates of *laissez-faire* to call for positive government initiative in this sphere.

SAY'S LAW, MACHINERY AND FLUCTUATIONS

The 'law' enunciated in this period by the French economist Jean-Baptiste Say provided another significant element in the Ricardian system. A good deal of imprecision surrounded its exposition by Say himself and its use by James Mill and others in Britain. However the basic proposition is that when an economy is in equilibrium, the aggregate demand for goods and services will be equal to the aggregate supply. The 'law' seeks to emphasise that the demands for the output of any industry depend upon supplies forthcoming from other industries. If these supplies increase, demands will increase.

The foregoing emphasis was usually interpreted to mean that supply creates its own demand. In this sense the 'law' was thought to demonstrate the impossibility of precipitating a business crisis through over-production. A general glut of commodities can never occur, since an increase of output by some industries means that the demands for the products of other industries are increased thereby. Individual entrepreneurs may err in forecasting the size of the market for their particular products. However, entrepreneurs as a group can never push the economy as a whole into chaos through their dedicated collective pursuit of the most profitable outlets for the employment of their capital.

Having embraced this principle, it was difficult for popular Ricardianism to recognise that commercial fluctuations may be inherent and recurrent in a *laissez-faire* situation. Any single business crisis could be construed as a random and quite temporary departure from the normal state of full employment in the economy. It was difficult to countenance the idea that boom and depression might be linked in a repetitive pattern.

Acceptance of Say's Law also enabled Ricardo and his followers to initially discount the phenomenon of technological unemployment as significant. Any displacement of workers by machines would be followed quickly by their finding employment in other fields. The expanded output in the sector or sectors of the economy in which machinery had been introduced would create employment opportunities in other sectors. Ricardo himself expressed doubts in the third edition of his *Principles* that employment opportunities would be forthcoming in all cases. However this potentially most important break with Ricardianism by its key figure did not shatter the structure of the orthodoxy he had built.[25] Even after Ricardo's change of mind, McCulloch continued to argue the validity of the earlier position.

CAPITAL AND REAL WAGES

Major emphasis was placed on accumulation of capital, i.e., saving and investing viewed as one indivisible activity, as the prime determinant of the national levels of production and employment. This emphasis was facilitated by acceptance of a concept of capital derived via Adam Smith from the agriculture-based treatment of production promulgated by the Physiocrats. Capital was seen as consisting, in the main, of a stock of subsistence goods accumulated with a view to earning profits.[26] This stock could be thought of as a given quantum in existence at the outset of any one period of production and from this source productive labour was sustained until its efforts yielded the output which afforded the substance of a new stock.

This approach glossed over the fact, emphasised earlier by Lord Lauderdale, in his *An Inquiry into the Nature and Origin of Public Wealth* (1804, second edition 1819), that capital could be treated as labour-replacing rather than labour-employing. Further it minimised the analytical importance of a distinction such as Adam Smith had drawn between fixed and circulating capital. James Mill endeavoured to explain away this minimisation on the ground that fixed capital can be considered 'as a product, which is regularly consumed and replaced by every course of productive operations. The capital, not consumed, may always be taken as an additional commodity, the result of the productive process.'[27]

According to Ricardo the long-run tendency of real wages is to a level which provides their recipients with a conventional minimum of subsistence. 'Despite occasional references to comforts and conveniences to be found in the modern cottage,' observes Oswald St Clair, 'Ricardo habitually thinks of the labourer's wage as affording him nothing but necessaries.'[28] Yet in the short run real wages might diverge from this level, and Mrs Marcet, James Mill and McCulloch introduced the wages-fund theorem which could help account for such divergence.

Real wages, at any one time, depend on the quantity of capital (subsistence) accumulated compared with the number in the work force. Thus a sudden decrease in the work force might result in a rise of real wages above the subsistence minimum. Similarly a decrease in the

accumulated fund leads to below subsistence wages. James Mill summar-
ised this approach as follows:

> Universally, then, we may affirm, that, other things remaining the
> same, if the ratio which capital and population bear to one another
> remains the same, wages will remain the same; if the ratio which capital
> bears to population increases, wages will rise; if the ratio which
> population bears to capital increases, wages will fall.[29]

In this analysis the ultimate determinants of the level of real wages were the
rates at which the capitalists saved and the workers reproduced their kind.

WAGES, PROFITS AND RENT

For Ricardo the question of the distribution of the national product
between labourers, capitalists and landowners was the central issue in
political economy, and the manner in which he and his followers
approached this issue involved considerable emphasis on the mutual
opposition of the three shares. In addition they endeavoured to demonstrate that there was a danger that the distributive process could operate to
diminish the effective use of capital in the nation.

Popular Ricardianism proposed a direct opposition between money
wages and profits. 'The profits of stock', explained James Mill, 'depend
upon the share, which is received by its owners, of the joint produce of
labour and stock; profits of stock depend upon wages; rise as wages fall,
and fall as wages rise.[30] Further, as Ricardo himself taught, over time
there could be a tendency for the incomes of landowners (rent) and of
labourers (wages) to expand at the expense of the incomes of those who
provide the funds for the employment of productive labour, i.e., at the
expense of profits. This tendency might well become evident in an
economy where agricultural production was given a substantial and
continuing degree of protection from the competition of foreign food
suppliers.

The expansion of rents and wages at the expense of profits occurs as
the pressure of increasing population extends land use to less fertile soils.
Because rental payments are premiums commanded by intra-marginal
(more fertile) land, rents rise as the margin of cultivation is extended. In
the process money wages rise also. The use of increasingly less fertile land
reduces the efficiency of agriculture and, hence, increases the unit cost of
production of food. However money wage rates must generally be
sufficient to afford their recipients a minimum of subsistence. As the cost
of food production rises the price of subsistence increases and money
wages must adjust upwards to meet that increase. With rents increasing and
wages increasing, the residual income item, profits, must decrease.

Within this analysis Ricardo offered no direct explanation of the genesis of profit. Income of this nature remained a residual, determined after rent and wages. As a devotee of the Ricardian school, Thomas De Quincey wrote: 'he [Ricardo] it was who first made it possible to deduce wages from rent — and therefore to deduce profits from wages . . . in one brief formula, it might be said of profits — they are the leavings of wages'.[31] J. R. McCulloch was unhappy with this analytical gap and endeavoured to fill it by characterising profits as the wages of 'stored-up' labour. In this he was followed by James Mill.[32]

Whatever might be the origin of profit, however, the Ricardians taught that in an economy which was assumed to be relatively frictionless, with high capital and labour mobility, a decline of profits pointed the way to secular stagnation. The desire to accumulate would be minimal where insufficient profit incentives were present. Existing capital would be transferred out of the nation to seek better profit prospects abroad.[33]

In the immediate historical background to Ricardo's reasoning on profits and rent was the drive to increase food production in Britain during the war years and the enclosure movement which had commenced in the 1790s. Both of these factors had served to enhance the significance of rent as a form of income. Further, in the realm of analysis, there was the conviction that since, as Adam Smith had taught, there is a tendency for a uniform profit rate to be established across all sectors of an economy, the rate of profit returned on capital invested in agriculture will influence the rate of return in all alternative employments of capital.[34]

POOR LAWS AND CORN LAWS

The possibility of the onset of an era of diminished profits in England was believed to be magnified considerably by two sets of laws currently on the statute books — the Poor Laws and the Corn Laws. The former, it was argued, encouraged improvidence and lack of moral restraint among the labouring classes, so that a higher birth rate than would otherwise have been the case was maintained. The higher rate intensified the pressure of population against the means of subsistence, thus encouraging the growth of less efficient agricultural undertakings. The protection from overseas competition which the corn laws afforded agriculture, Ricardo contended, directly encouraged the maintenance of inefficient domestic production in the rural sector, an unnecessarily high price of foodstuffs, higher money wages and rents and, hence, lower levels of profits and community well-being than would be achieved otherwise.[35]

In the course of his arguments on this issue Ricardo disputed long-standing notions concerning the continuing primacy of agriculture in any type of economy.[36] In fact, production in the agricultural sector, in contrast with manufacturing activity, was characterised by diminishing returns per unit resource input as population increased. Technical improvements in agricultural production methods could not compensate in any enduring fashion for the presence of diminishing returns. Further, there is a positive disincentive for landowners to introduce improvements since 'their immediate effect is to lower rent'.[37] On grounds such as these the Ricardians argued the case for unfettered development of a strong manufacturing sector. The material benefits were obvious and, as McCulloch declared, 'The Health, Morals and Intelligence of the population have all gained by the establishment of the present manufacturing system.'[38]

BULLIONISM

Ricardo believed that an ideal monetary system was one founded on an invariable measure of value. The precious metals, especially gold, provided the best approximation of such a measure.[39] Yet it was unnecessary and wasteful to rely on the metals as the exclusive media of exchange. Paper could be substituted given that there were adequate safeguards against inflationary action by the banking system. The best basis for the operation of a currency was afforded by the maintenance of the convertibility of issues of bank paper into bullion on demand.[40] If this course were not followed, i.e., paper was not convertible, then at least the currency should be regulated as if the paper was convertible.

For the Ricardians a system involving inconvertibility, such as had pertained in the Napoleonic war period, was to be opposed. Maintenance of inconvertibility almost certainly involved over-issue of bank paper which depressed the real purchasing power of money, and such inflation, like deflation, wrought social evil. On the other hand convertibility would prevent gross injustice by curtailing any attempted over-issue of paper by the banks. Excessive issue would raise the price level in Britain, turn the foreign exchanges against the nation and thus cause notes to be returned to the banks in exchange for bullion to settle international payments obligations.

MONEY, INTEREST AND USURY

Ricardian bullionism was accompanied on the analytical level by adherence to the quantity theory of money. According to this theory there was an universal and direct relationship between the money supply and the price level in the economy. These two variables always tended to move together in the same direction. Further, in the more rigid version of the theory which seems to have had the support of the Ricardians, alterations in the money supply were believed to affect all prices in equal proportion. Hence no major adjustments of domestic market relationships would result from such alterations.[41]

Related to this understanding of the role of money was the view that interest payments could be treated as transfers out of 'profits of stock'. Interest rates moved in the same direction with virtually the same magnitude as profits.[42] There was then an identification of interest with net profit or, as Joseph Schumpeter states, 'the money aspect of the interest problem is definitely reduced to a matter of form or technique'.[43]

The doctrine that profit determined interest provided a strong ground for attack on the policy of maintaining the Usury Laws which put a ceiling on interest charges. These long-standing provisions, which Jeremy Bentham had denounced in his *Defense of Usury*,[44] could be portrayed as interfering with achievement of an optimum allocation of capital in an economy and hence with maximisation of the rate of economic growth. They prevented interest from finding its true level in relation to the profitability of enterprise and as such they were a prime example of injudicious legislation which debarred society from enjoying the full benefits of *laissez-faire*.

In the realm of economic analysis the Ricardian understanding of the role of money and the determination of interest enabled the school to affirm that a quite sharp distinction could be drawn between monetary processes and 'real' processes. An illustration of this is James Mill's argument against David Hume's suggestion that inflation following an increased money supply in a community could act as a stimulus to greater production of goods.[45] Mill contends:

> This doctrine implies a want of clear ideas respecting production. The agents of production are the commodities themselves, not the price of them. They are the food of the labourer, the tools and machinery with which he works, and the raw materials which he works upon. These are not increased by the increase of money: how then can there be more production? This is a demonstration that the conclusion of Hume is erroneous.[46]

RICARDO'S METHOD

A general distinguishing feature of Ricardianism which provided a grave source for complaint and downright confusion among many of its critics was Ricardo's analytical method in relation to current economic policy issues. Part of the complaint and confusion was aroused by the unfamiliarity of the attempt at analysis in terms of a unified theoretical system. The very aspect of his writings which more than any other accounts for the continuing interest in Ricardo among professional economists, confounded a large body of his contemporaries.

Despite Adam Smith, the work of Ricardo presented the British intellectual with a novel phenomenon. As Maurice Dobb has pointed out, in Britain

until 1817, the year of Ricardo's *Principles*, there was nothing that could be called a single theoretical system of political economy, even as a preliminary sketch. A characteristic of the *Wealth of Nations* was its unsystematic character so far as theory was concerned . . . With Ricardo, however, we meet something rather different: an integrated theory of value, of profit and of rent . . . its aspects or elements having something of the neatness and precision of a mathematical demonstration, to which a major policy-corollary was most persuasively attached.[47]

Ricardo's contemporary readers also found it difficult to appreciate the time perspective within which he integrated his generalisations concerning economic forces. About that perspective he wrote to Malthus in 1817:

It appears to me that one great cause of our difference in opinion, on the subjects which we have so often discussed, is that you have always in your mind the immediate and temporary effects of particular changes — whereas I put these immediate and temporary effects quite aside, and fix my whole attention on the permanent state of things which will result from them. Perhaps you estimate these temporary effects too highly, whilst I am too much disposed to undervalue them.[48]

Even where this perspective was understood it was startling to many when the Ricardians drew firm policy proposals on concrete current issues out of generalisations concerning long-run equilibrium tendencies. Further, it was frustrating and annoying when empirical evidence concerning countervailing tendencies was dismissed as being related to ephemeral phenomena. Many critics, for example, drew attention to adjustment problems in the economy arising out of immobility of labour and capital but found those who had imbibed Ricardo's method able to discount the significance of such problems for policy by reference to principles which were invested with a status approaching that of eternal verities although postulated on the assumption of high factor mobility.[49]

THE LABOUR THEORY OF VALUE

At the very opening of the first section of Chapter One of his *Principles* Ricardo wrote:

The value of a commodity, or the quantity of any other commodity for which it will exchange, depends on the relative quantity of labour which is necessary for its production, and not on the greater or less compensation which is paid for that labour.[50]

He then went on in the same chapter to allow that this principle was 'considerably modified' by the presence in productive processes of capital with varying degrees of durability and with differing proportional applications. Nevertheless he affirmed that he would 'consider all the great variations which take place in the relative value of commodities to be produced by the greater or less quantity of labour which may be required from time to time to produce them'.[51] Thirdly, in the final edition of his book he added that 'to facilitate the object of this enquiry' he would assume gold to be an invariable standard of value 'and therefore all alterations in price to be occasioned by some alteration in the value of the commodity of which I may be speaking'.[52]

For both the sympathetic and the unsympathetic reader, as for Ricardo himself, Ricardo on Value posed a host of knotty conceptual problems. James Mill in his *Elements* was prepared to hold to the simple version of a labour-embodied theory of exchange value but, as Donald Winch has observed, 'Mill himself does not appear to have been eager to enter into extended controversy on this issue.'[53]

McCulloch, for his part, initially adopted the dualistic position of retaining for purposes of popular exposition 'a straightforward labour quantity theory of value' while, at the same time, developing 'a cost of production theory of value in which he recognized and was at pains to solve the problem of capital'.[54]

It is not possible then to designate a particular approach to the question of value as 'Ricardian' except inasmuch as less perceptive readers associated Ricardo with a simple labour theory and were encouraged to do so for a time by the desire of McCulloch and Mill to hold the line concerning the 'true principles' of the new science they promulgated. Modern scholarship concerning Ricardo on value (i.e., scholarship since Mr Sraffa's introduction to his edition of Ricardo's works) indicates that his interest in the problem of value was both idiosyncratic and logically developed. For example, Ricardo was not interested for its own sake in the question of why two commodities produced by the same quantities of labour might not have the same exchange value, although most of his contemporaries who considered themselves political economists would have professed a direct interest.[55] Rather Ricardo looked to the 'function of the theory of value of making it possible, in the face of changes in distribution, to measure changes in the magnitude of aggregates of commodities of different kinds or, what is even more important, to ascertain its constancy . . .'[56]

Problems of measurement associated with his development of a model which would show how the national product was divided among classes in society were the key problems for Ricardo in the evolution of his thinking on value.[57] The problem of a numéraire for his particular system, the question of the choice of a supposed invariable measure of value and the logical difficulties involved in its employment, was a central preoccupation for Ricardo. His interest was not well understood by fellow economists, whether supporters or critics. Even where there was some suggestion of understanding, his quest was generally dismissed as an attempt to attain the unattainable and as an exercise that was not necessary to establish the soundness of the economic policies he advocated. Yet, to the very eve of the onset of his short, fatal illness, Ricardo wrestled with this particular problem. That the question continued to loom so large for him is most indicative of Ricardo's cast of mind and the methodology suffusing his entire output as an economist.[58]

2 1819: Wage Labour, Taxation, and the Poor

Political Economy, when the simple principles of it are once understood, is only useful, as it directs Governments to right measures in taxation. We very soon arrive at the knowledge that Agriculture, Commerce, and Manufactures flourish best when left without interference on the part of Government, but the necessity which the state has for money to defray the expenses of its functions, imposes on it the obligation to raise taxes, and thus interference becomes absolutely necessary.

David Ricardo
to Hutches Trower, 12 November 1819.

This analysis of the economic content of parliamentary debate commences at a point marked by the assembly of a new House of Commons after a general election. During the year, David Ricardo joined the House to consolidate and extend the impact on policy making which he had exerted already through his publications. A third feature of our starting point is the onset of economic depression in a seemingly new and virulent form, a development which destroyed the promise of continuing prosperity which the revival of the British economy from the second half of 1817 had appeared to offer.

At the general election of 1818 there had been a return of 157 new M.P.s, involving a loss of about thirty seats to the majority supporting the Tory administration of Lord Liverpool. However, the losses were insufficient to suggest the unseating of that administration, especially as divisions among the opposition ensured that the Whigs were not a viable alternative as the governing body.[1] Liverpool's ministry included Nicholas Vansittart as Chancellor of the Exchequer, and Frederick Robinson as President of the Board of Trade. Thomas Wallace was Vice-President of the Board of Trade.

Ricardo was elected on 20 February 1819, in place of Richard 'Conversation' Sharp, who took the Chiltern Hundreds.[2] His seat was the

Irish pocket borough, Portarlington, a constituency numbering about twelve electors, and he retained it until his death in September 1823.[3] During his term in the House, Ricardo spoke on 126 occasions that are recorded in Hansard, and he voted regularly at divisions, for the most part in the minority. On this showing he proved to be far more active as a member than the vast bulk of his contemporaries in the Commons.

The unreformed House which Ricardo joined consisted of 658 seats, including 100 Irish members. Of these, 229 were occupied by baronets, Irish peers, and the sons of English and Scottish peers. Professional men numbered 253, including 105 with a background in law, and eighty-six career officers in either the army or the navy. The aristocrats and the professionals were both more numerous than men involved in commerce, trade and industry. The latter accounted for 147 seats and, allowing for multiple interests on the part of some twenty of these members, this total was made up as follows: bankers, 47; manufacturers, 13; nabobs, 17; India interest, 29; West Indies merchants, 7; West Indies interest, 26; miscellaneous mercantile activities, 28. As Ricardo could be classified by way of background in this last sub-category, it is evident that, from a vocational viewpoint, he was one of an insignificant minority in terms of numbers.

Ricardo was also in the minority as a non-graduate of a university. University graduates totalled 365 and, of these, 129 were the product of one college, Christ Church, Oxford. The dominance of Christ Church was paralleled by that of Eton among the public school men. This one school had educated 135 of the 310 then in the Commons who had attended such institutions.[4]

Historians who put great store on a man's vocational, educational and familial backgrounds in accounting for his impact on the decisions of his immediate contemporaries might be moved to suggest that, given these statistics, Ricardo could not have made much impression on parliamentary thought and action. Yet they would be wrong. Certainly, as this study shows, he failed to impress many of the more articulate commercial men in the House. However Ricardian theory offered aristocrats and professionals a rational basis for a voice in economic policy making. It equipped them with a set of general principles which they could use to compete, for influence in that area of government, with the partial analysis that constituted the wisdom of most men of business. Hence Ricardianism was a tool welcomed by some of those unfamiliar with the ways of economic enterprise and the inner life of the structures of commerce and industry.[5]

TWO MAJOR THEMES

When parliament opened, the Prime Minister's speech on 21 January remarked on the currently flourishing state of economic activity and the solidity of the nation's resources.[6] In the ensuing debate members showed no great disposition to question the validity of these observations. There was no strong hint of what was to become one of the two main themes for economic discussion in the following months — growing unemployment, desperate poverty and increasing sympathy for revolutionary action in the industrial centres.

There was a very strong hint, however, concerning the second main theme of economic debate. In the Lords the Marquis of Lansdowne raised the question of the state of the currency.[7] He drew attention to the fact that 'the act which restrained the Bank (of England) from paying in specie would expire in the course of the present year, and that the currency would then return to its former state.' For a number of years the government had delayed revision of the supposedly temporary wartime expedient of permitting the Bank to issue notes without the obligation to exchange those notes for gold on demand from their holders. Was the delay to continue? It was anomalous, Lansdowne proclaimed, to 'render it impossible for the richest country in the world to command the use of the precious metals, or anything of intrinsic value as a foundation for its currency'.

The Earl of Liverpool did not attempt to rebut the simplistic metallist doctrine of money involved in Lansdowne's thrust. Rather he replied that 'there was no man in the country more anxious than he was to see our currency restored to coin, or paper convertible into gold at the will of the holder'.[8] However given 'the present state of the exchanges' it would be impossible to undertake restoration by July of the present year. At this Lord Lauderdale called for an immediate enquiry into the operation of the existing currency arrangements.[9] Lauderdale added that 'until some alterations were made in the present Mint regulations, it was quite vain to expect the expiration of the Restriction Act.' At this point debate on the issue ceased, but it was soon to take up much of the time of both Houses as the session continued.

CHILD LABOUR LEGISLATION

In his observations on the Prince Regent's speech, Lansdowne in passing had expressed the doubt 'whether the effects of the revival of trade had as yet reached those to whom it was of greatest importance it should extend, namely, the labouring and agricultural classes'.[10] Shortly after, these general remarks were given specific content when the Bishop of Chester and Lord Kenyon, who had been Chief Justice of England and was active in the cause of law reform, presented petitions in the Lords requesting legislative restriction on the hours of work by children.[11] Kenyon moved for a committee to enquire into the subject and this drew fire from, among others, Lauderdale, who affirmed the principle that 'compacts between the employer and the labourer should be free'. The Bishop replied that 'much good had already been done by parliamentary interference; and that afforded a strong argument why parliament should go on to complete its work'. As a compromise the debate was adjourned for a fortnight.

When the Lords returned to the issue Kenyon proposed a committee to investigate the conditions of children in the cotton factories.[12] He contended that 'the children could not be considered as free labourers ... Nothing but a legislative enactment could afford them any effectual protection'. The motion was eventually carried with the support of Liverpool, who took Kenyon's point concerning lack of freedom. Earl Grosvenor protested this abrogation of 'the great principle of free labour', while Lauderdale professed to see in the move the baneful influence of the reformer- industrialist Robert Owen.[13]

Eleven days later the Lords continued on the same legislative tack with the successful second reading of a bill on chimney sweepers. Moving the reading Lord Auckland stated that the bill provided that 'after the 1st of May 1821, the use of climbing-boys, except for the purpose of examining chiminies, would be done away altogether'. This, he envisaged, would be 'a great step towards the total abolition' of child labour in the industry.[14] Lauderdale rose to oppose this measure also and he questioned the efficacy of forcing the introduction of machinery in place of manual labour.[15]

Later in the session the legislation on behalf of the climbing boys failed, but on 14 June the Lords assented to some measure of regulation of the hours and conditions of work for children in the cotton factories.[16] The significance of this latter has been underlined by Elie Halévy, who writes: '... for all its timidity the Act was by no means without importance. The political economy of laissez-faire had suffered a defeat in the very year when, in the matter of the Poor Law, Parliament was apparently preparing to embrace it'.[17]

POOR LAW REFORM

In the Commons on 9 February William Sturges-Bourne moved into a new phase of his lengthy campaign for a reform of the Poor Laws. Bourne, then member for Christchurch, proposed a further committee of enquiry into the operation of those longstanding social welfare provisions.[18] This proposal was immediately opposed by John Christian Curwen on the ground that, given the circumstances of many poor labourers, the House 'ought at once meet the question fairly'.[19] However, the House was reluctant to take any precipitate action, and a poor law committee was appointed. Three weeks later David Ricardo was added to the original list of committee members.

On 25 March Bourne requested leave to bring in a Poor Rates

Misapplication bill, and this afforded the occasion for Ricardo's maiden speech in the House. The bill sought to deny direct payments out of the poor rates to destitute parents of large families in cases where such payments were seen as justifiable only on the ground that there were many children in the family. To replace this type of assistance Bourne proposed that the children concerned should be taken away from their parents and placed in institutions where they would be put to work and educated. 'It must be recollected', said Bourne, in defence of his scheme, 'that persons in a higher sphere of life placed their offspring at some distance from their home for the purpose of instruction, and not unfrequently sent them out of the realm'.[20] He added that he envisaged that 'no relief should for the future be given to any able-bodied labourer in employment'.

Ricardo objected strongly to Bourne's scheme, although the forcible separation of parents and children seemed the least of his concerns. Ricardo's worry was that of a hard-line Malthusian.[21] At present in England, he declared 'the two great evils were the tendency towards a redundant population, and the inadequacy of the wages to the support of the labouring classes'.[22] He forecast that redundancy of population would be enhanced 'if parents felt assured that an asylum would be provided for their children in which they would be treated with humanity and tenderness'. Further, he felt that Bourne's innovation would not meet the problem of inadequate wage rates. Even if it led to a rise in real wage levels, 'they would still be no more than the wages of a single man, and would never rise so high as to afford a provision for a man with a family'. Obviously, Ricardo was looking for a more radical reform than that contemplated by Bourne.

Despite Ricardo's objections, leave was granted for Bourne to introduce his legislation and on its second reading John Curwen intervened again.[23] He was still entirely opposed to the idea of a poor law committee. He saw it as just one more manifestation of a political situation in which 'a weak, divided, and unpopular administration' was employing the committee technique to screen its inability to evolve meaningful economic and social legislation. Current circumstances, in his opinion, warranted direct parliamentary action on behalf of the labouring poor and he called for regulated wages and taxation reform. Increasing inequity in society had rendered obsolete the minimal government doctrine of the Ricardians. 'The writers on political economy', he affirmed, 'have not contemplated the state to which we are reduced. Whilst capital and labour bore a fair proportion to each other, there was no necessity for legislative interference'.[24]

David Ricardo did not trouble himself to counter the suggestion that the theories of the economists, having been formulated by reflection on an era of wartime boom, were lacking in relevance to the realities of post-war depression. He repeated his criticism that Bourne's bill would encourage increased population by its provision for the institutionalised care of children. 'In what situation would the country be placed in twenty years hence', Ricardo asked, 'when these children so educated grew up to manhood? The bill was only the plan of Mr Owen in a worse shape, and carried to a greater extent'.[25]

Joseph Hume, the nabob who was at this time member for Aberdeen, was even more blunt than Ricardo. 'Until the country looked the evil fairly in the face, and taught the labourer to depend more on himself', Hume instructed the House, 'no adequate remedy could be supplied'. Hume added that the present bill should have included a clause which stated 'that from and after the passing of this act, no child legitimate or illegitimate should be entitled to a maintenance from the parish'.[26]

The bill pleased neither the Ricardians, fearful of population increase, nor those who protested the inhumanity of enforced separation of parents and children. Nevertheless after a division it passed the second reading stage.

When the legislation came to a third reading, the most notable dissenter was Viscount Milton.[27] In particular, he objected to the non-extension of relief to able-bodied workers who were unable to find employment or were obliged to accept a below-subsistence wage. 'The object of the bill', as he understood it, 'was, by an indirect operation, to raise wages, and stimulate the labourer to increased exertions; but this was to be done by previously inflicting much pain and misery upon him'. A similar demur was expressed by Peter Moore who 'could not consent to deprive the labourer of a share of the poor-rates while he knew, that in Coventry and several other parts of the country, the poor were working 16 hours a day without being able to earn enough to support existence'.[28]

Despite these protests and those of Ricardians like George Philips who believed that the bill would remove 'all restraint upon improvident marriages' among the non-respectable poor, the legislation was passed.[29] Its proponents were doomed to disappointment however when, later in the session, the measure failed in the Lords.[30] Poor law reformers and abolitionists alike were obliged to wait until 1821 for another major assault on the structure of the welfare system (see Chapter 11).

THE INCIDENCE OF TAXATION

During the poor law debate of 9 February John Curwen claimed that parliament could best assist the bulk of wage earners by revision of existing taxation arrangements.[31] Particularly, it should do away with the present reliance of the public revenues on taxes raised from consumer expenditure on the basic necessities of life. A much more equitable system, he believed, would be one based on property taxation. This would decrease the incidence of pauperism among wage earners. At the same time it would facilitate a partial transfer of the financial burden for provision of the public relief from rural employers to 'the great bulk of the monied interest, and the whole of the trading community'. Under the poor law system, organised on a parish basis and financed out of local rates, it was undeniable that agriculturalists carried a disproportionate burden when compared with rentiers and traders.

Curwen's suggestion concerning a property tax was revived in the budget debate in June by John Mansfield, the new member for Leicester.[32] Ricardo came out against the proposal, claiming that it would have 'bad effects', the exact nature of which he did not specify at this point.[33] However, as Ricardo understood the relationship of the current state of the public finances to the existing depression in industry, 'the evil of the national debt' provided the crucial link. He was against any system of taxation which enabled the government to go on from year to year meeting the substantial interest charges on the debt without pressure to reduce the size of the liability. The maintenance of the large debt, which had accumulated over twenty-five years of warfare, was most debilitating for the economy. That debt, Ricardo believed 'destroyed the equilibrium of prices, occasioned many persons to emigrate to other countries, in order to avoid the burden of taxation which it entailed, and hung like a mill-stone round the exertion and industry of the country'.

Ricardo's solution was a radical one - a once-ever discharge of the debt by means of a levy on all holders of accumulated wealth. He admitted that 'a great sacrifice should be made'. However he was confident that 'the sacrifice would be a temporary one, and with that view he would be willing to give up as large a share of his property as any other individual'.[34]

Later in the same month, Ricardo had cause to correct the whig Lord John Russell on the taxation question. Rather like Curwen, Russell contended that further taxation would, if imposed on commonly consumed commodities, depress wage earners' standards of living below their existing low level.[35] Ricardo explained that this would not be the case. Such taxes, he argued, fell, in the main, on the employers of labour:

> If, indeed, they were imposed on the luxuries of the labourer, they might in some measure diminish his comforts; but the more the articles taxed approached the nature of necessaries, the more completely would they fall on those who employed labourers. It had been said, that these taxes would fall upon the poor-rates; but that amounted to the same thing; for the poor-rates formed, in reality, a fund destined to support labour, however inconvenient it might be to pay it in that way.[36]

W.H. Lyttelton of Worcestershire then queried whether or not a tax on a commodity like malt, and hence a rise in the price of beer, could not be said to fall directly on its major consumers, the poor.[37] In reply Ricardo stated that his point was that taxes on the necessities of life would not be 'particularly borne by the labouring classes'. These taxes 'would be only prejudicial to the labourers in the same way as most other taxes would be, inasmuch as they would diminish the fund employed in the support of labour'.[38] In Ricardo's understanding, the welfare of workers was directly related to a minimisation of all forms of taxation. Governmental retrenchment and parsimony were preconditions for maximisation of employment opportunities.

REGULATION OF WAGES

In their desire to see an improvement in the lot of the workers there were some members who were prepared to urge action by parliament to influence the conditions under which wages were determined. John Curwen was one of these, and on 9 February he argued the injustice of the laws against combined action by employees to establish rates of pay.[39] 'If when laws were made to punish combinations amongst the men', said Curwen, 'their provisions had also been directed against combinations amongst the masters, he would have agreed in the justice of the enactment'. In his experience, bargaining power (as Adam Smith had observed forty years before) was weighted heavily on the side of the employer. This was especially the case in the rural sector, Curwen believed, since there, labour was 'dispersed abroad'. The worker was totally dependent on his employer, but the latter 'might do without him, till he should be starved into submission, without injury'. As a partial remedy Curwen looked to the introduction of a system of localised minimum wage determination, at least in respect of agricultural labour. 'It would be wise', he said, 'if the minimum wages to the agricultural labourer with reference to small districts, were regulated at petty sessions.'

A somewhat similar proposal was introduced later in the session by Peter Moore, but on this occasion the focus was manufacturing industry.[40] Moore, during May, in response to petitions from his electorate of Coventry, moved for 'leave to be given to bring in a bill for the better Regulation of Persons employed in the Silk Manufacture in Great Britain'.

The wages of ribbon weavers in Coventry had fallen to a very low level with the onset of the new trade depression. The remedy which Moore proposed was 'a standard regulation to be appointed, by which a due remuneration might be paid to the artisan for his labour'. He was not requesting the establishment of a fixed minimum wage, he claimed, but rather the application to Coventry of legislation for wage determination similar to that pertaining in silk manufacturing at Spitalfields in London. Wages at Spitalfields were set within a framework of systematised collective bargaining supplemented by recourse to arbitration by local magistrates.

Frederick Robinson of the Board of Trade found the suggestion quite unacceptable.[41] In a doctrinaire speech, devoid of analytical content, Robinson declared '. . . it was inexpedient to allow the wages of labourers, of whatever denomination to be settled by any other means than by the natural demand for their labour. Indeed, he was almost ashamed to use so trite and acknowledged a principle - a principle maintained by every able writer on the subject of political economy'. If the House acceded to Moore's propositions, he continued, there was a real possibility of 'an end to the system of free labour in this country'.

The other member for Coventry, the newly elected entrepreneur Edward Ellice, supported Moore, as did Dugdale Dugdale of Warwickshire and Thomas Fowell Buxton, the businessman and reformer. However Thomas Wallace reiterated the argument of his colleague at the Board of Trade, and George Philips, a most consistent exponent of *laissez-faire*, observed that he failed to see 'any reason why labour should not be just as fair a commodity of sale and purchase, as anything else sold or bought in this country'.[42]

The debate ended when John Curwen counselled Moore to withdraw his motion for the time being. Thus perished an early attempt to evoke direct legislative response to the mounting misery of a new business depression.[43] The requested response ran counter to 'the true principles of political economy', and those principles frequently offered a ready escape route for an administration clearly disposed to inaction. They also offered a partial camouflage for the government's lack of expertise in commercial and industrial matters. Merchants, entrepreneurs and bankers might distinguish problem areas in the economy and suggest remedies, but the literature of political economy could often be relied upon to yield a generalisation that questioned the wisdom of the practical man of business.

THE COMBINATION LAWS

Earlier in the session, we have seen, John Curwen had raised the matter of the injustice of the existing laws against combination of workmen. Now, a new and more comprehensive critique was offered from a different quarter when Joseph Hume, who had previously given notice of motion for repeal of the Combination Acts, presented a petition concerning them. According to the petition, those laws: prevented the achievement of wage justice; encouraged the use of combinations by wage earners; had given rise to 'universal distrust, jealousy, and oppression' in employer-employee relations; and forced workers to go outside the law of the land to seek better wages. In addition it was stated 'all laws which interfere with the wages of labour are injurious to the general prosperity of the country'.[44]

It was this latter point which Hume was concerned to stress. Repeal of the combination laws was a blow in favour of greater freedom of trade. In addition it was in accord with a doctrine of minimal legislative intervention in society, as Ricardo and Bentham taught. 'All laws which interfered with the rate of wages', declared Hume, 'were hostile to the best interests of trade, and were the source of constant complaint and litigation'. From the Ricardian viewpoint, laws against the formation of trade unions were in the same category as the poor laws.

This petition did not move the government, but three other members of the Commons spoke to it, each in support. Edward Ellice characterised repeal of the combination acts as 'the first step toward re-establishing the principle of free labour'. In his opinion it had been 'the repeated violation of those principles, which had produced the distressing effects from which the manufacturing classes were now suffering'.[45] Ricardo did not speak, nor was he called upon to vote in this particular debate. Yet he made his position clear in response to a query from J. R. McCulloch, in a letter written the following year. The combination laws, he informed his Northern disciple,

> appear to me to be unjust and oppressive to the working classes, and of little real use to the masters . . . The true remedy for combinations is perfect liberty on both sides, and adequate protection against violence and outrage. Wages should be the result of a free compact, and the contracting parties should look to the law to protect them from force being employed on either side; competition would not, I think, fail to do all the rest.[46]

REVIEW

In the discussion of labour and social welfare issues during the first six months of 1819 it is evident that some members of the aristocracy plus a small group of entrepreneurs and rentiers - notably Curwen, Moore and Ellice - were anxious to have parliament take legislative initiative to improve the lot of the labourer. These men were not averse to the introduction of new types of measures or the elaboration of old, if the occasion seemed to demand it.

On the other hand the Ricardians were wedded to the belief that the interests of workers were best served by the reduction of parliamentary intervention to a minimum. The initiatives they looked for were those in the direction of repeal of existing statutes. Hence, Sturges-Bourne's innovation of asylums for destitute children was to be resisted, while abandonment of the Combination Laws was encouraged. In this latter instance both the Ricardians and the articulate men with experience in business found themselves in the same camp.

Liverpool's administration stood aloof from both sides, in the main, although the Prime Minister lent some support to the argument for protection of children in cotton factories and Robinson found the *laissez-faire* banner convenient to wave at the advocates of legislation for wage regulation. The Cabinet, at this time, seems to have had a passionate devotion to inaction on welfare issues. Their passivity suggests a large measure of indifference in the matter of the politically impotent poor, although it must be allowed that the tenor of parliamentary events had obliged the government to give a great deal of its domestic policy attention to another set of economic problems. This second set was bound up with what was termed 'the state of the currency'.

3 1819: The Bank and the Chancellor

The corporation of the Bank of England had, during a period of twenty-two years, accumulated an enormous mass of wealth at the expense of the public, without the performance of any public service that could entitle them to that exclusive benefit ... they had accumulated wealth during a shorter period, and to a greater amount, than any body of men had been ever able to do in any banking or commercial country, since banking or commerce had been established in the world.

Pascoe Grenfell
House of Commons, 26 January 1819

On the morning of Sunday, 26 February 1797, an emergency meeting of Cabinet had sanctioned a striking innovation in the British monetary system. The previous day had seen a run on the coin and bullion reserves of the Bank of England, a run engendered by fear concerning the invasion of Ireland by the French. With the Bank expecting it would not be able to meet its liabilities when trading resumed on the Monday, Cabinet issued an Order in Council which restrained the Bank from paying gold on demand to holders of its notes. The Order received immediate support from a meeting of London merchants who undertook to accept bank notes and use them in payments, despite their non-convertibility. Confidence returned speedily, and the Bank began the issue of one-pound notes to supplement those of larger denomination to which its paper currency had been confined previously.

The Order in Council was confirmed by Act of Parliament in May and this initiated a series of Acts which, over the next twenty years, repeatedly deferred resumption of the pre-1797 system. Then, in September 1817, the Bank announced that as of the following month it would be willing to exchange specie for any of its notes which were dated earlier than 1 January 1817. Implementation of this policy was accompanied by an outflow of over £2.5 million in gold from England over the next few months. The bulk of the gold was widely believed to have been transferred to France in consequence of public loan raisings by the French Government.

The British Government reacted in May 1818 with yet another act which restrained the Bank from undertaking cash payments. This new act set the date for removal of the restraint as 5 July 1819, so when parliament assembled again the question of resumption loomed large. Was parliament to continue to temporise on this issue or, now that peace had been firmly restored, was it to rid the nation of a wartime expedient which, some members believed, had been the occasion for exploitation of the country at large by the Bank and the Chancellor of the Exchequer?[1]

PASCOE GRENFELL ATTACKS

In the opening debate of the session the Prime Minister, as seen in the previous chapter, expressed the opinion that it would be impossible to return to cash payments by July. This statement incensed a large segment of the opposition, including the member for Great Marlow, Pascoe Grenfell, who five days later moved for presentation of data on the note circulation and on dealings between the Bank and the government.[2]

Grenfell launched an attack on the privileged postion of the Bank under the continuance of the legislation of 1797.[3] 'For twenty-two years,' he declaimed, 'twenty-four merchants of the city of London, as the directors of this corporation, had, without check and without control, the unlimited power of issuing a forced paper currency on the country for their own exclusive benefit.' The Bank had amassed great wealth over a short period, particularly because of the terms under which it granted accommodation to the government.[4] Parliament, said Grenfell, had given the Bank an 'exclusive credit', and that monopoly power had been exercised in a manner injurious to the nation.

The Chancellor of the Exchequer offered no objection to presentation of the information requested and Grenfell's motions were agreed to. Then, three days later, Grenfell took up his campaign with the contention that the Chancellor's 'system of forcing a circulation of paper pounds' had led to the creation of a higher price of silver in the market than that offered by the Mint.[5] Thus it was profitable for individuals to melt silver coin and export the product. 'The silver coin', he forecast, 'would follow the course which the gold coin had already taken, and entirely disappear.' This would go on despite the existence of a law which made such a practice illegal. That law, in Grenfell's opinion, was 'impolitic, absurd, and ridiculous', and it had been criticised by all the best authorities on monetary policy since John Locke.

William Wellesley-Pole, the Master of the Mint, replied that the anomaly of which Grenfell complained arose out of an arrangement of which

Grenfell approved, namely 'that one precious metal (gold) should be made the standard of value, and that the other metals (including silver) should be considered as counters.'[6] Pole did not think the present situation as serious as Grenfell contended but he allowed that if the price of silver continued at its existing level a committee of enquiry should consider the matter. The same committee might also consider the law against the exportation of silver bullion, a law which Pole agreed 'was worse than foolish.'

Lord Archibald Hamilton and George Tierney questioned the relevance of Pole's analysis.[7] The latter recommended that Pole read a recently published pamphlet addressed to Robert Peel on the currency question.[8] Pole, who was obviously floundering with the range of issues at hand, offered no substantive argument in reply and called for an investigating committee.

THE BUSINESS COMMUNITY REACTS

During the foregoing debate Thomas Wilson, a new member for London, expressed the fear that should parliament decide to restrict the ability of the banking system to issue notes 'the trade of the country would suffer in proportion.'[9] Merchants of a similar mind hurried to petition parliament and on 1 and 2 February petitions were received from businessmen in Leeds, Halifax and Liverpool.[10] The first two were presented by James Stuart-Wortley and the third by George Canning. The Leeds petition read, in part:

> . . . so great a diminution of the circulating medium would be caused by the necessary restrictive measures of the Bank of England, and of private banks, as must occasion stagnation in trade and manufactures, depreciation of property and general distress, throwing a considerable portion of the population out of employment, injuring the revenue, and hazarding the prosperity of the empire.

As events unfolded the businessmen of Leeds must have been confirmed in the belief that their prognosis was all too accurate. However when full-scale debate commenced in parliament few of the members, and certainly not David Ricardo, seemed to believe there was much substance in their forebodings. Distrust of the Bank of England added to the lingering influence of the old metallist doctrine of money served to distract the House from reflection on the deflationary implications of resumption of cash payments.

TIERNEY MOVES FOR A COMMITTEE

George Tierney, who was whig leader in the Commons, believed that in the controversy concerning resumption he had an excellent opportunity for embarrassing the tories.[11] Accordingly, following the presentation of the petition from Liverpool he moved: 'That a Committee be appointed to inquire into the effects produced on the Exchanges with Foreign Countries, and the state of the Circulating Medium by the Restriction on Payments in Cash by the Bank, and to report whether any, and what reasons exist for continuing the same beyond the period now fixed by law for its termination.'[12]

At the outset Tierney avowed his allegiance to the principles laid down by the Bullion Committee of 1810.[3] He knew of no good reason for delaying return to 'the ancient and wholesome circulation of the country'. Neither was there a good reason 'why property in this kingdom should not be subject to the same test of measurement which is applied to it in every country under heaven'. With an inconvertible paper currency, he continued, society was at the mercy of the machinations of 'gamblers, speculators in the funds, stock-jobbers, and all those who were living upon the losses of the honest and industrious'. Such a system might lend the appearance of national prosperity but 'one piece of paper piled upon another' could not contribute to genuine well-being. Particular sympathy, Tierney thought, should be shown to whose who had invested their money in government stock and who were now suffering from the effects of inflation and a low rate of interest. 'Was it not high time', he queried, 'to take some steps that should put an end to a system which secretly destroyed the foundations of national prosperity?'

In reply to Tierney's rhetoric Nicholas Vansittart, the Chancellor of the Exchequer, did not attempt to exploit the intellectual bankruptcy of his whig opponent's monetary opinions. Rather was he intent on minimising any political advantage the opposition might gain as sole champions of the cause of resumption. Vansittart announced that the government was now in favour of a committee of enquiry, but that it ought to be a secret committee.[14] Further, Tierney's motion ought be amended to focus more precisely on the question of the ability of the Bank to resume cash payments.

The first speaker in this debate to address himself meaningfully to the economics of the problem of resumption was Viscount Castlereagh.[15] He was concerned to counter the simple metallist outlook of sections of the membership. 'Nothing, indeed, could be more fatal to the interests of a great country', he warned them, 'than the fact of the whole of its property, more or less, being incapable of being represented by nothing but metallic money, more or less'. To force the country to accept a purely metallic currency would be 'to destroy the principles of reproduction'. The main sufferers would be the poor, 'that class of men who, from their wants, become the superior objects of legislative concern'. There was a strong possibility that lower prices following such a currency revision would lead to unemployment.

Castlereagh urged caution in the matter of cash payments. He 'was of a very different opinion' from those who believed the time for resumption had arrived. At present, some foreign governments, acting in terms of 'wide and impracticable theories' were endeavouring to restore metallic circulations. These endeavours 'operated unnaturally and violently on the money markets of Europe', and it was imperative that the Bank of England was not exposed to the pressures thus engendered in international financial arrangements. Castlereagh also reminded members that although 'the effect of a war was to hoard in this country a great accumulation of capital', there had been considerable capital outflow since the peace.

George Canning, for the government, was another to speak against hasty action.[16] The Bank, he revealed to the House, had approached the government with a request to delay resumption. In addition he pointed out that public opinion was sharply divided on this question, as witnessed by the 'new flight of pamphlets [which] had lighted on the town.'[17] This division was bound up with a number of controversial problems in analysis, including whether or not 'the amount of the issues by the Bank regulated the rate of exchange, and that if the issues were diminished, the exchange would turn in our favour.' Even if the foreign exchange rate did turn there was the even more difficult question of the social cost at which this might be achieved. Canning concluded that an enquiry was warranted and, in the public interest, it should be secret since 'the safety and credit of the Bank' was at stake. He recalled that the recent 'partial experiment of opening the Bank' had been a failure. A similar error was to be avoided now.[18]

William Manning, a director of the Bank of England, then rose to announce that the institution had already set itself on a deflationary course in expectation of resumption.[19] This announcement may have been welcome to many members but it was greeted with alarm by Alderman William Heygate of London. Heygate pronounced himself in disagreement with the recommendations of the Bullion Report (a form of heresy among Ricardians and in many non-business circles) and he challenged the view that currency appreciation would, of itself, improve the foreign exchanges. Heygate stated:

> The exchanges could only be turned in our favour by such a fall in the prices of labour and of all articles of manufacture as would force exportation till our exports exceeded our imports; but when he considered the evils with which this operation might be attended, he hesitated with regard to the policy of bringing about such a state of things, and thought a return to cash payments on such conditions would be paying too dear for the advantages contemplated.[20]

At this stage George Tierney returned to sum up and, politically outmanoeuvred, directed his invective at Vansittart. He declared that he 'would not be satisfied with the nomination of the committee by the chancellor of the exchequer, surrounded as he was, by day and night, by Jew brokers, speculators, and other interested adventurers.' Tierney believed that the costs of resumption would be minimal, although even he allowed that 'such payments could not commence until there had been some sort of jar with the public.'[21]

Despite these final words Vansittart's motion for a secret committee was agreed to, rather than Tierney's. The whigs had failed to gain their expected political victory.[22] Robert Peel was appointed as chairman of the committee and the twenty other members included Tierney, Castle-reagh, Vansittart, Canning, Robinson, Huskisson, Grenfell, Frankland Lewis and Stuart-Wortley. The Lords also appointed a secret committee with Liverpool, Lansdowne, King, Grenville, Lauderdale and eight others as members.

EDWARD ELLICE ON THE CHANCELLOR

Undoubtedly in parliament at this time there was not only deep distrust of the Bank but also of the motives and activities of Nicholas Vansittart. This latter emerged plainly on 3 February in the speech of Edward Ellice of Coventry who, as a new member, had not entered the debate for a committee of the previous day's sitting. However unlike most of the Chancellor's critics, Ellice had a broad background of business experience plus considerable analytical skill to support his arguments. When a petition was received from the merchants of Bristol requesting parliament to avoid 'an hasty and premature' return to cash payments, Ellice took the opportunity to demand that the Chancellor discontinue further issues of exchequer bills so as to prevent a further increase in the paper circulation when a return to convertibility was being contemplated.[23] Failure to discontinue would swell the future burden on the economy of the public financial liabilities. 'Would it not prove the height of mockery', he asked, 'that stock to be purchased with bank-notes, should be repaid in gold?'

During the following week Ellice extended his attack on what he termed Vansittart's 'vicious system of finance'.[24] He began by explaining the trade boom of 1818 in a manner reminiscent of the approach of John Maynard Keynes over a century later. An increase in the money supply had lowered the rate of interest at a time when expectations were high as to the profitability of a variety of business ventures, so that increased investment in trade had resulted. Ellice stated:

> He (Vansittart) had, in fact, created that trade by his loans from the Bank, and his excessive issues of exchequer bills, which forced the Bank to extend their issues, and enabled every man who wished to extend his dealings, to have any command of money he pleased, at a reduced rate

of interest. No man who imagined he saw a chance of profit in any branch of trade, could be at a loss to obtain the funds at a reduced rate of interest. All this had increased the trade of the country.

Yet, continued Ellice, last year's boom had collapsed. 'There had been a fall in all commodities of 20 or 30 per cent', he claimed: 'There was not a manufacturer in Coventry, who by working fourteen or fifteen hours a day at present could earn more than six shillings a week.'

The immediate cause of the substantial fall in commodity prices was a shortage of liquidity. 'Those who had lent money to the merchant', Ellice explained, 'now called for it again. The consequence was, that he was forced to bring his commodities to market at a time when money was scarce. The price ceased to afford the manufacturer an adequate return, and consequently his stock went down.' The liquidity shortage, itself, had been engendered by the transfer of funds overseas. The fact was that both France and America were at present offering much higher rates of interest on public loans that the British government. Reflecting on this sequence of events Ellice concluded: 'If the chancellor of the exchequer continued to borrow one day for the purpose of raising the price of the public funds, and to issue paper merely for the purpose of producing a temporary prosperity, it was impossible that things could proceed.' As later debate was to indicate, many members were prepared to agree with this diagnosis of the ills of the immediate past.

4 1819: Evidence and Report on Cash Payments

I see, that they have adopted a scheme of one Ricardo (I wonder what countryman he is) who is, I believe, a converted Jew. At any rate, he has been a 'Change-Alley-man for the last fifteen or twenty years. If the Old Lord Chatham were now alive, he would speak with respect of the Muckworm, as he called the 'Change-Alley-people. Faith! they are now become everything. Baring assists at the Congress of Sovereigns, and Ricardo regulates things at home.

William Cobbett
Cobbett's Weekly Political Register, 4 September 1819

The Lords committee on the resumption of cash payments heard evidence from 8 February to 30 April and the Commons committee from 11 February to 1 May.[1] David Ricardo appeared as a witness before both bodies and his plan for resumption emerged as the major focus for discussion. Its chief features were the adoption of a system of payments of notes in bullion rather than in coin, and a graduated return to convertibility by means of a reduction of the price of gold in terms of notes according to a scale fixed over time. Eventually the mint price of gold would be established as its permanent price.[2]

Ricardo entertained no serious doubts concerning the desirability of setting his plan in motion as speedily as possible. However this was contested by some other witnesses drawn from the world of banking and finance. By far the most significant of the latter was Alexander Baring. His evidence to both committees provided the most telling intellectual opposition encountered by Ricardo and the other advocates of resumption, at either the committee stage or in the parliamentary debates which ensued. Hence it is appropriate to concentrate in this study on the divergent approaches of Baring and Ricardo.

RICARDO BEFORE THE COMMITTEES

The Commons committee heard Ricardo's evidence on 4 and 19 March.[3] Ricardo was certain that the paper currency of England could be said to have depreciated and he believed that the sure test of such depreciation was the increase in the price of gold. He distinguished between 'depreciation' and a fall in the value of the currency. Replying to the seventy-eighth question put to him he stated:

> ... the term 'depreciation', I conceive, does not mean a mere diminution in value, but it means a diminished relative value, on a comparison with something which is a standard; and therefore I think it quite possible that a bank note may be depreciated, although it should rise in value, if it did not rise in value in a degree equal to the standard, by which only its depreciation is measured.

To restore the currency to a sound footing it was essential to ensure its stability. At the same time it was highly desirable to avoid the need for employing a large volume of precious metals in domestic circulation. The best system was one involving a paper currency, the volume of which in circulation was regulated so as to maintain a fixed value of that paper in terms of gold. This would not ensure absolute stability, since gold itself could vary in value. Nevertheless gold was the least variable standard that could be adopted. Silver, for example, was liable to greater degrees of variation, especially as the world supply of silver was soon to expand because of increased mechanisation in its mining.[4]

One of Ricardo's questioners challenged that since his plan required a reduction of the market to the mint price of gold, it must involve a contraction of the note issue of the Bank of England and hence a downturn in the level of economic activity (Question 47). At this, Ricardo pleaded ignorance. Under his plan for resumption he believed commodity prices would fall by about five or six per cent, i.e., by the extent of the existing difference between the market and mint prices of gold. Just what effect this would have on an economy which was already in a state of depression, he did not know. 'I am not engaged in trade,' he explained, 'and it does not come much within my own knowledge.' He continued (Question 52): 'An alteration in value of five per cent does not appear to me very formidable; but of this matter I do not profess to know much; I have had very little practical knowledge upon these subjects.'[5]

Although professedly ignorant of some of the wider implications of the deflationary course he was advocating, Ricardo was quite confident that an inconvertible paper currency encouraged 'over-trading' (Questions 91 and 92). He could not be drawn into any precise definition of what he meant by 'over-trading', but he felt that its presence could be indicated by the degree to which bankruptcy was prevalent. Further, the connection between this phenomenon and inconvertible paper was given by the fact that 'men rely more confidently on renewing the discounting of their bills' when the link between paper and gold was severed.

Ricardo was also quite confident that deflation would not be accompanied by any tendency in the community to hoard money (Question 103). 'No man', he assured the committee, 'would willingly lock up his money ... he would be glad to lend his money at interest during the interval that it was necessary for him to keep it.'

Before the Lords committee on 24 and 26 March Ricardo remained adamant concerning the desirability of the swift introduction of his plan.[6] He was convinced (Question 117), than only 'gross misconduct on the part of the Bank' could give rise to difficulties for the economy during the period of transition from a higher to a lower market price of gold in terms of notes.[7] Among the alternatives to his plan which he explicitly rejected were the adoption of a silver standard or the introduction of a bimetallic system which gave the Bank the option of meeting its notes with payments of either gold or silver bullion.

During his first session with the committee Ricardo was involved in an exchange with one of its members (most probably Lauderdale) on the question of the role of effective demand in relation to the general level of economic activity (Questions 58–76). Despite Lauderdale's persistence Ricardo held to the view that increased activity depended on increased investment of capital rather than stimulation of consumer demand. Assuming, as was his habit, that full employment must generally prevail, Ricardo also denied that expansion of credit could have any impact on production in the aggregate. He allowed that the pattern of use of credit facilities could influence the pattern of employment of capital and hence the composition of output. However there was no getting away from the fundamental reality that commodities were produced by commodities.

Lauderdale (assuming it was he) attempted to stress the role of credit in enabling entrepreneurs to create new combinations of resources which led to increased output in the aggregate.[8] Against this, Ricardo invoked his belief in the necessary equality of savings and investment, the impossibility of general over-production and the reality of the assumption of full employment. Neither protagonist seems to have moved the other.[9]

Later Ricardo was able to reiterate that monetary factors could not help provoke greater employment and output (Questions 98 and 99). He allowed that expansion of the money supply in the era of restriction of cash payment may have served to increase profits at the expense of wages. However even this effect was doubtful.[10] It was certain that there had been no impact on the general level of activity. Then, when challenged to explain the growth of the British economy over the previous twenty years (Questions 114 and 115) Ricardo put this down to 'the discovery of improved machinery, and to the industry and ingenuity of our people'. The growth could not be attributed in any way to the activities of those who had indulged in the (undefined) practice of 'over-trading' (Questions 100–103).

THE EVIDENCE OF ALEXANDER BARING

Ricardo's intellectual toughness, as well as some of the starker unrealities of the theoretical system he had fashioned, are most vividly displayed in the above evidence.[11] Experienced bankers, such as Gurney and Attwood, appeared before the committee and endeavoured to counteract Ricardo's influence with predictions of the economic distress that would follow any precipitate attempt to resume cash payments.[12] However the major counterweight to Ricardo's unrealities was provided by the evidence of Alexander Baring.[13] During March Baring gave evidence to both the Lords' and the Commons' committees and in this he touched on most of the points of criticism which, after the passage of the bill for resumption, continued to dog Ricardo for the remainder of his parliamentary career.

Baring was not averse to resumption as a longer-term policy goal and he was positively enthusiastic about that aspect of Ricardo's plan which looked to establishment of a paper currency convertible into bullion. The arrangement was no great novelty and had some foundation in successful business practice.[14] Outside of this, Baring, who drew on a wide range of first-hand knowledge of monetary practices, took a very different view from that of Ricardo on the question of resumption. In his evidence he stressed the relevance of a variety of economic variables that were given scant attention in Ricardo's reasoning.

Baring stated his basic policy goal with regard to the currency as follows: 'I always consider the great desideratum to be, to keep out in circulation as much paper as possible, provided it can be secured from depreciation.'[15] In marked contrast with Ricardo he was prepared to allow that an inconvertible paper currency carried some definite advantages for an economy. The absence of convertibility tended to foster expansion of the money supply and increasing commodity prices which favoured the entrepreneur as against the rentier. Economic growth could be promoted thereby.

Here Baring, by focusing on the dynamics of the forces involved, was affirming what Ricardo had been anxious to deny in the face of Lauderdale's questioning (discussed above). Baring explained:

> . . . Benefit has been derived during the gradual progress of the increase of prices, arising from the increased and unvaried abundance of money; but the benefit is already enjoyed, and more to be found in the progression, than in the actual state of things. The paper system is

undoubtedly particularly favourable to one class of people, viz., to
enterprising speculators; and may be said to be unfavourable to persons
of large capitals. But at the same time it is impossible to deny, that
much of the aggregate wealth of the country has been derived from that
spirit of enterprise.[16]

Despite this major advantage Baring thought a return to a currency
regulated in terms of a fixed metallic standard was highly desirable. He felt
that the constant threat of inflation was too high a price to pay for the
'ease and facility' of the paper system.[17] Nevertheless he made it clear to
both committees that resumption must act to dampen the level of activity
for a period, that it should be undertaken gradually, and that the present
was a most inappropriate time to contemplate taking the step.[18]

As an authority for his view that resumption would have depressive
consequences Baring cited David Hume's *Essay on Money* (1752). In
commending Hume's analysis Baring emphasised the point that the
important consideration was not the size of the money supply at any one
time but rather the rate and direction of change which that variable was
undergoing.[19] Rapid contraction could result in serious dislocation of
business. Summing up on this theme in the Lords committee Baring
stated: 'I feel so much apprehension of the difficulties that attend this
return (to cash payments), and the probable impatience of the country
under an operation so painful, that I have always rated the difficulty of it
higher than I found public opinion generally to do.'[20]

Baring strongly dissented from Ricardo's view that on resumption
commodity prices would fall by only five or six per cent, i.e., to the degree
by which the present market price of gold was in excess of its mint price.
The fall would be considerably greater, he predicted, because of two
factors which Ricardo persisted in ignoring. One of these was the impact
of resumption on world commodity prices. The second was the climate of
uncertainty and the check to business confidence that the change would
evoke.

England's demand for substantial amounts of gold, Baring argued, when
added to the concurrent demands of Austria, Russia, Denmark and the
other states which were attempting to return to metallic currencies, must
serve to depress commodity values in terms of the precious metals
throughout Europe.[21] Further, within England, the new status of the
Bank of England after resumption must engender a degree of deflation.
Baring stated:

> I further think that, the uncertainty as to the accommodation to be
> afforded in time of distress, may make the same amount of money go
> further in a country at one period than at another; and I cannot
> conceive any state of things under a liability to pay in cash which can
> make the public feel a confidence in the same extent of facility, in the

event of occasional distress, as can exist under the present paper circulation, because at every period of distress the bank must feel that distress itself as well as every other establishment, and of course, be unable to afford them assistance; not only the bank will feel the distress really but for the maintenance of its credit will always be taking precautions much beyond what necessity may require.[22]

In making this last observation Baring anticipated the over-reaction of the Bank of England which in fact occurred when parliament legislated for resumption. The Bank set out to accumulate gold, an over-reaction which amazed Ricardo and became a major ground for his recriminations concerning the institution and its directorship from that time on. This was a case where, given his extraordinary propensity to abstract from the state of expectations or business confidence as meaningful economic variables, Ricardo was ill-equipped (by comparison with the sensitive and wide-ranging Baring) to act as a guide to the monetary realities of his time. Hence, Ricardo had no conception of the degree of deflation he was striving to have parliament impose on the British economy. Baring's estimate was to prove far nearer the mark.

As to the time of resumption, Baring thought that four or five years, at least, were necessary to permit the Bank to build up the stock of bullion which would permit it to carry out its normal business functions under convertibility. Such a period of preparation for the change would also help minimise the deflationary impact of the measures required to accumulate a large amount of gold. Further, Baring was certain that to commence even cautious moves towards resumption in the current year would be disastrous. The short-run problem here was created by the phase in the trade cycle at which the British economy now stood:

> The present distress has its origin in one of those fluctuations in commerce, which every five or six years usually occur. Its immediate cause is the great decline of the prices of some of the principal articles of trade, and more particularly the article of cotton, some qualities of which have fallen near 50 per cent. The distress is so considerable, that I think it will take several months before it will be got over; and certainly any considerable diminution of circulation during the period of its existence would tend both to aggravate and prolong it.[23]

Not only should the committees pay attention to the business cycle, according to Baring, but they should also recognise that the economy would be forced to contend with the phenomenon of hoarding if they sanctioned resumption. 'No man', Ricardo had assured his questioners, 'would willingly lock up his money.' However Baring was confident that 'a good deal of gold would be hoarded, a practice which the late experience of the country, as to the depreciation of paper is likely to promote and increase.'[24]

Baring and Ricardo also differed on the crucial issue of the most appropriate criterion for regulation of the size of the money supply. Ricardo insisted on referring to the market price of gold as the means of judging whether or not that supply was excessive. Baring challenged the validity of this view in that it failed to take account of the monopsonistic position of the Bank of England. 'Undoubtedly,' said Baring, 'if the transactions in bullion were quite free, and there existed a general competition, the price of gold bullion would be the most correct mode of estimating the depreciation of paper; but in London, there exists only the bank broker in bullion, and of course no competition . . . '[25] Under these circumstances 'the rates of exchange are a better criterion to judge of the depreciation of paper, than the price of bullion.'[26]

While advocating this latter criterion Baring thought it should be supplemented by a second type of consideration. The appropriate volume of the money supply should be determined by reference to the needs of business for financial accommodation as well as to the rates of exchange. 'Circumstances may have arisen,' observed Baring, 'and perhaps may arise, of commercial difficulties in the country, when the bank may, under the system which has so long been continued, think it right to afford assistance, without immediate reference to the state of the exchanges.'[27] The needs of business, he felt, could be a criterion particularly relevant during any period of transition to full restoration of cash payments. 'Should any particular circumstances of distress occur,' he told the Lords' committee, 'such as exist at the present moment, I should hope, that the measure for a return to bullion payments, however important such an event may be, would be made to give way to the necessary relief of commerce; at the same time, however, that necessity must be very manifest.'[28]

Baring was prepared to give a degree of discretion to the directors of the Bank of England which Ricardo, distrusting their competence, could not allow. Baring was critical of the directors for having denied, 'the principle of the par value of paper being dependent upon the amount of its issue.'[29] Nevertheless, if parliament was to set a date for resumption, 'it should always be with the understanding that the bank should resume earlier if their situations permitted it . . . '[30] Then again, the Bank should be left free to come to the aid of the business community when there was manifest need for accommodation.

Because of these considerations Baring was completely opposed to that aspect of Ricardo's plan for resumption which would have parliament impose on the Bank a fixed time scale for a progressive return to convertibility of its notes at the mint price of gold. When asked for his opinion of Ricardo's proposal, Baring replied: 'I should fear that the Bank would, in its practical operations, be tied down more than would be consistent with the public interest.'[31] Further, he did not believe that Ricardo's provision for a gradual reduction in the price at which notes were exchanged for gold gave the least protection against substantial, short term contraction of the note issue. Baring affirmed: 'I believe that the bank, to pay at the present market price of gold, would require nearly as large a stock of that metal as to pay at the mint price; and that the trade of the country would be put under the same restrictive system which would be required to return to the old state of currency.'[32]

Drawing on his experience of the French monetary system Baring proposed that England should eventually adopt bimetallism so that the Bank would have the option of changing its notes for silver as well as gold. Such an arrangement was anathema to Ricardo, but Baring was moved to suggest it because of his belief in the desirability of maximising the money supply subject only to the constraint of avoiding inflation.[33]

Despite his experience and authority it is questionable whether any members of either committee seriously considered implementation of Baring's proposal. It is also doubtful whether many of them were moved by his 'practical' criticism of the Ricardo plan, or by his devastating exposure of the weaknesses of Ricardo as a monetary theorist. The general impression one gains of the committees is of groups of men who were not particularly interested in canvassing a wide spectrum of possibilities for a future monetary system. As Professor Fetter has observed: '. . . both in the selection and questioning of witnesses the committees secured an appearance of unanimity of public opinion that was not in accord with facts.'[34]

PEEL'S FIRST REPORT

The chairman of the Commons' committee, Robert Peel, reported initially to the House on 5 April.[35] His purpose was to secure passage of an act which would 'restrain the issue of sovereigns for fractional payments under 5l. in consequence of notices issued in the course of 1816–17, in which they (the Bank directors) undertook to pay all notes dated previously to the 1st of Jan. 1817.' Peel explained that the partial resumption set in train by these notices had resulted in a substantial drain of gold from England to France. Further drain must be stopped to make the full restoration of cash payments a possibility. 'Whenever the time came for removing the restriction,' Peel argued, 'a large sum in cash would be necessary; that sum considerably exceeded the sum which the Bank had at present in its possession.'

The Whigs Henry Brougham and George Tierney fulminated at the proposed legislation.[36] The measure was merely designed to protect the private interests of the Bank. That institution had lost its gold through its own folly in continuing to issue notes and through its complicity in the machinations of Vansittart, the Chancellor of the Exchequer. It should be obliged to make good the undertakings of which it had given notice.

Castlereagh replied that the new bill was brought forward in the public interest, 'in the purest spirit of contributing to the resumption of cash payments at the earliest period'.[37] Then Ricardo came in on the government side in oppostion to the whig line.[38] Ricardo agreed with Brougham and Tierney that the conduct of the Bank had been 'improvident'. He also agreed that it could not expand its note issue further but must reduce the issue to obtain an adequate supply of gold. 'But then,' he continued, 'that reduction ought to be gradual and in order to enable the Bank to resume its cash payments, such a measure as that now proposed appeared to him essentially necessary.'

By this Ricardo indicated that he could not be made a tool of the whig campaign for short-run political capital on the currency question. In fact, he went so far as to suggest that the current whig posture was such as to promote a set of circumstances which must encourage the unscrupulous to break the law of the land by secretly exporting or melting gold coin.

The bill was duly passed by the House, having been given only token readings on its second and third commitments.[39] However at the third reading Hudson Gurney raised the spectre of the measure's impact on business confidence. Ricardo and other previous speakers had abstracted from the presence of that dimension of the question.[40] Gurney predicted:

> The measure would be productive of more evil, than could be compensated by any good that might be expected to accrue from it. It was brought forward at a moment of great commercial pressure, and great suspicion in the monied part of the community, and appeared likely to occasion a degree of alarm extremely to be deprecated.

Gurney believed that the legislation was singularly ill-timed. It was designed in terms of events which had ceased to exercise a significant influence on the domestic economy. 'The three reasons given for gold having reached an adventitious price', he pointed out, 'were the large issues of Bank notes, the demand for gold for France in consequence of the payments to the allied powers, and the great importation of corn. The Bank issues were lessened. The demand for France was over. — The ports were closed against the importation of corn; and now, surely, if ever, gold might be expected to find its natural level in this country.'

Any attempt by the legislature to reduce the market price of gold to its mint price, Gurney warned, would be fraught with danger 'under the burdens contracted during the late war'. Such action could not be undertaken 'without dragging down the prices of all other things to a degree which would render those burdens absolutely unbearable'.[41] With this statement Gurney touched on a theme that was destined to become a major one in the debates of subsequent years.

THE COMMITTEES' PLAN

The Secret Committees reported to their respective Houses on 6 and 7 May. By the end of the same month both Lords and Commons had agreed to a plan for gradual resumption of cash payments. At the same time the long-standing laws concerning prohibitions on the melting and exportation of the coin of the realm were repealed.[42]

The agreed resolutions of the Committees envisaged four stages of progression to full restoration of cash payments. The first was to extend from 1 February to 1 October 1820, and in it the holders of Bank notes could obtain bullion at a fixed price of £4 1s 0d per ounce. It was also provided that the bullion should take the form of bars weighing 60 ounces, and that these could be exchanged only for notes equivalent to the value of 60 ounces.[43] Silver coins would be used to exchange for notes involving values in excess of the 60 ounces equivalent, but less than 40 ounces in excess of the same.

The second stage of the plan, 1 October 1820 to 1 May 1821, retained the same arrangements, except that the price of bullion was reduced to £3 19s 6d per ounce. In the third stage, 1 May 1821 to 1 May 1823, the only change would be a further and final reduction of price to £3 17s 10½d per ounce. Then, on the latter date, provisions for payment in bullion only (or bullion plus silver coins) were to cease. At this juncture, there would be full and free exchange of gold coinage against notes on demand from the holder.

These reports represented a signal victory for Ricardo, and the Lords committee, in particular, put particular emphasis on the virtues of his proposals 'in preference to a simple resumption, in the first instance, of cash payments by the Bank'.[44] Ricardo wrote to McCulloch (8 May 1819): 'The Committee have deviated in two points from the plan as originally suggested — they think that the bars of bullion delivered by the Bank, in exchange for notes, should be assayed, and stamped, at the Mint; and they have advised that after 1823, at the latest, we should revert to the old system of specie payments. Perhaps, in both instances, they have done right . . .'[45]

5 1819: The Debates on Resumption

No country in the world had ever established a currency without a fixed standard of value ... It might be gold, it might be silver, it might be copper, or even iron. It might be anything that had real value in it; though the metals had been preferred for this purpose by the general consent of all nations. But it could not be paper, which has no value, and is only promise of value'.

The Earl of Liverpool
House of Lords, 21 May 1819.

The Ricardo Plan for resumption, as recommended by the Secret Committees, was debated in the Lords on 21 May. However before the debate proper, Lauderdale introduced a petition from the merchants of London requesting retention of the restriction on cash payments.[1] The Earl was most sympathetic to the viewpoint of the petitioners inasmuch as 'they objected to the plan of the Bank committees, as tending to produce a forced diminution of the circulating medium, and thereby to cause the greatest distress ...'

Immediately after this Lauderdale called for presentation of a recent letter to the Chancellor of the Exchequer from the directors of the Bank of England. The Prime Minister agreed, and the letter was read.[2] In it the directors stated that the course of action advocated by the parliamentary committees was 'fraught with very great uncertainty and risk'. The directors were concerned particularly that they should in no way appear to acquiesce in a plan 'which seems to take away from the Bank anything like a discretionary consideration of the necessities and distresses of the commercial world'.

THE PRIME MINISTER'S ADDRESS

Seemingly unmoved by the forebodings of much of the business opinion of London and the provinces, the Earl of Harrowby, the Lord President of the Council, brought forward a series of six resolutions necessary to give effect to the proposals of the Secret Committees.[3] Lauderdale countered with seven resolutions by way of amendment. The thrust of these amendments was most evident in the seventh which stated that, 'an alteration of our mint regulations, such as will approximate the mint values of our silver and gold coin to the market values of these metals, is a necessary preliminary step to the restoration of our currency to a satisfactory state'.[4] As his remarks on the merchants' petition had indicated, Lauderdale was worried about a 'forced diminution' of the money supply. If the mint price of gold was raised to its present market price, rather than the market reduced to the mint price as Ricardo's plan required, then the diminution might be avoided.

Liverpool then spoke at length to the measures before the House.[5] His first basic consideration was the inadvisability of continuing with a set of arrangements which allowed the Bank 'the power of making money, without any other check or influence to direct them, than their own notions of profit and interest'. Secondly, state control of the note issue was not a welcome alternative. 'Nothing could be more unwise', he stated, 'than for government to erect itself into a company of bankers'. Thirdly, the country needed a standard of value and that standard must consist of something that 'had real value in it'. Paper could not be a true standard since it has 'no value, and is only promise of value'.

With these three points Liverpool had touched on some of the leading beliefs conditioning the thought of many of his contemporaries on the monetary aspects of the structure of an economy. In the first place there was the assumption that private pursuit of maximum, individual gain would maximise public welfare (as Adam Smith had taught), but not in the case of outright monopoly. The Bank could not be criticised for acting in the best interests of its proprietors, but those interests could not always coincide with the national interest while the Bank enjoyed its existing degree of freedom from legislative check. Secondly, a government-run central bank of issue did not appear practicable, given the prevailing philosophies of government and the realities of the organisational structure of public administration. Finally, the concept of a managed paper currency was an affront to the post-medieval European acceptance of the myth of metallism, i.e., the belief that money to function effectively as money must consist of a material that has a value independent of its function as money.

The viability of the British economy during the years of coincidence of war and restriction on cash payments had given some thinkers cause to question metallism in a thorough-going manner.[6] However other factors conspired to keep the old myth alive, even if only in a much modified form such as bullionism. Among these factors was the desire for a practical safeguard against depredation of personal wealth by inflation. More fundamental still was the prevailing notion of property as a 'sacred right', property (including money in balances) being understood as possessions inherited or gained by personal expenditure of 'labour'.

Given these basic considerations, the Prime Minister was willing to recommend adoption of the committees' plan. Like Ricardo, he was optimistic that only a small contraction of the note issue would be necessary to ensure 'return to the fixed and ancient standard of value', since the present difference between the market and the mint prices of gold was a mere 3 per cent. Liverpool admitted that a degree of controversy surrounded the question of the impact on business activity of a decrease in the money supply. However the controversy was understandable since 'the commercial world would be always against the resumption of cash payments; as it would diminish the facilities with which they at present obtained accommodation'.

At this point Liverpool took up the evidence tendered to the committees by Baring. He allowed that he had 'never heard anything more intelligent and comprehensive' on the issues at hand.[7] Liverpool agreed that suspension of cash payments had been beneficial in war and carried some definite advantages in peace. Not the least of those advantages was the enhanced ability of the Bank to check the onset of economic difficulties by continuing to grant accommodation to businessmen with liquidity problems. Nevertheless he felt that the advantages of an inconvertible paper currency were outweighed by its disadvantages. Despite the force of Baring's arguments, Liverpool believed the existing system 'was too often an encouragement to speculation, to unsound dealings, to the accumulation of fictitious capital . . . on the long-run it tended to destroy that solid and secure foundation on which the commerce of a great nation ought to rest'. It was true that the effect of a return to cash payments 'might be in some degree to limit mercantile transactions, but it would be to place them on a firm and honourable basis. People would know where they were'.

Having rebutted Baring with this hollow rhetoric, the Prime Minister added that those who feared contraction of the currency generally overlooked the fact that, in a modern economy, hoarding was virtually non-existent. Further, they forgot that banking as a business had been subject to 'the same spirit of enterprise and talent which when directed to mechanics had discovered the powers of the steam-engine and the spinning-wheel'. The result of this latter was that a much greater volume of transactions could be supported by the same quantity of money now as compared with earlier decades. Hence, Liverpool was confident that their lordships 'would see the ancient standard of the country restored without material distress to any class of his majesty's subjects'.

LAUDERDALE OBJECTS

The Earl of Lauderdale congratulated Liverpool on his emphasis concerning the need for a fixed standard of value. At the same time, however, he found the Prime Minister to have grossly underestimated the difficulties involved in reaching that goal. Particularly, Lauderdale questioned the belief of the advocates of Ricardo's plan that the market price of bullion would be necessarily reduced by the impact of a reduction in the note issue on the foreign exchanges. He doubted whether the Bank, in this fashion, could exercise 'a command over the exchanges'.[8]

Lauderdale also contended that silver rather than gold was the operative standard of value for England. He pointed out that in March 1817, when the new silver coinage had been issued, there had been the coincidence of a nominally unfavourable turn of the foreign exchanges against the country. Yet, since that time, silver had continued to flow into England, a fact which indicated that in reality the exchanges were favourable. The latter were nominally unfavourable in terms of gold but 'the real exchanges had been uniformly favourable when calculated in silver, the only metallic coin in circulation'. Lauderdale added that if the paper currency of England had really depreciated then silver would not have continued to be imported.

The proposed plan for resumption was extremely dangerous in Lauderdale's opinion, if introduced without adjustment of the Mint regulations. He repeated his earlier call for the mint to 'approximate the mint values of our silver and gold coin to the market values of these metals'. This step would ensure an adequate metallic circulation in the country and thus facilitate resumption without ill effect to business.

Lauderdale also found much of the current reasoning on resumption faulty in that it ignored the existence of the need to satisfy a transactions demand for coinage. More generally, that reasoning ignored the problem of effective demand as a whole. In the first place, he criticised the views of Adam Smith:

> On the subject of productive capital Dr. Smith's work contained some absurd ideas: holding all circulating medium to be unproductive capital, he said that if a part of the gold in circulation were to be sent out of the country, manufactures and materials of greater use were obtained instead.

Yet, continued Lauderdale, gold 'performed a very important duty as an equivalent for ordinary payment' and to obtain it from overseas 'a new demand must be created for our manufactures'.

This latter, Lauderdale admitted, would be seen by some as a non-problem. It would present no difficulty for those who 'entertain the notion of Mr. Ricardo, that whether there was an extension or diminution of demand, was a matter of perfect indifference, because the quantity of manufactures must always be the same'.[9]

FURTHER SUPPORT FOR RESUMPTION

Lords King and Grenville, and the Marquis of Lansdowne then came out against any delay in the restoration of cash payments. King welcomed the deflationary tendency of the committees' plan because it would favour rentiers at the expense of entrepreneurs. The former had suffered injustice through inflation during the years of restriction. Now the balance would be redressed. For too long, he believed 'wealth was taken in part from those who did not actively employ it, and given to those who did'.[10]

King also welcomed the legislation as tending to discourage the practice of 'over-trading', which he thought had been all too prevalent. This practice he defined as 'increasing shipments to an extravagant amount in one year, while in the next a proportionate diminution of demand below the average, and a proportionate languor ensued.' King's remarks on this subject indicates that he, like many other parliamentarians of the day, had very little grasp of what was entailed in the operation of a laissez-faire, enterprise economy. In particular they seemed incapable of appreciating the role played by the expectations of entrepreneurs concerning the future state of effective demand.[11]

Lord Grenville urged an even speedier return to cash payments than that proposed by the Secret Committees.[12] He looked to the earliest possible dissolution of 'the ominous and dangerous confederacy between the government and the Bank'. At the same time, in an obvious reference to Ricardo, he praised the plan for resumption in that 'it came recommended by a name which of all others in Europe would be most likely to recommend any question of political economy.' He utterly rejected the viewpoint of Alexander Baring to which the Prime Minister had lent some credence. However he applauded Liverpool's emphasis on the necessity of restoring gold as the standard of value. 'Without value', he reasoned, 'it was impossible to represent value: it was as absurd as it would be to attempt to measure weight by that which had no weight or to measure length by that which had no extent.' Strengthened by these naive physical analogies, Grenville concluded that there was no alternative except a return to 'the sacred standard of metallic value . . . which could alone restore its native vigour to our finance.'

Apparently most of the peers were impressed by the sanctity of the object of Ricardo's plan. After a speech by Lansdowne, which included an attack on Lauderdale's claim that silver was the true standard, Lauderdale's resolutions failed to gain assent and the committees' recommendations were approved.

At this there was an immediate reaction throughout the business community. *The New Times* reported (24 May 1819): 'No sooner was it known that the Resolutions in favour of Mr Ricardo's novel and visionary scheme passed the House (of Lords) without a division that an actual panic took place on the Stock Exchange.' The mechanisms triggering such an event had been given scant attention by Ricardo in his theoretical schema and he commented to his friend Trower: 'The alarm that prevailed in the City is incomprehensible.'[13]

PEEL LEADS IN THE COMMONS

On 24 May Sir Robert Peel (the elder) introduced in the Commons the petition of the merchants of London against resumption.[14] No member, apart from Sir Robert, lent support to its sentiments and then Robert Peel, as Chairman of the Secret Committee of the Commons, rose to present the Committee's findings to the House.[15]

Peel began by admitting that in 1811 he had voted against similar resolutions stemming from the report of the Bullion Committee. Nevertheless, he had since reversed his opinions, especially because of evidence and discussion in the present committee. Now he accepted that 'the true standard of value consisted in a definite quantity of gold bullion'. The best test of whether or not the money supply was excessive or deficient was the price of gold in the market.[16]

An inconvertible paper currency encouraged over-trading and led to economic fluctuations which 'deranged all the relations of humble life'. Further it involved parliament's abrogating its public responsibilities in favour of a private body, the Bank. 'The House had too long transferred its powers', declared Peel, 'Let it recover the authority which it had so long abdicated.'

Peel continued that those who argued that gold was an unreliable standard of value because its market price could vary considerably, were guilty of confusing 'price' and 'value'. 'When people talked of gold rising in price', he challenged, 'were they prepared to show that it had risen in intrinsic value? Let them not talk of its price in paper, but in any other commodity of a real or fixed value.' Another fallacy among the opponents of a gold standard was the idea that 'the circulating medium should increase with the trade, taxation, and revenue' of the nation. This was invalidated by the train of events since 1792 which demonstrated that 'a much less circulation was necessary, and would perform transactions to a greater amount, at one time than at another.'

Before moving the committees' resolutions, Peel attempted to answer Lauderdale's points concerning silver and the mint regulations.[17] Then, without division, the House agreed in principle to a gradual resumption of cash payments and to a gradual repayment of £10 million to the Bank on account of prior loans to the government.

A SPEEDIER RESUMPTION PROPOSED

A series of amendments to Peel's resolutions was moved by Edward Ellice.[18] He wished to see the possibility of an earlier full resumption than that allowed for in Ricardo's plan and to that end he suggested that the Bank be given the option of meeting its notes in coin, as well as in gold at the mint price, after 1 May 1821. In addition, parliament should oblige the Bank to pay in coin after 1 May 1822. He also moved that the government should rapidly repay its loans from the Bank and that it should be limited in any future use of financing by way of exchequer bills. The stated rationale of these amendments was to prevent Vansittart, the Chancellor of the Exchequer, from engaging in the monetary practices of which Ellice had complained on previous occasions (see Chapter 3).

These amendments had the support of George Tierney, who acknowledged that he was the only member of the Commons' committee who had not agreed to the details for gradual resumption.[19] 'There was no security for the empire but in a recourse to a metallic currency,' declared Tierney: 'No man's property could be safe, or even have a value until that wholesome state was restored.' As he saw the question of the timing of resumption, it was one of direct conflict between the true principles of political economy and a sectional business interest: 'The issue then was between statesmen and philosophers, acting upon solid principles of political economy, and Bank directors who considered only their own peculiar convenience, and private interests.'

Nicholas Vansittart then rose to commend the committees' plan, although he admitted that 'public clamour had been excited against it.'[20] His main ground for supporting the plan was a decidedly vague one and he put his argument in such a way as to suggest that his commendation was half hearted, at best. Vansittart stated: 'However desirable the resumption of cash payments was, the public had hitherto experienced no inconvenience from the paper currency, as it had answered internally every purpose of metallic payment. The proposed plan, however, would prove highly advantageous by providing against any unforeseen event, arising from public alarm, or sudden commotion'.[21]

The Chancellor also joined those other speakers in both Houses who had paid tribute to the quality of Baring's evidence before the Secret Committees. That evidence, he affirmed, 'was certainly the most important of any, from the details of facts and reasonings into which that gentleman had entered.'

Speaking next, William Manning, the Bank director, was able to be much more free than Vansittart in expressing his distaste for the Ricardo plan.[22] 'The resolutions, if passed in their present shape,' he warned, 'would have the effect of fettering the Bank so as to cause an inconvenient reduction of the currency.' Manning's main worry was that the aspect of the plan which obliged the Bank 'to pay at the intermediate times in bullion, at a certain price, without reference to circumstances, might have a mischievous effect on the country'. This was the feature which Baring in his evidence had found so objectionable, and Manning was prepared to allow that even Ellice's amendments, aimed at swift resumption, offered a procedure preferable to that envisaged by the committees. Manning concluded by predicting that the Bank would be able to achieve a complete resumption by 1821 if it was not hampered by the inflexibilities of Ricardo's scheme.

RICARDO'S GREAT HOUR

Ricardo followed Manning with a speech which, so the Hansard record suggests, produced the greatest measure of acclaim that he was to receive on the floor of the House during his entire parliamentary career. When he concluded shortly before 2 a.m., the reporter notes that, 'the hon. member sat down amidst loud and general cheering from all sides of the House.'[23] It was a great moment for the principles of political economy as against the supposedly self-interested wisdom of the world of commerce. Subsequent events do not suggest that this triumph of lawyers and aristocrats over bankers and entrepreneurs was such a great moment for the vast bulk of the populace.

Ricardo moved straight into an attack on the competence of the Bank directors and the reliability of governmental monetary policy. As he saw it, it was a case of 'ministers and the Bank on one side, and the country on the other'. Parliament would be failing in its duty to the people if it left discretion concerning resumption in the hands of the Cabinet and the Bank.

The basic monetary reality involved in this debate was quite clear, according to Ricardo. He stated:

> Those who had the power of regulating the quantity of the circulating medium of the country, had the power of regulating the rate of the exchanges and the price of every commodity. This power clearly resided in the hands of the directors of the Bank, and it was a most formidable one.[24]

The basic monetary policy required was also clear and the measure was far from draconian:

> The difficulty was only that of raising the currency 3 per cent in value. And who could doubt that even in those states in which the currency was entirely metallic, it often suffered a variation equal to

this, without inconvenience to the public . . . By withdrawing paper, so as to restore the note to its bullion value (an alteration, by the bye, only of 3 per cent), the House would have done all that was required.

This alteration, he believed, could be effected with little risk of dislocation of existing commercial arrangements, if the House agreed to implement the committees' resolutions. The House should not countenance the alternative of restoring cash payments in terms of gold coin, as Edward Ellice proposed. Ellice's amendment would give rise to an unnecessary degree of deflation. 'An extraordinary demand would take place for gold, for the purpose of coinage,' Ricardo predicted, 'which would enhance the value of the currency 3 or 4 per cent in addition to the first enhancement.' Ricardo was also opposed to the idea of the government repaying its previous advances from the Bank. This particular motion was unacceptable because 'the Bank was a cautious and timid body, and if they had no other means of supplying the requisite amount of circulation but by discounting bills, he feared the public might suffer from a scarcity of money.'

Ricardo continued on this anti-deflationary theme with advice to the Bank directors that they ought to use caution in the manner in which they reduced their note issue during the transition period specified by the Secret Committees. At the same time they should not buy bullion but rather, 'should boldly sell. Every sale would improve the exchanges, and till gold fell to 31.17s.6d. there would be no necessity for the Bank to make any purchases.'

The committees' plan, Ricardo assured members, was 'perfectly safe and gentle', except for the omission of one provision. Ricardo was 'sorry that the Bank was not to be obliged by the resolutions to buy all the bullion offered to them at 31.17s.6d. lest through excessive caution they might starve the circulation.' Such a provision was desirable to cover the possibility of a short fall in the circulation during the period between the Bank's contracting its note issue and the coining of gold at the Mint.

Returning to the subject of the past behaviour of the Bank, Ricardo charged that 'the indiscreet language' of its directors concerning the reduction in the money supply had created business panic. He professed himself 'quite astonished that such an alarm prevailed at a reduction of perhaps one million in four years.' If parliament had come to lose confidence in the Bank, he added, it was 'from a conviction of its total ignorance of the principles of political economy'. The Bank directors should give up the attempt at playing the role of cabinet ministers and concentrate instead on serving the interests of the proprietors of that institution.

In conclusion, Ricardo briefly dismissed as irrelevant the fears which Lauderdale and Grant had expressed concerning silver and the mint regulations.[25] He also was highly optimistic concerning the outcome of the plan for resumption:

> A most fearful and destructive depreciation had at one time taken place; but from that we had so far retraced our steps. We had nearly got home . . . He would venture to state that in a very few weeks all alarm would be forgotten, and at the end of the year, we should all be surprised to reflect that any alarm had ever prevailed at a prospect of a variation of 3 per cent in the value of the circulating medium.

This optimistic statement was, in later years, to provide a ready base for criticism of Ricardo in parliamentary debate and in the press. At this time, however, the Commons were eager to accept his assurance. 'The phenomenon of that night', so Mallet records, 'was Ricardo; who notwithstanding his slender footing in the House, his jewish name and his shrill voice, obtained the greatest attention, and was cheered throughout his speech . . .'[26]

A RALLY AGAINST RICARDO

When debate resumed the following day, Heygate, Gurney, Lord Folkestone and Joseph Marryat assailed Ricardo's position. Alderman Heygate led off with the claim that there had been no depreciation of the currency, as Ricardo had contended, and he asked his fellow legislators to 'pause before they imposed on the Bank the necessity of constantly referring to the price of gold, as the only standard for the extension or diminution of its issues.'[27] Empirically, he pointed out, it was not the case that, 'the price of gold might always be regulated by a reduction of paper.'

Heygate cited Alexander Baring, 'who was perhaps the most enlightened merchant in Europe', in support of the contention that resumption now would give rise to such a contraction of the money supply as to cause 'general embarrassment and distress' throughout the economy. The country was in the grip of depression, and the distress would be intensified by resumption, since every businessman would be trading in fear of the possibility of a run on the Bank engendered by the activities of foreign speculators. 'There must, consequently, be but little employment for labour, and a great increase of the poor rates', Heygate deduced: 'He knew this to be the feeling and expectation of a large proportion of that part of the community engaged in carrying on our agriculture, commerce, and manufactures.'

The Alderman not only pinpointed Ricardo's habitual neglect of the state of expectations, but also his tendency to abstract from capital immobilities in rural and in secondary industry. Merchants, bankers and bullion dealers did not face the same immobility problems as farmers and industrialists, Heygate claimed, yet acceptance of the Ricardo plan by the Secret Committees was based on evidence drawn almost exclusively from representatives of the first three categories of business. In Heygate's opinion. 'those who had studied this subject had been guided too much by theory and too little by practice.'

Gurney found Ricardo's obsession with the sanctity of the current mint price of gold to be a major stumbling block.[28] He believed that great economic instability had been created already by 'this erroneous determination, that an ounce of gold should under the taxation of a debt of 800 millions, pass for no more than 31.17s.10½d. happen what might — from whence the necessary consequence has followed, that it has gone where it would purchase more.' Gurney then launched the first of many attacks to come on the relevance of Ricardo's statement that 'the difficulty was only that of raising the currency 3 per cent in value'. That small existing difference between the mint and market prices of gold, said Gurney, 'merely proved the depression of price in all other articles; and it must be obvious that under this depression we could not go on.'

Rather like Lauderdale, Gurney looked to a revision of the mint regulations concerning the price of gold. It was courting disaster, in his opinion, to attempt to appreciate the currency over a three year span as Ricardo urged. To do this, he contended, 'was the equivalent to working upon a three years falling market; and instead of three per cent, he feared we must calculate whether our farmers and manufacturers could afford to drop 20 per cent upon their prices, and pay their taxes, their workmen, and their rents.' This view gained immediate support from Lord Folkestone who was particularly concerned about the increased burden on the economy of interest payments on the public debt and of fixed personal income payments out of the public purse in an era of deflation.[29]

Joseph Marryat was another to express his complete lack of sympathy with Ricardo.[30] Under the plan for resumption, he believed, the Bank was exposed to a run on its reserves in the event of any crisis of business confidence. To preserve its position, the Bank would be forced into a sudden contraction of its issues and the economy would be plunged into depression. Ricardo's 'whimsical advice' to the committees of enquiry compared most unfavourably with the evidence of Baring on this as on other points. Of Baring, Marryat stated that, 'no man's authority stands higher upon all matters of commercial intelligence.'

Marryat was particularly scathing concerning Ricardo's urging the Bank to deplete its existing bullion reserves so as 'to turn the foreign exchanges in our favour, and thus bring it (the bullion) back again with advantage'. The notion of gaining an adequate gold reserve in a short period by selling stocks of that very commodity he found 'a most paradoxical proposition'. One of the main flaws in Ricardo's argument, according to Marryat, was the unreal supposition that the foreign exchanges were unaffected by factors other than the size of the note issue. In fact the state of the exchanges depended upon the 'balance of trade and payments' which in turn was a function of the 'enterprise of our manufacturers and merchants'. Because that enterprise would be damaged by the introduction of Ricardo's plan, concluded Marryat, the payments situation would deteriorate and the exchanges move against England. The expected inflow of bullion would not follow reduction of the note issue.

Vitiating all of Ricardo's economic reasoning, in Marryat's opinion, was his false methodology. His approach was that of a philosopher and not that of a 'practical man'. As an illustration of this basic defect Marryat cited Ricardo's attitude to the present climate of uncertainty in the business community:

> The commercial part of the community find their capital daily diminishing, by the depreciation in the value of all commodities; their warehouses are full, their purses empty, and failures among them continually taking place ... An honourable member (Mr. Ricardo) says there is a great panic abroad; but that though men are frightened, they ought not to be frightened. This is very philosophical; but putting the case fairly between the philosophers and the alarmists, I really think the latter will be found to have reason on their side.

The underlying defect of the Secret Committees, Marryat thought, was in their permitting the views of philosophers like Ricardo to predominate. Such views could not be trusted, since they were based on a scientific spirit of fascination with experimentation rather than on a genuine concern for human welfare. Marryat reminded the House of Edmund Burke's anathema regarding the persons concerned:

> These philosophers consider men in their experiments, no more than they do mice in an air pump, or in a recipient of mephitic gas. They are carried on with such a headlong rage towards their desperate trials, that they would sacrifice the whole human race, to the slightest of their experiments.[31]

THE RICARDO PLAN PREVAILS

Sir Henry Parnell and Robert Wilmot-Horton both hailed the committees' resolutions as a 'triumph of sound principles of political economy'.[32] Castlereagh too came to the defence of the legislation and paid tribute to Ricardo as a member 'who was not less clear in his opinions than happy in illustrating them'.[33] Like Ricardo he could find no ground for the current alarm in the business world and he was confident that it would quickly disappear. However, he differed from Ricardo on the question of the depreciation of the note issue. He accepted that notes were depreciated in terms of gold but 'the diminution of value was not positive but relative only . . . diminution or depreciation was never such as to be experienced in the purchase of home commodities, manufactures, or product.' Further, unlike Ricardo, he was complimentary concerning the past conduct of the Bank, although he admitted that its present opposition to the plan for resumption was 'by no means warranted or reasonable'.

This much said, Castlereagh then allowed that 'it was impossible to disguise from themselves the impossibility of returning to a metallic currency without causing some pressure to the country.' He proceeded to make it plain to the House that at least some members of Cabinet did not find the present an appropriate point in time to begin the move to cash payments. The state of money markets on the Continent and the outflow of British capital both told against resumption. Ministers, however, 'were diverted from that circumstance by the determination of parliament itself and the public anxiety.' The matter having been taken up by parliament at such length it could not be left unsettled.[34]

When Castlereagh concluded, Ellice withdrew his earlier amendments. Several members attempted to speak, but loud calls of 'question' made this impossible. Eventually Canning managed to restore some order and, after a brief reply by Peel, he asked for 'an undivided vote' on the issue for the sake of 'tranquillising men's minds'. At this there was some protest, but Canning renewed his request for 'an acquiescence in the unanimous determination of parliament, that the country should return, as speedily as possible, to the ancient standard of value in the establishment of a metallic currency.' Hansard records that this statement was received with 'loud and universal cries' of assent. The resolutions were passed 'without a dissentient voice'.[35]

AMENDMENTS AND REARGUARD ACTION

When the bill was read a third time in the Commons on 14 June Edward Ellice moved for the inclusion of a clause that would give the Bank the option of short-circuiting the process of graduated return to full convertibility.[36] The clause allowed the Bank to begin exchanging its notes for coin at 1 May 1821, if it should so desire. This amendment was accepted by the Commons, but the Lords altered the relevant date to 1 May 1822. Less than two years later (March 1821) the government itself introduced Ellice's option and the Bank took it up. Hence the Ricardo plan was never permitted to run its projected course.

Ellice also moved for deletion of those clauses of the bill which provided for resumption by intermediate steps. In this he was unsuccessful and when the matter came to the vote he was one of the small band of twenty-three who did not give their assent to the bill as it stood. Others in this minority were William Heygate, Joseph Marryat, J. P. Grant and the Bank directors William Manning and John Pearse.

Two days later Peel asked for leave 'to bring in a bill to establish regulations for the purchase of government securities by the Bank'.[37] This bill would provide for the necessity of parliamentary authority for any future advances to government by the Bank. Peel indicated that sales of exchequer bills were included. The measure immediately drew fire from Ricardo who saw it as an unwarranted interference with legitimate private enterprise. 'The Bank', said Ricardo, 'ought not be in any way shackled in the management of their own affairs. Great inconveniences, in the diminution of the circulating medium, might result from establishing too strict a limit on this subject.'[38] Despite this protest, the bill eventually passed in the Commons on 25 June.

In the Lords on 15 June, Lauderdale made an unsuccessful attempt to revive the issues of the silver standard and the mint regulations.[39] However when the bill for resumption was brought in for commitment on 21 June, Lauderdale welcomed it.[40] He was especially pleased in that he believed that it returned from the Bank 'what was once considered as the greatest power and pride of the prerogative of the Crown — the right of regulating the currency of the country'.

The Marquis of Lansdowne also welcomed the measure and he expressed the hope that 'the country would never again hear of the theories founded on the abstract idea of a pound sterling as a unit'.[41] Liverpool was somewhat more restrained and he repeated Castlereagh's reservation that the government would have preferred to delay resumption had not the wishes of the nation been against it.[42] Nevertheless the government was now clearly resigned to the legislation and, as there were no further speakers, the bill was committed. On 23 June the bill was read a third time and passed in the Lords. Two days later it received final assent in the Commons.[43]

REVIEW

None of the speakers in these debates expressed outright support for the indefinite suspension of cash payments.[44] None except the Prime Minister (who regarded the idea as quite impractical), canvassed the idea of a managed paper currency under the control of a government-run central bank. For all of them, then, it was a question of the timing and manner of return to some form of arrangement which related paper to metal.

From first to last, prominent members of the Cabinet took the view that initiation of a movement towards cash payments should be delayed by at least one more year. The Bank of England remained hostile to the committees' proposals, but spokesmen for the Bank, like Manning and Pears, found even less sympathy in parliament than did the Cabinet. Those few members who feared resumption must lead to sudden contraction of the note issue and a depression of the level of economic activity lent some assistance to the Bank's position.

Ricardo came to be cast in the role of the main intellectual authority, among those then in parliament, on the technique of resumption. 'I had the courage to set myself foremost in the battle', he wrote to Trower (28 May 1819), 'and was amply rewarded by the support of the House . . .'[45] His most able critic, by far, was Alexander Baring, but Baring did not participate in the debates and thus could not enhance the already substantial impact made by his evidence in committee. In the Lords, the idiosyncratic Lauderdale was able to offer some meaningful criticisms. In the Commons members who, like Baring, had a strong commercial background, provided the best analyses of the weaknesses of Ricardo's stance. Gurney, Marryat, Ellice and Heygate were able to articulate some of the grounds on which entrepreneurs felt threatened by this exercise in applied Ricardianism.

In both committee and debate Ricardo remained very much his own man. He was anything but a spokesman for the business community, setting himself firmly against its representations. Rather he clung religiously to those monetary principles he had enunciated some years before when the British economy was on a wartime footing. A rugged independent, he was critical of many aspects of government policy but could not be used by the Whigs to serve their political fortunes. Again, he was scathing concerning the policies and pretensions of the Bank, but he was prepared to defend it against Peel's motion to limit its freedom to conduct what he regarded as legitimate banking business. Although his plan for resumption was not followed in detail, and some of the blind spots of his theoretical system were probed in debate by a few perceptive critics, the entire episode enhanced Ricardo's personal stature and political significance as an independent voice with which many members could find themselves in agreement on a fundamental policy issue.

6 1819: In the Wake of Peterloo

Swellfoot: Out with your knife, old Moses, and spay those sows
    That load the earth with pigs; cut close and deep,
    Moral restraint, I see, has no effect,
    Nor prostitution, nor our own example,
    Starvation, typhus fever, war, nor prison —
    This was the art which the arch-priest of Famine
    Hinted at in his charge to the Theban clergy —
    Cut close and deep, good Moses.
Moses: Let your Majesty
    Keep the boars quiet, else —
Swellfoot: Zephaniah, cut
    That fat hog's throat; the brute seems overfed;
    Seditious hunks! to whine for want of grains.

                        Percy Bysshe Shelley
       Oedipus Tyrannus; or Swellfoot the Tyrant (1820)

There was a growing conviction across the country that the interests of the vast bulk of the people would not receive adequate recognition from the legislature until the franchise was widened. Agitators for parliamentary reform were not slow to capitalise on the increasing discontent and, during June and July, a wave of mass protest meetings swept through major industrial centres. On 16 August upwards of 50,000 persons assembled for a meeting in St Peter's Fields at Manchester. Proceedings were hardly under way when dragoons and yeomanry intervened and in ten minutes eleven of the crowd were dead and some hundreds injured.[1]

In the words of one historian: 'A howl of execration arose throughout the length and breadth of England.'[2] New protest meetings were organised and the movement spread to Scotland in early November, with large assemblies in major cities. Parliament was recalled on 23 November.

The government reacted with repressive zeal. The Blasphemous and Seditious Libels Bill, the Misdemeanours Bill, the Seditious Meetings Prevention Bill, the Training Prevention Bill, the Seizure of Arms Bill, the

Newspaper Stamp Duties Bill — all six acts were introduced in an attempt to stifle expression of dissent.[3] However, in the debates of November and December the more perceptive members of both Houses drew attention to the links between social unrest and the new structure of the British economy. Some of these members, in defiance of the minimal government hypothesis of the Ricardians, believed those linkages warranted new legislative initiatives in economic life.

LANSDOWNE ON THE NEW ECONOMIC ORDER

In the Lords on 30 November Lansdowne moved for an enquiry into the state of the country with particular reference to regions where manufacturing predominated.[4] Current unrest, he observed, was located almost exclusively in those regions, its root causes were economic and those causes were related to trends over the past two decades. His analysis was such as to call into question fundamental Ricardian assumptions concerning factor mobility and supply response.

Firstly, Lansdowne noted the trend to increased accumulation of fixed capital. This had given rise to decreased mobility of that factor. 'The greater that capital was,' said Lansdowne, 'the greater became the difficulty when any derangement of its usual course of employment took place, of throwing it into new and productive channels.' Secondly, the extension of the division of labour had rendered labour itself less mobile:

> That very division of labour, too, which was another consequence of social improvement and high civilization, formed, on such occasions an additional evil; for the workman became a part of the same fixed capital, inasmuch as the talent and ingenuity he had acquired in his particular art or manufacture could not be otherwise employed. It was in every sense of the word, in his hands a fixed capital, which he could not remove to any other productive source of employment.

Thirdly, where manufacturing activity was being conducted on a large scale there was not a ready adjustment of supply to fluctuating demand. In fact when demand decreased there was not merely a lag in the diminution of output, but output actually increased. Lansdowne explained that in the face of falling demand, 'the master-manufacturers lowered the rate of wages: this reduction induced the labourers to work a greater number of hours; and thus more goods were produced, which served only to add to the evil.'[5]

The general tenor of Lansdowne's speech was to endeavour to make their lordships aware that they were living in a new form of society, one which had begun to be shaped by economic forces of which many of them seemed only dimly conscious. Wartime prosperity, he reminded them, had been accompanied by rapid population increase. At the same time there was a most significant increase in the proportion of industrial to rural workers. Hence in the recent past 'the population which had been raised by commercial speculations during the war was thrown back upon the country, in a very different situation from that in which the population stood at the commencement of hostilities.'

There was no doubt that industry was depressed and in these circumstances, said Lansdowne, he 'might be induced to depart from those principles of political economy which, under other circumstances, he should be disposed to hold sacred.' If the depression could be considered a temporary one he would support a direct parliamentary grant to assist the populace in the distressed regions.

GRENVILLE'S ALTERNATIVE ANALYSIS

The idea of direct financial grants to relieve the sufferings of the unemployed was quite unacceptable to Lord Grenville.[6] Such grants, he argued, merely divert capital to uses which are 'avowedly less productive to its employer, and consequently less beneficial to the community'. The policies which he might countenance, under current conditions, were cautious revisions of the taxation system, the poor laws, or the restrictions and duties on foreign imports.

Grenville also adopted a rather different view from that of Lansdowne concerning the causes of the depression. He took the (quite popular) line that long engagement in war must bring a measure of economic calamity, even to the victor. Some, like William Wilberforce in the Commons, were even prepared to explain the depression in terms of a Divine warning against future engagement in armed conflict.[7] Grenville did not go so far. Shortage of capital and a departure from some supposedly 'natural' order concerning its use were his chief candidates as the agents subverting the national economy.

During peace, according to Grenville, there is a tendency for capital 'to increase in a more rapid proportion than the population'. During war, the reverse holds:

> In war, large amounts of capital are continually and utterly destroyed. Much is also diverted to channels of employment, wholly or comparatively, unproductive; from whence, on the return of peace, it cannot be transferred into its natural course, without much difficulty, delay, and loss.[8]

Over the past twenty years in Britain these processes had been accentuated by restriction of cash payments and continuance of the poor laws. 'An excessive and forced paper currency [had] contributed to arrest of the natural increase of capital, and perhaps, in some of the last of those years, to effect an actual diminution of it.' Again, population had expanded, partly because of 'the artificial and improvident system of our poor laws'. These considerations led Grenville to conclude: 'No art, no wisdom, no power of man can make our diminished capital equally productive as before of employment and subsistence for our augmented numbers.'[9]

CALLS FOR ACTION: BENNET, BARING, AND ELLICE

In the Commons on 9 December Henry Grey Bennet moved for an enquiry into the state of the manufacturing districts.[10] Bennet had personally researched the situation in those areas and, after a detailed account of the low wages and starvation which prevailed, he assured the House that the social unrest there would subside if only the people had 'food and work'. He strongly recommended the introduction of a comprehensive public works programme and urged the government to repeal the existing laws against the emigration of skilled workers. 'There were too many', he observed with regret, 'whose absence from their country would be felt rather as a blessing than a loss, at the present moment.'

Baring too was impressed by the reality of the plight of the industrial workers. He found a wide range of policy initiatives appropriate in the current circumstances. Direct aid to the unemployed and starving, minimum wage provisions, and extension of credit facilities were desirable measures.[11]

Underlying the present misery and unrest, according to Baring, was a flight of capital engendered by the type of commercial panic he had feared in connection with precipitate resumption of cash payments. He also believed that there was exploitation of workers by 'small capitalists'. Concerning the first factor, he stated:

> There never had been a period when so much of the capital of the country was withdrawn for the purpose of being invested in foreign securities, as during the last three weeks. A sort of panic had seized the public mind — there was a general *sauve qui peut* amidst monied men, each endeavouring to outrun the other in removing capital from the kingdom . . . a considerable degree of the present distress arose from this insecurity on the part of many capitalists.

The transition from war to peace had given rise to some uncertainty among business men, and now expectations were further depressed by 'the want of tranquillity and security in the manufacturing districts themselves'.

Lack of tranquillity, and hence poor expectations, were attributable, in part, to the impact on workers of those who preached a doctrine of class conflict. Baring himself rejected the idea of necessary enmity between worker and capitalist as 'wicked and unfounded'. Nevertheless, he believed there was some substance to the thesis: 'He would not deny that the desire and policy of men engaged in trade was (whatever might be said of its inhumanity) to screw down the price of labour as low as possible.' At this point, however, an important distinction was to be made. The incidence of the desire to 'screw down' wages depended on whether short-run or long-run profit maximisation was the employer's aim. 'The great manufacturer', Baring thought, was generally exempt from this form of exploitative behaviour, since he was concerned with the long run. The problem was with 'the small capitalist, who cared not what the world thought of him, went on a different system, and got together the scrapings of work-houses, whom he employed at from 2s. 6d. to 3s. per week. From those causes, the wages of the operative labourers were so materially reduced.'

Given the existence of exploitation, Baring saw scope for government action. 'Humanity' ought to take precedence over economic theory. 'Notwithstanding the principles of the political economists, which were generally unexceptionable', Baring admitted, 'he was, he must confess, for the sake of humanity, an advocate for the establishment of a minimum with respect to wages.' Further, as a short-run palliative to help those in desperate need, 'he should not hesitate to give his vote for the application of one or two million from the public fund for that object.' To these policies Baring allied that of a monetary reform which would increase 'the facility of commercial speculation'. As in his evidence before the Secret Committees (Chapter 7), he urged legislation for a bimetallic system.

Edward Ellice found himself in broad agreement with Baring.[12] He too found the theories of the Ricardians lacking in relevance to contemporary conditions:

We had deviated too widely from the principles of political economy to render it an objection to any propostion that it was hostile to those principles. At present it seemed to him, that while one part of the kingdom was labouring under the greatest distress from an insufficiency of the prices of labour, another part was supported by means of the poor-rates.

Ellice envisaged that some form of minimum wage legislation could be helpful and he agreed that the existing arrangements concerning the currency had served to depress the economy. Again, he allowed that there was a danger of a continuing flight of capital because of uncertainties evoked by social unrest derived from poverty and unemployment. Ellice added that there was an urgent need for taxation reform.[13]

THE IMPOTENCE OF LEGISLATION

Castlereagh was scornful of the notion of direct government intervention to promote employment.[14] 'Was it possible', he asked, 'for any fund to be established that would secure employment, amidst all the fluctuations of commerce, and manufactures?' George Philips found Baring's minimum wage proposal to be equally objectionable.[15] In Philips' opinion there was no scope at all for action concerning the depression: 'the evil, he apprehended, was to be met only by natural means, and could not be removed by legislative measures.'

James Stuart-Wortley was of a similar mind, although he admitted the existence of class conflict.[16] 'Between the labouring mechanics and the master manufacturers', said Wortley, 'there was an opposition of interests, and violent disputes which had lasted for years.' Such was the gulf between these groups there was no basis for parliamentary intervention. 'The factions', he declared, 'put it out of their power, by the violence of their conduct, to conciliate.' Like Marx, Wortley believed that class conflict was both simplified and intensified by the transition from an agricultural to an industrial society:

> It was not as in the agricultural counties where the peasant looked up to the farmer, the farmer to his landlord, the proprietor to the peer, and the peer to the Crown, thus forming a connected chain which bound the highest and lowest classes of society together. On the contrary the operative weaver saw no gradation. There was only himself toiling, and his employer apparently enjoying all the luxuries of life: no wonder he repined at his condition, and at observing that all labour was exhausted but for this single end.

Another to advocate no action was Robert Peel.[17] The causes of the distress, he was convinced, 'were entirely beyond the control of parliament'. In the fashion of a fundamentalist Malthusian, he denied that any genuine benefits would flow from direct parliamentary grants in aid to the starving populace. Such a policy, said Peel, 'would rather tend to counteract the natural checks of increasing population, which, though affording a tardy remedy, was the only one he could discover of affording effectual and lasting relief.' Further, both public works programmes and minimum wage legislation would do more harm than good.

Peel's attitude appalled John Smith, the member for Midhurst.[18] 'He had listened to the speech of the right hon. member for Oxford with the utmost pain,' said Smith, 'the conclusion to be drawn from which was that the wretched sufferers could hope for no relief.' Smith then raised an additional issue, the problem of technological unemployment, which had lingered on the fringe of the debate to this point. He alluded to, 'the rapid inroad which machinery had made upon manual labour within only a few years . . . it was an undoubted fact that it had thrown a great many hands out of employment.'[19]

MR OWEN'S PLAN

Bennet's motion for a committee of enquiry was lost, but exactly one week later (16 December) Sir William De Crespigny moved for a committee to consider 'the plan of Mr. Owen for ameliorating the condition of the lower classes'.[20] The 'plan' was that proposed to the Poor Laws Committee of 1817, and it involved the establishment of small, self-contained communities in which the members shared a moderately communalised life style. Productive activity was to be a blend of agricultural and industrial pursuits, but the use of machinery in the latter was carefully controlled.

Much of the thrust of De Crespigny's advocacy of Owen's scheme turned on the problems created by technological unemployment. He was anxious that the House should 'investigate the consequences arising from that mechanism which had within the last few years so extensively superseded human labour . . . that mechanism should always be made subservient to human labour.' Increasing use of machinery had not only given rise to unemployment, but had introduced the very real danger of over-production. This second problem was not dealt with in earlier economic thought. 'At the period when Adam Smith wrote his treatise on the Wealth of Nations', De Crespigny argued, 'the great object was to increase the wealth of the country. This object had been since achieved by the increase of machinery, so as almost to increase the production of some articles much beyond consumption.'

Investigation of Owen's plan was opposed by the prominent whig Henry Brougham.[21] He expressed considerable regard for Owen as a man, but very little for his theories. The basic weakness of Owen's scheme was its assumption that population increase was beneficial. 'On the contrary', said Brougham, 'he had no hesitation in stating that the excess of population was one of the great causes of the distress which at present afflicted the country . . . it was amongst the most melancholy malpractices of the low part of the press, to depreciate this, which was the soundest principle of political economy.'

RICARDO ON THE DEPRESSION

Ricardo, like Brougham, was opposed to Owen's scheme, since it 'was built upon a theory inconsistent with the principles of political economy.'[22] The plan dismissed, he took up the issues of unemployment and over-production through the use of machinery. He said:

> It could not be denied, on the whole view of the subject, that machinery did not lessen the demand for labour; while, on the other hand, it did not consume the produce of the soil, nor employ any of our manufactures. It might also be misapplied by occasioning the production of too much cotton or too much cloth; but the moment those articles ceased in consequence to pay the manufacturer, he would devote his time and capital to some other purpose.

High mobility of capital, then, would prevent serious over-production.

However, here Ricardo appears to admit that technological unemployment was a very real possibility. The introduction of machinery in manufacturing was not the universally benign event he had hitherto claimed it to be. Yet the seeming change in Ricardo's stance at this stage was probably a case of misreporting. An alternative version of Ricardo's speech as published in the *British Press* is quite consistent with his earlier view.[23]

The machinery question examined, Ricardo declared that what the country now required was 'a demand for labour', and he turned to a general review of the causes of the current economic ills. The primary disease was 'insufficiency of capital'. The immediate problem was to retain existing capital in the nation at a time when several factors militated retention.

Basically, retention of capital in one country as against another depended on the relative degrees of security of property and the relative rates of profit offered by the countries concerned. England was particularly reliant on the security element, since the rate of profit was lower there than in some other countries. This was the case because profit depended on the relationship of three variables: quantity of capital; 'extent of soil'; and direction of population change. In England the first of the three was large, the second 'limited', and the third postive, hence the rate of profit must be relatively low.

The situation then was such as to encourage a flight of capital and the existing state of the laws of the country was in large measure to blame. One set of harmful laws was that protecting domestic agriculture. The corn laws permitted high prices of grain which inflated money wages and hence diminished profits. Also debilitating in this respect was the range of other prohibitions against importation of foreign goods. Thirdly, there was the problem of the high level of taxation required to meet the interest payments on the large national debt accumulated during the war. This taxation diminished the already relatively low profit margin a capitalist could expect to achieve.

Sound policy involved a gradual retreat from the whole apparatus of the corn laws and import prohibitions.[24] In the case of the national debt, there was no need for gradualism. The debt could be discharged by a direct levy on the accumulated wealth of individuals. The massive transfer of wealth, Ricardo assured the House, would not damage the economy, since 'the stockholder would be eager to employ his money, as he received it.'[25]

Ricardo had no sympathy for the policy of promotion of public works to relieve the current depression. The advocates of this course 'appeared to overlook the fact, that capital thus employed must be withdrawn from some other quarter.' However if his policies were adopted, Ricardo concluded, there was the greatest potential for expansion of the domestic economy. Far from any prediction of the imminence of an era of economic stagnation, Ricardo ended his review with the statement that he was 'convinced that the country had not yet nearly reached the limits of its prosperity and greatness.'

Given some of the leading assumptions of Ricardo's theoretical system — diminishing returns in agriculture, full employment of available capital, the finely tuned responsiveness of market mechanisms, and the like — this was a superbly logical address. Those who understood his theories and were sympathetic to his assumptions may well have found his conclusions irresistible. Yet it seems most probable that this speech was politically damaging to the Ricardian cause.

At the least, most members of the House, lacking the necessary background in Ricardian theory, were almost certainly bewildered. Earlier in the year they believed they could appreciate Ricardo's reasoning on the question of the resumption of cash payments, but the new proposals were based on far less seemingly obvious grounds. More than this, Ricardo's statements on the corn laws must have immediately disaffected the vast majority of the large contingent of country gentlemen in the Commons. One of their number, Viscount Althorp, was quickly on his feet at the conclusion of Ricardo's speech and protested that the nation 'could not secure a supply at home in time of war unless by imposing some tax on corn of foreign growth.'[26]

The most damaging element of all in Ricardo's proposals was the plan for discharge of the national debt. A variety of contemporary and near-contemporary sources suggest that, during his lifetime, Ricardo's political status was never to recover from the distaste aroused by that plan. In his diary J. L. Mallet noted sadly: 'His [Ricardo's] speech on paying off the national debt has very much damaged him in the House of Commons, which cannot but be regretted.'[27] And it is little wonder that Ricardo's contemporaries were shocked. As Edwin Cannan later observed, 'Few more drastic "democratic" financial proposals have ever been made than this one of laying an immediate tax of six or seven hundred millions upon property in order to get rid of about thirty millions of annual taxes on consumable articles.'[28]

STARVATION IN SCOTLAND

De Crespigny's motion for a committee of enquiry failed, as had Bennet's motion of the previous week. Ricardo was one of eighteen members who supported the motion, his ground being an interest in Owen's ideas concerning 'spade husbandry'.[29] Immediately after this failure, John Maxwell, the recently elected member for Renfrewshire, raised the issue of the conditions prevailing in the industrial areas of Scotland. Maxwell asked that the House should 'sanction some relaxation from the strict principles of political economy, in order to alleviate the evils which now confessedly existed in different parts of Scotland.' His specific requests were for direct parliamentary grants to the distressed, revision of taxation burdens in favour of wage earners and landholders, and financial assistance to those who wished to emigrate.[30]

On behalf of the government Vansittart replied that this matter was of definite concern to the ministry and that the Prime Minister had undertaken to consider loans for public works in districts of high unemployment, provided 'reasonable security can be given for ultimate repayment'.[31] William Huskisson, the Chief Commissioner for Woods and Forests, was inclined to favour a less direct response to the problem.[32] 'The parliament could do but little by direct relief', he said, 'but much could be done by restoring that confidence and security to the capitalist which recent measures had so much shaken.' Distress he attributed to 'the over-growth of population' in some areas, and to 'the state of the foreign markets, particularly that of America, one of the greatest consumers of British manufacture.'

The Commons returned to the Scottish problem five days later (21 December) when Lord Archibald Hamilton introduced a petition on the issue. Castlereagh then announced that the government was willing to lend a sum of £500,000 by way of relief, if 'any visible security' for the loan was offered by the gentlemen of Scotland.[33] At this, Scottish members again expressed their dismay at the inadequacy of the government's response and they were joined in their protest by Edward Ellice of Coventry. Ellice provided a pithy account of the achievements of parliament since its recall in November.[34] The legislature had passed coercive bills which were merely 'temporising expedients'. It had taken no meaningful action to mitigate the destitution which was at the root of the social unrest.

RICARDO UNDER ATTACK

The Blasphemous Libel Bill was passed by the Commons on 24 December and immediately there followed one further attempt to spur the government to consideration of the state of the economy. The attempt was unsuccessful, but it gave a number of members the opportunity for expressing their dissatisfaction with the performance of the ministry. Some of them, mainly businessmen, also voiced their dissatisfaction with the advice which Ricardo had been tendering.

John Irving, the member for Bramber, introduced a petition from a group of London merchants which urged the necessity for parliamentary enquiry.[35] The petition did not specify measures that ought to be considered, but in his introduction Irving distinguished 'the change in the currency of the country' as a major depressant of the level of activity. He also expressed the opinion that little stimulus, if any, would flow from adoption of Ricardo's suggestions concerning the corn laws, poor laws, and national debt redemption.

This wholesale rejection of his policies goaded Ricardo to a restatement of his position.[36] He utterly rejected the view that the depression was linked to implementation of his plan for resumption of cash payments and he repeated that the main problem was one of capital flight engendered by low profits.[37] He also repeated his call for swift discharge of the national debt. Ricardo added that the economy would also benefit materially if the government began working towards removal of all types of restriction on trade. This, he admitted, must be a gradual process.[38]

Kirkman Finlay, the Glasgow factory owner and spokesman for that city's manufacturers, found Ricardo's analysis of the causes of the depression to be quite invalid.[39] Finlay attributed the slump to general over-production, a phenomenon which was non-existent in the Ricardian canon. 'The distress of the country at present', was due to 'over speculation, over importation, and over manufacture.' The position in the cotton industry made nonsense of Ricardo's reasoning: 'In the cotton trade, the manufacturers of which were the most distressed at present, we were enabled to undersell all the foreign manufacturers in their own market. What then became of the hon. gentleman's [Ricardo's] theory as to taxation and low wages and their effects?'

Finlay also had reservations concerning that freedom of trade which Ricardo advocated. It was 'a sound principle in theory', but the difficulties of putting it into practice were generally underestimated by its proponents.

Speaking next, Brougham, the lawyer, found some points of agreement between himself and Ricardo who, he allowed, was 'an oracle' on matters of currency and trade.[40] However his professional experience suggested a major drawback to Ricardo's plan concerning repayment of the national debt. 'The effect of such a measure', said Brougham, 'would be to place the property for five years at the mercy of all the solicitors, conveyancers, and money-hunters, in the country.'

Alderman Heygate, whose remarks concluded discussion of the merchants' petition, was convinced that monetary factors were responsible for the depression.[41] Ricardo denied such a relationship, but Heygate 'imputed the distresses to the great diminution of the currency, which had been for a long time gradually going on.' The diminution had led to a crisis of confidence, according to the Alderman, although he believed that expectations had begun to revive. To assist the revival of confidence within the business community the government should come out with a firm statement as to the limit beyond which it would not permit further contraction of the money supply.

REVIEW

The post-Peterloo debates ended with the government unwilling to seek any other course of action apart from legislation for repression of dissent.

Despite its intellectual (or maybe moral) bankruptcy, Liverpool's administration was able to survive in the face of sharp divisions among its critics concerning the causes and cures of business depression.[42] Some diagnosed a severe shortage of capital due to 'natural' trends which only time could reverse. Ricardo attributed the misery to a capital flight encouraged by low profits. Only the correction of past errors by Cabinet and parliament could rectify the situation. Businessmen identified a number of debilitating influences including general over-production; factor immobilities; a collapse of expectations; and deflationary policy.

As the economy floundered Ricardo's political credibility slumped. Most of those commercial men who were not already disaffected by his plan for resumption found his views on repayment of the national debt to be ludicrous. The country gentlemen, who did not seem to have seen any threat to their interests in adoption of a gold standard, were ready to bristle at the merest suggestion of repeal of the corn bill of 1815. However, it must be recognised that Ricardo was of some use to the ministry. He could be counted upon to staunchly uphold a policy of inaction when Baring, Lansdowne, Ellice, Maxwell and others brought forward suggestions for measures such as public works programmes and minimum wage legislation. *Laissez-faire* was often a useful doctrinal posture for a dilatory Cabinet, and Ricardo's powerful logic could cloak the posture in the garb of true statesmanship.

7 1820: A Campaign for Free Trade

> Freedom from restraint is calculated to give the utmost extension to foreign trade, and the best direction to the capital and industry of the country ... the maxim of buying in the cheapest market and selling in the dearest, which regulates every merchant in his individual dealings, is strictly applicable, as the best rule for the trade of the whole nation.
>
> Petition of the Merchants of London
> House of Commons, 8 May 1820

The death of George III on 30 January gave rise to the dissolution of the old parliament and the need for a general election early in the year. The election did not materially alter the state of the parties in the House, nor did it occasion a major Cabinet reshuffle. When parliament assembled on 21 April, Vansittart was still Chancellor of the Exchequer, Robinson continued as President of the Board of Trade, and Liverpool, as First Lord of the Treasury and Prime Minister, maintained a significant role in the shaping of economic policy.

Throughout the year there was a steady decline in the prices of agricultural produce, and most sectors of manufacturing remained depressed. Violent expressions of social unrest were not on the scale of some of the previous post-war years, but particular incidents manifested the continuing tension. In February a police spy unmasked the plot of the Cato Street conspirators to murder Cabinet ministers and the plotters were executed.[1] In April a clash between workers and militia at Kilsyth in Scotland led to the execution of three of the dissidents.

Both parliament and the public at large diverted their attentions from basic social ills when, during the second half of the year, the estrangement of the new King, George IV, and his wife, Queen Caroline, developed into a political *cause célèbre*. The Queen arrived in England in June and the King, alleging gross misconduct on her part, insisted that the government introduce a bill of pains and penalties to deal with her. Liverpool eventually agreed and, at considerable cost to the government (and far greater cost to the country), the parliament was obliged to debate the issue from July through to November. Before the onset of this pathetic exercise, however, both Houses were able to consider some initiatives of greater significance ₁or the future welfare of the people.

THE MERCHANTS' PETITION

With the economy in difficulties and with some indications in the recent past that the Prime Minister was not unsympathetic to a more liberal line in commercial matters, a group of London merchants decided that the time was right to suggest that what was in their particular interest as businessmen was also in the interest of the country as a whole. Accordingly they petitioned parliament for a greater measure of freedom in the arrangements governing the conduct of foreign trade. The petition came forward to the Commons on 8 May and was given the prestige of an introduction by Alexander Baring.[2]

Fundamental to this document was the assertion that national economic policy should be determined by analogies with the dictates of private business calculus. 'The maxim of buying in the cheapest market and selling in the dearest, which regulates every merchant in his individual dealings', the petition declared, 'is strictly applicable, as the best rule for the trade of the whole nation.' Further it rebutted traditional protectionist arguments concerning the necessary diminution of domestic production that must follow importation, and concerning the need for international reciprocity, i.e., the mutual, simultaneous lowering of barriers by potential trading partners. Unilateral action to remove import prohibitions was recommended as the wisest course, especially as there was 'a strong presumption that the distress which now so generally prevails is considerably aggravated by that system (of protection).'

In commending the petition Baring first took up the question of the prevailing distress.[3] The extraordinary stimulus given the economy by war, he pointed out, 'had been followed by a langour as remarkable'. Like the vast bulk of his contemporaries he found this langour puzzling, but he identified a shrinking volume of foreign trade, the burden of a massive public debt and the recent decision to resume cash payments as major elements in the country's difficulties. The fundamental requisite for recovery, he believed, was establishment of domestic tranquillity so that those with capital could 'employ it without apprehension'. Greater freedom of trade would also help, although Baring added the rider that this cause should be promoted only 'as was compatible with other and important considerations'. Unlike the petitioners, it would seem that Baring did not accept the strict analogy between the conduct of national policy and the logic of business success.

Baring concluded by advocating a number of highly desirable liberal-isations of trade. These were: repeal of the duty on imported wool; substitution of duties for direct restriction on imports of certain other commodities; greater freedom to import with a view to exporting the same goods; and abolition of the Navigation Laws which forbade the carriage of imports in other than British ships or those of the exporting nation.

Replying on behalf of the government Robinson urged extreme caution in any movement towards freer trade.[4] In particular he set himself against abolition of the navigation laws and against any suggestion of revision of the corn laws. The former, he admitted, might harm the flow of trade to some extent 'but the injury so sustained was but a feather in the scale compared with the great advantage derived from those laws in the protection and safety of the country.' As far as agricultural protection was concerned, 'he did not feel that there was anything so radically wrong in the present system as to induce an alteration.'

RICARDO AND HIS CRITICS

On the oppostion benches Lord Milton also thought that the navigation and corn laws ought to be maintained, although other forms of restriction might be progressively relaxed.[5] Taking up the general issue of the current depression, he noted that it had brought greater relative hardship to wage earners than to other groups in the community. Further it had involved 'a tendency to absorb capital from the general body of the people, and to accumulate property in a few hands.' Like Baring, he attributed the malaise, in part, to legislation for a return to cash payments. In Milton's opinion, many members, including Ricardo 'had formed too low an estimate of the pressure which a change in our currency would create.'

Ricardo immediately denied that the measure he advocated successfully during the previous year could account for the degree of 'pressure' of which Milton complained.[6] The market price of gold had moved only from £4 2s 0d when the Secret Committees were sitting to £3 17s 10½d at present. 'A small degree of embarrassment', Ricardo admitted, however, could be anticipated from the decision to return to the old gold standard.

The principles embodied in the Merchants' Petition were most satisfactory to Ricardo, but he saw two main difficulties in their implementation. The first was the need for revenue on the part of government, and the second was the desirability of avoiding 'the absolute ruin of those who vested large capital on the faith of laws so long established as the restrictive laws'. He looked for a gradual movement to freer trade, 'allowing those who had their property invested, to turn it into other channels'. As to the corn laws, he favoured the removal of all protection of agriculture save countervailing duties which compensated rural producers for the obligation of carrying the burden of payment of poor rates and tithes.

Ellice, speaking next, adopted very different views from those of Ricardo concerning the currency question and the relevance of the petition before the House.[7] 'Since the return to cash payments was finally settled, to the present time', he contended, 'every staple article or produce connected with manufacturers had experienced a fall of from 30 to 50 per cent.' Given this degree of deflation, 'the state of the [national] debt and the finances, rendered it impossible, without some great alteration, for the House to pay much attention to the petition before them.' For Ellice, free trade was no panacea in present circumstances.

Baring and Ricardo then returned for a passage of arms which rehearsed some of the conflicts between their submissions to the Secret Committees of 1819.[8] Baring charged that Ricardo overlooked the fact that the currency alteration had created a scarcity of money, 'augmented by the difference in the facility in the negotiation of paper, which carried the change in the state of the monied world much beyond the differences of prices [of gold]'. According to Baring 'on an average during the war as compared with the present time the difference in the currency was at least 25 per cent.' In reply, Ricardo allowed that the latter might be true, but the relevant consideration was that in 1819 the degree of depreciation of the currency was a mere 4 per cent.[9]

Baring also revived his suggestion of 1819 that England should adopt a bimetallic currency system. This, he felt, would help counter the deflation by expanding the circulation. Ricardo rejected the proposal on the grounds that it would involve an unacceptable degree of fluctuation in the standard of payments. Baring replied that, in practice, there would be little fluctuation because of the use of both gold and silver. His opponent, Baring implied, lacked the experience that could temper deduction by empiricism. At this point, after a notice of a petition from Edinburgh in the same vein as that of the London merchants, debate ended.

TWO FURTHER PETITIONS

On 16 May the Commons received petitions in favour of free trade from the Chamber of Commerce of Glasgow and from the woollen manufacturers of Hawick. The first was introduced by Kirkman Finlay, who stated that the petitioners believed that there was a direct link between the present state of the economy and the restriction of trade.[10] In their opinion 'the distresses of the commercial and manufacturing interests of this country were much increased; if not in a great measure caused by the various restrictions which impeded our imports from and exports to foreign countries.'

Finlay himself added to the calls for liberalisation, as raised in the earlier debate, by way of a protest against the continuance of the usury laws. He also proposed that the East India Company should be asked to consent to a modification of some of its monopoly rights.[11] He further commented that, in presenting the London petition, Baring had been too gloomy in his assessment of the opportunities for economic recovery. Finaly concluded with the observation that Adam Smith would have gained 'inconceivable pleasure' from the manner in which the Glasgow document embodied his doctrines.

Having been challenged, Baring stated that he was worried by trends in the international economy.[12] 'New and great difficulties had arisen,' he said; 'the situation of other countries presented serious difficulties to the encouragement of British commerce.' The war had given British industry an advantage over that of other countries in respect of accumulated capital, quality of machinery and exercise of enterprise. To maintain that advantage in peace would require 'nothing but the most watchful and active exertions, and the wisest laws'.

Baring also indicated that a degree of unfavourable reaction to the free trade petitions had begun to assert itself in sections of the business community. Only that morning he had attended a large gathering of shipowners who were concerned about the manner in which the navigation laws might be modified. They were particularly anxious that British shipping retain its monopoly of the trade with India and the colonies. They were also disturbed that there might be alterations in the regulations relating to the timber trade. In the face of these problems it was Baring's hopeful conclusion that 'when gentlemen inquired into the particular points they would not find so much difference of opinion, as they first imagined to exist.' From these remarks it is apparent that if the government was to entertain the principles of the free traders, it must expect swift reactions from powerful interest groups should those principles be applied. The strongest opposition to free trade in practice would come from within the business community, as Adam Smith had taught.[13]

COMMITTEES ON FOREIGN TRADE

The weight of the potential opposition to liberalisation was almost certainly in the forefront of the mind of the Prime Minister when the Marquis of Lansdowne opened a debate in the Lords on 26 May. Speaking on the distress, Lansdowne came out strongly in favour of the thesis that the path to economic recovery was the path to freer trade.[14] The Marquis argued that the major problem in domestic policy was that of creating new employment opportunities. He explained the origins of the problem as follows:

> Long wars had been carried on, and nations had expended a
> considerable portion of their capital, instead of limiting their expendi-
> ture to their income. An artificial system had thus been established, and
> the consequence of this state of things was, that a numerous population
> had been called into existence by the great demand for labour. It was,
> however impossible that this expenditure could continue, but the
> population remained when the expenditure diminished; and this
> unemployed and unproductive population, or in other words, the
> quantity of labour beyond the demand for it, was the great cause of the
> existing distress.[15]

Unemployment could be overcome by stimulation of effective demand for
goods and labour, and further 'the most obvious mode of creating that
demand was, to encourage and to extend our foreign trade by removing
some of those restrictions by which it was shackled.'

Lansdowne's specific proposals for liberalisation were much the same as
those of Baring and Finlay. However they included, in addition, a request
for reconsideration of the existing duties on timber from northern Europe
and on wines and silks from France. Reduction or abolition of the silk
duties, he allowed, would cause immediate hardship for the domestic silk
industry. In this case parliament ought to vote a large sum in aid of the
workers who would be affected.

In conclusion Lansdowne moved: 'That a Select Committee be
appointed to inquire into the Means of extending and securing the Foreign
Trade of the Country.' He stressed that this was preferable to appointment
of any body with a brief for wider investigation of the economy's
problems. Broader terms of reference would prevent the emergence of a
practical outcome from the committee's work.

The Prime Minister replied that he felt 'no inclination to oppose the
motion'.[16] Then, by way of preface to a review of the state of the
economy, he expounded on a theme which was to be reiterated by speaker
after speaker in the debates of this year. 'All the great interests of the
country are intimately and inseparably connected', said Liverpool, 'and
that while on the one hand, what is for the benefit of one, must be
beneficial to the rest; on the other hand, any attempt exclusively to favour
the one, must be prejudicial to all.' He deplored the tendency, evident in
some of the recent petitions received, to display 'a disposition to separate
the interests of the one from the interests of the others, and to represent
them as at variance, and as capable of being separately benefited'.[17]

Reviewing the economy Liverpool first set out to demonstrate that the
depression could not be due to a failure of domestic demand. For proof he
referred members to the statistics concerning the consumption of such
dutiable articles as tea, coffee, tobacco, malt and spirits. The figures
revealed increases, or only slight decreases, for the year ending 5 April

1820, as compared with the averages for the period 1817—19. The state of the domestic market was in marked contrast, however, with that for exports. Official statistics showed there had been a substantial decline in exports, and the major factor underlying the decline was the condition of the American economy.[18]

Liverpool explained that, as the principal neutral power during the recent war, America had experienced a rapid expansion of commerce and industry. Now with the coming of peace that country had lost its comparative advantage. At this juncture, America 'must retrograde to a certain point . . . until she has returned to that which is her natural condition.' He saw the American case as a major example of 'the nature of the distress at present existing, and that it can be remedied by time alone.' Liverpool continued: 'If the people of the world are poor no legislative interpostion can make them do that which they would do if they were rich . . . our manufacturers must wait with patience until the supply and the demand adjust themselves to each other.'

These remarks set the stage for a staunchly conservative set of pronouncements on economic policy. Although the Prime Minister had acknowledged the basic validity of the principle of free trade for some years,[19] in this instance he urged caution and gradualism: 'We have risen under a very different system than that of free and unrestricted trade. It is utterly impossible, with our debt and taxation, even if they were but half their existing amount, that we can suddenly adopt the system of free trade. To do so, would be to unhinge the whole property of the country . . .'

He also urged no alteration in the corn bill of 1815 or in the plan to resume cash payments. To revert again to an inconvertible paper currency would lead to 'the creation and extension of fictitious capital, and of the appearance of prosperous trade, without the reality'.[20]

Liverpool foresaw that a revival of the economy would soon commence. Nevertheless he was not confident that economic growth could proceed smoothly along a full employment equilibrium path in time of peace. He warned that the country must be prepared to face the possibility that fluctuations would prove to be concomitants of growth. 'But that which I know alarms many men — and, men of great practical experience on these matters', he observed, 'is, that we may be subject to the danger of a periodical revulsion of the same nature every three or four years . . . '

Concerning Lansdowne's proposals for derestriction of trade, Liverpool commented that the economy would derive no great benefit from the suggested abolition of direct prohibitions on the import of a range of commodities. Further, in the case of the silk trade, although he wished England had never encouraged the development of that industry, the Prime Minister was opposed to its destruction and to the idea of financial support for the workers who would be displaced. Summing up, Liverpool proclaimed himself a friend to *laissez-faire* but an enemy of those demanding its swift implementation: 'I firmly believe that, on all commercial subjects, the fewer the laws the better. I am sorry to see so many on our Statute book; but the evil is not one of easy remedy ... constant fluctuations in our legislation on such subjects can only be productive of disorder and ruin'.[21]

The Earl of Lauderdale found much to commend in Liverpool's speech.[22] He concurred in the Prime Minister's sentiments concerning the corn laws, paper currency, and the need for caution in an approach to freer trade. Lauderdale also agreed that economic revival was not too distant and he added that this depended to some extent on the self-education of the *nouveau riche*. 'The country at large was not impoverished', said Lauderdale, 'though the distribution of property was different, and time would soon teach men how to apply what they had acquired.' Another variable bearing on recovery, in his opinion, was stimulation of effective demand. Lauderdale's interest in this variable was expressed in connection with criticism of the government's intention to maintain the sinking fund method of retiring the public debt. That fund, he stated 'was nothing more nor less than a forcible assumption of five millions of taxes to be converted into capital. Now, if this sum were not so forcibly applied, it might be employed by all who paid it in the purchase of manufactures, and at the present moment such an addition would be of incalculable advantage.'[23]

When the debate concluded Lansdowne's motion was agreed to, and a committee appointed which included Liverpool and Lauderdale. A similar committee was established by the Commons on the motion of Baring on 5 June. Thomas Wallace, the Vice President of the Board of Trade, was chairman.

The Lords' committee reported on 11 July, recommending a reduction in the degree of protection given imports of Canadian as against Baltic timber.[24] Presented seven days later, the Commons report concentrated on liberalisation of aspects of the navigation laws and of the regulations governing re-exportation. On the navigation laws the report recommended 'admitting the importation into the United Kingdom, of the produce of every part of the world, without reference to the place of their growth or product, provided such importation be made in British ships.'[25] Concerning the re-export trade, it was stated that parliament should contemplate 'giving the most unlimited extension to the Warehousing system'.[26]

When he presented the report to the Commons Wallace hailed the projected reform of the navigation laws as 'the first and most material step of this country to a departure from the course of restrictive policy which its legislature had hitherto pursued'.[27] Further, expansion of warehousing would be a significant step toward the goal of maintaining England as 'the great emporium and the great mart of the world'. Many members seem to have shared his enthusiasm and Hansard records that Wallace 'sat down amid considerable cheerings from both sides of the House'. As in the case of resumption of cash payments parliament, as a parliament, rejoiced in the prospect of asserting itself against a vacillating Cabinet and powerful vested interests in the community at large. Nevertheless, no specific legislation came forward on the committees' recommendations in this session in either the Commons or the Lords.

THE SPECIAL CASE OF IRELAND

On 2 June the general issue of free trade had been raised in the Commons in the context of a discussion of a petition against the continuance of the duties protecting the Irish linen industry. Vansittart was prepared to defend the duties on grounds which suggested his acceptance of the 'infant industry' argument as a legitimate modification of free trade doctrine.[28] In the Chancellor's opinion Irish manufacturers required a few more years before they were ready to face open competition.

Ricardo retorted that the duties had been in existence for twenty years, 'which surely was a period quite long enough to give the Irish manufacturers an opportunity of preparing for their repeal, if any such opportunity were necessary.'[29] Ricardo called for the protection to be discontinued, but he was opposed by William Huskisson who believed that, 'the immediate repeal of those duties would be productive of the worst effects in Ireland.'[30] Some 'further continuance' was justified in this case, although Huskisson sympathised with Ricardo's general sentiments.

The same issue re-emerged on 8 June, when Vansittart moved for gradual reduction of duties on the import of certain English goods into Ireland. Ricardo welcomed this as a step in the right direction and expressed the hope that Irish linen would soon be treated in like manner.[31] At this, William Vesey-Fitzgerald, the Chancellor of the Irish Exchequer, protested in terms that were to become increasingly familiar whenever 'the true principles of political economy' were considered in relation to the Irish situation.[32] Fitzgerald agreed with Ricardo's 'general principles', but claimed that Ireland was a special case. 'The situation of Ireland was, indeed, very peculiar', said Fitzgerald, 'as far as related to the provisions of the Union, for the protection and encouragement of the manufactures of that country.'

The belief in the special position of Ireland was again demonstrated just eight days later (16 June) when Vansittart, against the trend of domestic economic policy for England, moved successfully for a grant of £500,000 to increase the money supply of the Irish economy.[33] Eleven banks in the south of Ireland had suspended payments and to meet the crisis the government proposed to make loans to businessmen whose securities were substantial but who were experiencing liquidity problems.[34] The proposal was agreed to, despite the protests of some members that it was simply a device to support failed speculators who had been guilty of 'over-trading'.

8 1820: Farmers and Labourers in Distress

> His hon. friend, the member for Portarlington, had argued as if he had dropped from another planet; as if this were a land of the most perfect liberty of trade — as if there were no taxes — no drawback — no bounties — no searchers — on any other branch of trade but agriculture; as if, in this Utopian world, of his hon. friend's creation the first measure of restriction ever thought on was that on the importation of corn . . .
>
> Henry Brougham
> House of Commons, 30 May 1820

In the three years 1819—21, parliament received some twelve hundred petitions on the subject of agricultural distress. The inundation was particularly pronounced over the early weeks of the current session and even some of those sympathetic to rural interests found the campaign annoying. Lauderdale, for example, pointed out that the recent crop of petitions was the work of George Webb Hall who 'had taken so active a part in setting the agricultural interest against the manufactures'.[1] Hall had been appointed Secretary of the Board of Agriculture and Lauderdale remarked that 'if a motion for suppressing this board were to be brought forward, that was a question of economical reform which he should be very much inclined to support.' Long a supporter of the principle of corn laws, the Earl found 'the doctrines now afloat' regarding them to be quite unacceptable.

The presentation of one of these petitions in the Commons provoked Ricardo to state that 'the object of the petitioners seemed to him to be nothing else than to get a monopoly of the English market. The consequence would be that the price of corn would be raised and laid generally on all the other classes.'[2]

A COMMITTEE ON AGRICULTURAL DISTRESS

Scattered comments such as these gave way to full-dress debate in the Commons on 30 May when George Holme-Sumner moved for a select committee on the subject of agricultural distress.[3] Since 1814, Sumner claimed, the condition of the rural sector had been deteriorating and it was imperative to reverse the trend. Those who advocated the purchase of cheap corn overseas were ignoring the dangers inherent in dependence on foreign suppliers for basic commodities. Again, they were ignoring the interdependence of agriculture and manufacturing in any economy. 'If the manufacturer were to buy his bread where he could procure it at the cheapest price', Sumner reasoned, 'the consequence would be that the farmer could not purchase his manufactures, and thus both would suffer.'

Robinson then replied for the government with a speech that indicated considerable sympathy for the Ricardian analysis of the situation.[4] The immediate cause of agricultural distress, he admitted, was a low price of corn due to diminished demand. Nevertheless it must be remembered that during the war 'an immense capital was embarked in the cultivation of the land, which would never otherwise have been so employed.'[5] Robinson continued:

> It appeared to be thought by some that the natural level of the price of corn, was that which would pay the cultivator of the worst land actually in cultivation ... [Yet] it was not by any act of the legislature that that land had been called into cultivation, and it was not therefore to be expected that by any act of the legislature it should be continued in cultivation.

The corn laws, he concluded, should not be revised with a view to ensuring a remunerating price for production at the extensive margin.

Even more Ricardian in tone was the analysis of Thomas Frankland Lewis.[6] He began his attack on the corn laws by drawing a sharp contrast between manufactures and agriculture; a contrast created by the supposed prevalence of increasing returns in the first sector and decreasing returns in the latter. 'The former', he affirmed, 'were susceptible of the highest degree of cheapness; but the latter, when extended, must, by being driven to inferior land, have its produce deteriorated in quality and raised in price.'[7] Further, the corn laws not only encouraged productive effort of low productivity, but they subjected the rent-paying farmer to a profit squeeze:

> The landlord had but one object, that of obtaining the highest rent; but the tenant, whatever might be his interest under an existing lease, could derive no advantage from protecting prices when that lease expired. As a permanent system he must lose rather than gain by it, because whatever tended to raise the price of labour must diminish the profits of stock.

The existing protective legislation added to the farmer's woes by preventing him from exporting grain, exposing him to sudden influxes of foreign produce in seasons of domestic scarcity, and setting him at the mercy of combinations of corn merchants who were able to exploit the present system of calculation of official average prices of corn. The country as a whole suffered from the legislation, because its tendency to depress profits encouraged both capital and labour to leave England.

Neither Alexander Baring nor Charles Callis Western of Essex found himself living in the conflict-torn society that Lewis' Ricardian vision seemed to reveal. Both these speakers stressed the interdependence of the rural and manufacturing sectors.[8] The prosperity of the one depended upon the vitality of the other. Western observed that recently each sector had been in decline at the same time and this he attributed, in part, to 'the diminution in the issues of the Bank of England paper, and the consequent and sudden subduction of a country paper currency to the amount of many millions.'

RICARDO ON THE CORN LAWS

When Ricardo joined the debate he treated the House to a most optimistic prognosis for the British economy.[9] The only serious difficulties were within the power of parliament to eliminate. 'This would be the happiest country in the world', he prophesied, 'and its progress in prosperity would be beyond the power of imagination to conceive, if we got rid of two great evils — the national debt and the corn laws.' Once the debt was discharged and food was cheap 'the prices of articles would become natural and right.' Given 'natural' prices, 'this country, possessing the greatest skill, the greatest industry, the best machinery, and every other advantage in the highest degree, its prosperity and happiness would be incomparably, and almost inconceivably, great.'[10]

Ricardo repeated the arguments against the corn laws which he had used in his publications. Those laws encouraged the cultivation of poor soils, the maintenance of high food prices and money wages and hence, a low rate of profit which drove capital out of England. Turning to the arguments put forward in favour of corn laws Ricardo endeavoured to refute the claim that there was danger in dependence on foreign supplies of grain. He also denied that the laws could be justified by the existence of higher levels of taxation in England as against other nations.

In denying the need for national self-sufficiency in corn production Ricardo stressed the dependence of the foreign corn supplier on the British market, once trading links had been established for some time. Since the demand for corn was price inelastic, any habitual exporting country which retained its surplus production for political reasons would bring ruination on its own economy.[11] Ricardo added that England was likely to import corn from a variety of nations and it was improbable that England would ever be at war with all of them at the same time.[12]

Concerning higher taxation as a rationale for the corn laws Ricardo produced a highly complex counterargument which must have baffled most of his listeners. 'Some gentlemen', he observed, 'seemed to think that taxation made a difference in the state of the question, as to our intercourse with foreign nations . . . but, if all articles were taxed alike, commerce in general would not be affected.' Ricardo set out to prove this point with reference to the law of comparative advantage, which he had enunciated in the chapter on foreign trade in his *Principles of Political Economy and Taxation* (Chapter VII). Assuming that commodity taxes were set as fixed proportions of commodity prices, he reasoned as follows:

> If, for instance, this country produced corn and cloth, and that the production of each commodity was equally taxed, the amount of taxation would not make any difference in the relative advantage which one species of production had over the other, nor consequently in the choice of the commodity which we might supply to other nations, or be supplied with by them. It would be said, however, that taxation would make all things dearer: he admitted that — but though we might thus for a time cease to sell to other countries, we should not cease to buy of them till the reduction of the quantity of money we possessed reduced prices also, and brought us to a level with them. It was one of the evils of the national debt, that it stood in the way of a reduction of the taxes in the same ratio as the currency was reduced.[13]

Ricardo's argument here is a prime example of his methodology in action on the floor of the House. This use of economic theory as decisive in determining the best course of action on a burning political issue was soon to be condemned by Henry Brougham, among others. Further, the suggestion that 'commerce in general would not be affected' by the high levels of taxation was far from welcome to the whig opposition. It seemed as if Ricardo might be giving the government some measure of defence against those who called on the ministry to reduce the burden of taxation or resign.

BENNETT, HUSKISSON AND BROUGHAM ON RICARDO

Bennett of Wiltshire was unmoved by Ricardo's case for dependence on foreign supplies of corn.[14] Against Ricardo he set Adam Smith as an authority in favour of national self-sufficiency in this respect. He also inferred from Ricardo's line of reasoning on taxation that steps should be taken to discourage emigration of labour and to encourage population growth. It seemed to Bennett that Ricardo was saying that the country must rid itself of the national debt before the corn laws could be repealed. If this was so, then the first requirement was to increase national output and hence taxable capacity to meet the debt. That increase could come only through the employment of a larger domestic labour force. 'The productiveness of the country', said Bennett, 'was not carried half its length. It was capable of supporting double the population it now contained.' Bennett did not approve of the existing Corn Law, but he looked to the parliament 'granting some more efficient protection'.

William Huskisson was prepared to defend the existing arrangements in opposition to Ricardo's case for their abolition.[15] There were three grounds on which he had supported the Corn Bill of 1815, and he retained these grounds. They were: prevention of loss of a great proportion of the capital that had been invested in agriculture during the war; avoidance of overdependence on foreign nations for the necessities of life; and recognition of the special position of Ireland 'which had previously received encouragement from our demand, to withdraw which would have been most injurious to that country'.

Huskisson also disapproved of Ricardo's plan to discharge the national debt by a levy on personal wealth. The plan would 'have the effect not of bringing capital into the country, but of removing a great portion of capital out of it: for in the supposed case, everyone who could, by going out of the country with their capital avoid the payment, would endeavour so to do.' Summing up, Huskisson thought the best course was to leave these matters as they were, in the realisation that the present evil of inadequate demand for labour 'was to be remedied only by time'.

Henry Brougham's criticism of Ricardo was more fundamental than that of either of the two previous speakers.[16] He raised the issue of Ricardo's methodology, in much the same vein as had Joseph Marryat the previous year (see Chapter 5). According to Brougham, grave social injustice could arise if Ricardo's abstractions were used as the bases for policy making on concrete issues such as rejection versus retention of corn laws. 'His hon. friend, the member of Portarlington', Brougham charged, 'had argued as if he had dropped from another planet . . . as if all classes of the community were alike — as if all trades were on an equal footing; and that, in this new state, we were called upon to decide the abstract question, whether or not there should be a protecting price for corn.'[17]

In reality, Brougham pointed out, a variety of manufacturing activities was protected and manufacturers were not subject to the same range of taxes as farmers.[18] It was true that during the war relatively infertile land had been brought under cultivation, but it was also true 'that this land was now under cultivation — that it contained the capital, he might also say the life, of the cultivators.' Could one reason as if the life of those cultivators was of no account? Rather, said Brougham, it was 'as sound a principle as any principle in political economy, that the destruction of one portion of the community could not be considered a benefit because another portion gained by it. This was a proposition which no philosopher, or political economist, had ever attempted to deny or dispute.'[19]

Brougham then questioned the realism of Ricardo's concept of the presence in the rural sector of a tendency for production to expand or contract in a pattern governed by the relative fertilities of different soils. Fertility, he believed, was just one among many factors bearing on land usage:

> Even if the Corn Bill were repealed much bad ground would still be cultivated, and much good ground left uncultivated; because local circumstances, such as navigable rivers, canals, etc. had great influence over persons in the disposal of their capital. If these theorists, after the repeal of the bill, would go about the country, they would soon see that their theories were not verified.

Having thus struck at the Ricardian notion of the extensive margin, Brougham concluded by denying that protection of agriculture necessarily encouraged capital to leave England. The events of 1816, he thought, indicated the manner in which the well being of manufacturing depended upon the viability of agriculture. Farmers were the consumers of manufacturing output and there would be no outflow of capital where there was strong effective demand from the rural sector.

A LIMITED INQUIRY

There was no direct reply to Brougham's critique that night or when debate was continued the next day (31 May).[20] Even Robert Wilmot-Horton, a firm believer in the true principles of political economy, was prepared to take Brougham's point concerning the limitations of Ricardo's method as a tool in the formulation of policy.[21] He stated:

> He agreed with remarks that had been made by the hon. member for Portarlington; but yet he thought they were rather theoretical than practical. The principles of political economy might serve as beacons to enable us to direct our course; but as, in mechanics allowance must be made for friction and resistance, so in legislation reference must be had to the actual situation of affairs.

Horton was against any substantial change in the Corn Bill of 1815, but he thought that the operation of that act could be improved by altering the manner in which the official averages of corn prices were arrived at for purposes of the act. This same line was taken up by Castlereagh who urged that any parliamentary investigation should be confined to the question of establishing average prices.[22] Castlereagh's view prevailed and Holme-Sumner's original motion was amended to set up a committee with the narrow terms of reference desired by the government.

The committee reported in July, but no action was taken on its recommendations until the next year when Robinson brought in a resolution on 26 February which aimed at simplifying the method of striking the averages. Ricardo had been nominated, together with Baring, to serve on the committee but neither was appointed. However since the government had succeeded in preventing that body from considering any significant change in the existing corn laws, their non-appointment could not have been a serious disappointment to either member.

A PLEA FOR THE LABOURERS

Despite the continuing and widespread misery among wage earners the vast majority of parliamentarians seemed loth to consider the possibility of undertaking direct action to relieve the distresses of the workers. Two notable exceptions, however, were Philip Henry, the fourth Earl Stanhope, and John Maxwell of Renfrewshire. In the Lords on 16 May Stanhope moved: 'That a select committee be appointed to consider the practicability and the means of providing employment for the poor, particularly in the manufacturing districts.'[23] His speech in support of this motion revealed a conception of society in marked contrast with that of the Ricardians.

Stanhope began by linking the existence of agitation for violent overthrow of the present political order to the fact of lack of employment in manufacturing areas. He then declared his disenchantment with the factory system and with the government's encouraging that system through protection from overseas competition and relatively light taxation. Out of the growth of the factory system there had arisen the evils of exploited child labour, localised instances of 'superabundant population', and the need for workers to choose voluntary exile in colonies. In addition, by bringing large groups of labourers together, the system gave the disaffected 'every possible means and opportunity of combination and conspiracy'.

The wisest course, in Stanhope's opinion, was to limit the growth of manufacturing and to encourage employment in agriculture. Already the expansion of manufacturing had exposed workers' employment opportunities to the vagaries of the state of demand in foreign markets. A high and stable level of industrial employment could not be maintained in other than a war economy. The only genuine security for the poor now was in agricultural production.

To this end Stanhope called for retention of the corn laws, which also had the advantage of reducing the degree of dependence for subsistence on foreign countries. He also looked to some relief of the burden on the landed interest stemming from the poor rates, although this relief should not be sought by way of neo-Malthusian policies. 'Whatever may be the truth or falsehood of the theory which Mr. Malthus has attempted to establish', said Stanhope, 'I disapprove entirely of the measures which some of his followers have recommended.' Taxation burdens must also be reduced. By a zeal to ensure 'the maintenance of public credit' the government had weakened that credit through the imposition of new taxes which discouraged productive activity. Pressures on producers had been intensified recently by the decision to return to cash payments.

The great aims, according to Stanhope, were 'that of providing permanent employment for the poor, and that of enabling them to secure an independent subsistence'. These could be achieved mainly by encouraging the cultivation of waste lands through small-scale mixed farming which afforded the participants subsistence, plus a modest marketable surplus.[24] Such a policy, the earl realised, was open to objections from the Malthusian camp and he hastened to refute the potential criticisms.

Small-scale independent farmers, Stanhope believed, would not be prone to contract 'imprudent marriages'. This problem, which worried Malthus and others, arose in situations where the worker knew from experience 'that his own exertions whatever may be his industry or good conduct will not suffice for his support, and will not enable him to subsist without receiving parochial relief.' Yet if the worker was in a situation where his own exertions could foreseeably yield him 'comfort and independence', he could be expected to exercise the same prudence concerning marriage and size of family as did 'the middle and higher classes of society'.[25]

To further promote the welfare of workers Stanhope saw a need to regulate the use of machinery which was labour-replacing. Such machinery had already destroyed the domestic industry of the rural poor and was now threatening the livelihood of industrial labourers. Stanhope admitted that many articles could be produced at lower cost through the use of machinery or by importation, but, for him, the critical question was 'will you deprive of employment a considerable number of your artisans?' The introduction of new machinery ought to be regulated with a view to its impact on employment.

Stanhope found that those writers on political economy who advocated the widest possible use of machinery usually supported their case by reference to a fallacious principle, namely, Say's Law of Markets. He continued:

> It is true, that in general, and when trade is allowed to take its natural course, the supply will be equal to the demand; but the converse of that proposition, the principle upon which the manufacturers seem to act, that the demand will be equal to the supply, is false, and is contradicted both by theory and by experience.

The problem of ensuring an adequate effective demand, he believed, would be less severe where limitations on machinery helped maintain a continuity of employment of labour. 'Though the price of some manufactured goods would be somewhat increased', he allowed, 'the means of purchasing them, and the number of purchasers, would also be increased.'

There was no support in the Lords for this attempt to engender reaction against the factory system in a regime beginning to approximate *laissez-faire*. Stanhope's proposals were rejected completely by the Prime Minister who was the only speaker in reply.[26]

Liverpool told the House that there was too much waste land in cultivation already, and that limitations on machinery would severely prejudice the growth of the greatness of the nation. Then, in a statement which illuminated Liverpool's overall stance in regard to the miseries of the postwar years, he informed his peers that social distress must be a concomitant of progress:

> All experience proved that, wherever there had been great wealth there also had been at the same time great poverty; and that, wherever great enterprise had existed that enterprise had always been found forcing itself beyond its natural level, and not returning to it until it had experienced great distress and misery. To that state the enterprise of the country had at present reduced it. But were their lordships therefore prepared to say that they would retrograde to the first ages of society, and give up all the benefits which had since accrued to them from the exertion of human ingenuity?

This statement was quite consistent with Liverpool's view that cyclical fluctuation may be necessarily associated with the process of economic growth (see Chapter 7). Progress, he believed, must be purchased by human suffering. He was not reactionary enough to count the cost too great, but he was sufficiently conservative to resist legislative initiatives that might alleviate the miseries engendered.

ON BEHALF OF THE COTTON WEAVERS

A second attempt to focus attention on the plight of wage earners came from John Maxwell in the Commons on 29 June. Maxwell moved: 'That a Select Committee be appointed to inquire into the means of relieving the Cotton Weavers, which may be attempted without injury to the community.'[27] There was as little support for this motion as for that of Stanhope in the Lords. Ricardo was one to explicitly condemn Maxwell's views.

Maxwell began by deploring the fact of glaring social inequity. 'While the master manufacturers, and other classes of society, were rioting in every species of luxury', he claimed, 'the poor operative labourer was placed in a situation degrading to the character of the country.' He further deplored the attitude prevailing in the Commons: 'Many individuals in that house treated circumstances of this kind with the utmost coolness. They said it was no use to interfere. Things must find their level.' Yet investigation could reveal that it may be possible to improve the lot of the disadvantaged and benefit the nation as a whole at the same time.

Maxwell suggested four lines of action to improve the workers' position: taxation of machinery; repeal of the combination laws; subsidies in aid of greater mobility of labour; and government sponsorship of land settlement schemes. The first of these would help redress the competitive dis-advantage of man relative to machine. 'The capital of the poor man, which consisted in the labour of his two hands, must bear the burden of taxation', said Maxwell, 'since those articles without which he could not exist were taxed; while the large capital of the wealthy manufacturer, which he invested in a machine, was suffered to escape any contribution to the revenue.' The second line of action would give labourers some means of countering the effects of the ability of employers to combine to depress wages.

For the government, Frederick Robinson replied that the committee Maxwell envisaged would serve no practical purpose. It would merely 'propagate delusion'.[28] One of the points which, in Robinson's opinion, told against its appointment was that the mover had 'professed to echo the language of his constituents'.

In a brief but revealing speech, Ricardo also rejected Maxwell's request.[29] Ricardo protested against Maxwell's disregard of the principle of *laissez-faire*, of class divisions in society, and of private property rights. The government, Ricardo observed, could encourage industrial develop-ment 'only by removing the obstacles which had been created'. Secondly, Ricardo claimed, 'the recommendations of the hon. mover were in-consistent with the contrast between one class and another.' Thirdly, 'the principles of the hon. mover would likewise violate the sacredness of property, which constituted the great security of society.'[30]

REVIEW

After his success in the matter of cash payments in 1819, this new session had been one of frustration for Ricardo. The deterioration of his status in the House was manifest in June when he was not included as a member of the Select Committee on Foreign Trade, a committee established for the purpose of liberalisation. In his frustration Ricardo wrote McCulloch (13 June 1820): '. . . I am treated as an ultra reformer and a visionary on commercial subjects by both Agriculturalists and Manufacturers. Do you not observe that even Mr. Baring, the professed but I think lukewarm friend of free trade, did not nominate me on his committee.'[31]

Prominent members of the opposition — Milton, Ellice and Baring — had attacked Ricardo's views on the currency. Government spokesmen — Liverpool, Robinson and Huskisson — showed no sympathy for abolition of the corn laws or speedy discharge of the national debt. On both sides of the House — Brougham, Wilmot-Horton and Vesey-Fitzgerald — Ricardo's methodology was seen as inhibiting the usefulness of his doctrines as guides to the formulation of realistic policies.

For the most part Liverpool's ministry watched and waited while the economy languished. The political paralysis was depicted by Alexander Baring as follows:

> Ministers were balancing one party against another, and trying how they could keep their places from one year to another; neglecting in the meanwhile all those great commercial and national questions to which their most lively attention ought to be directed ... they went on from year to year, trusting that the next year would be spontaneously productive of some favourable change, and apparently with very indistinct notions of what the real condition of the country was.[32]

A not dissimilar charge could have been levelled at the opposition as a group. Leading figures in the whig party were also playing a waiting game.[33] Both whigs and tories stayed their hands in anticipation of the political crisis that was almost certain to break when the new King was confronted by the arrival of his wife in England. That crisis took almost all of parliament's attention from July to November. Economic debate ceased.

9 1821: Fundholders and Landholders

He dreaded the possibility of a conflict of which they had already seen some symptoms between the landed and the funded proprietor, as to the share which each should bear in the general calamity . . . One of the most baneful consequences, first of the vast creation of monied capital by the paper system; and secondly, of the great comparative depreciation of all other property, was, the increased influence of the monied interests on the institutions and government of the country.

Edward Ellice
House of Commons, 9 April 1821

The conflict between King and Queen dragged on. The affair continued to demand the attention of both Houses and to prejudice the chances of survival of the government. On three occasions during this year, parliament was to be obliged to debate the question of the inclusion of the Queen's name in the liturgy, and the current of social unrest which accompanied these debates was not to subside until the Queen's death on 7 August 1821. As members gathered early in the year for the opening of the new session, the whigs were optimistic about their chances of a return to power. The ministry had lost the confidence of the King because of the manner in which it had handled the royal scandal. The able George Canning had felt it necessary to resign his Presidency of the Board of Control. In addition, the tories were extremely unpopular in the country at large. Liverpool's administration had clearly reached a major turning point.

Towards the end of 1820 there had been signs of revival in cotton manufacturing in both Lancashire and Scotland.[1] The situation continued to improve throughout 1821 and other areas of secondary industry seemed to have begun to recover from the slump during the year. Nevertheless, the difficulties of the rural sector continued. Prices remained low and harvests were inferior to those of 1820. These trends were reflected in

parliamentary debate, as puzzled agriculturalists tried to come to grips
with the new but shadowy power structure that was groping towards the
shaping of English society into a more perfect vehicle for industrial
revolution.

Among intellectuals, Ricardo's reputation gained ground. Indicative was
the query of Thomas De Quincey in his *Confessions of an English Opium
Eater:* 'Could it be that an Englishman, and he not in academic bowers,
but oppressed by mercantile and senatorial cares, had accomplished what
all the universities of Europe and a century of thought, had failed even to
advance by one hair's breadth?'

Some of those who were willing to answer this question in the
affirmative joined the newly launched Political Economy Club which in
the opinion of at least one of its founders, James Mill, was to act as a
platform for the dissemination of the Ricardian gospel. The decision to
start the Club was taken at a meeting in London during April. As well as
Mill, those present included Tooke, Torrens and Mushet of the Mint.[2]

In this year a third edition of Ricardo's *Principles* was published, and
James Mill gave a 'popular' exposition of the new creed in his *Elements of
Political Economy*. Potential believers who might find either of these
books difficult were offered a fourth, and improved, edition of Mrs
Marcet's *Conversations on Political Economy*, as well as a series of simple
expositions of Ricardo's teachings in *The Champion: Weekly Review of
Politics and Political Economy*. Ricardianism did not go unchallenged in
the literature of political economy, with works by John Craig and 'Piercy
Ravenstone' providing some of the most notable opposition. Mill's treatise
was not regarded favourably by all reviewers in contemporary periodicals.[3]

A PETITION FROM BIRMINGHAM

In the Lords on 5 February Earl Grey introduced a petition from
Birmingham concerning the distress which prevailed there.[4] Grey claimed
that the data included in the petition showed that the problems of the
nation's secondary industries were no longer those of transition from war
to peace. Rather he detected the emergence of a pattern of industrial
fluctuations governed by variations in expectations concerning the state of
foreign markets. This, he believed, was a totally new phenomenon. The
problems of agriculture, on the other hand, were different in origin. These
stemmed from a heavy weight of taxation which had been aggravated by
parliament's attempt to prevent further depreciation of the currency.

The next speaker for the opposition, Lansdowne, attacked the idea that
rural difficulties were due to over-production of food.[5] It was absurd to
claim that 'the country, which did not grow enough for its own
consumption when prices were high, should all at once grow too much
when they had fallen.' The fundamental problem in the economy (as he

had stated the previous year) was exhaustion of capital. The government could play its part in aiding recovery by adopting a policy of stringent economy in public expenditure and by removing obstacles to foreign trade. 'The tranquilization of the world', affirmed Lansdowne, 'rested on the prosperity of trade.'

CURWEN AND BARING ON THE DISTRESS

When the Birmingham petition was considered three days later in the Commons, John Curwen found it indicative of the situation in many parts of the country.[6] Curwen believed that the only effective remedy for the distress was 'a decrease of the interest to the fundholder'. Curwen contrasted the position of the farmer with that of a person living off the proceeds of investment in public funds. The farmer suffered, but the fundholder was free, from the burden of poor rates and the deflationary consequences of the decision to resume cash payments. The relatively privileged position of the interest-earner could not be maintained. If the government did not act to establish a measure of equity, Curwen warned, 'men of property and consequence might feel themselves compelled to resort to measures at which they would now tremble.'

Robinson strongly deprecated the idea of a reduction of interest and characterised such a step as 'a breach of the public faith', and as 'neither honourable nor useful'.[7] Baring, too, found this proposal highly objectionable.[8] Neither was he in favour of a return to an inconvertible paper currency. Rather he looked to retrenchment of public expenditures plus the introduction of a bimetallic currency system in place of a gold standard.

According to Baring, the country's problems were no longer due to the return to peace. He also denied that the basic difficulty was the decline in exports (as the Prime Minister had claimed, and as the free trade petitions of the previous year had suggested). Instead he directed the attention of members to 'the nature of the currency'. Years of inflation and escalation of the public debt had been succeeded recently by deflation. This alteration had dealt a blow to entrepreneurs, while it had favoured rentiers. It had served to enhance the 'means of the man of fixed income' at the expense of 'the productive classes' of society: 'It was the drones in society whose means of enjoyment were increased, while the interests of all who were actively engaged in commercial and agricultural pursuits were depressed.'[9]

The levels of employment and investment were now at a low ebb because entrepreneurial expectations concerning prices and profits had not been realised, while the real burden of fixed-interest public and private debt obligations had increased. Underlying the simultaneous decline of prices and increased weight of contractual obligations was a substantial contraction of the money supply. In the process consumer demand had failed, except the demand emanating from those on fixed incomes.

Entrepreneurs would be given some assistance by a reduction of taxation consequent on greater economies in public expenditure. Above all, however, Baring urged 'the expediency of giving to the Bank the option of paying either in gold or silver, that the value of the two precious metals might be rendered more equal, and the present pound sterling, which was somewhat too high, relaxed. He wished to relax a cord which was at present stretched somewhat too tightly.'[10] Among the advantages of this step would be its impact on confidence within the financial sector itself. The move into bimetallism, he argued 'would have the effect of removing a great deal of uncertainty which at present prevailed. There was hardly a country bank which knew what to do, from the uncertainty as to what was to become of the system.'

RICARDO REPLIES

Ricardo rose to defend parliament's course of action in 1819 'when the plan which he had the honour to recommend was adopted by the House'.[11] At that time, Ricardo explained, the basic goal was to establish a fixed currency standard, a standard that could not be altered continuously to the detriment of the public interest by the Bank of England. There was nothing sacrosanct about returning to the old gold standard, but it was convenient and expedient to do so in 1819 because the then market price of gold was only four per cent above the old standard.

Baring must be wrong, Ricardo thought, in placing so much emphasis on a variation of a mere four per cent as a cause of economic distress. 'When a few years back we had so much greater variations,' observed Ricardo, 'we had no such distress.' Again, although it was true that there had been a substantial fall in commodity prices recently, that was the case throughout Europe. These facts indicated that the legislation of 1819 was not to blame. In support of this contention Ricardo also pointed out that commodity prices in England had fallen by different proportions.[12] The very considerable proportional falls in grain prices, he continued, could be attributed in part to the existence of the corn laws. These indirectly prevented the high-cost agriculture of England from competing on the export market in seasons when the domestic harvest was abundant.

A bimetallic system, such as Baring proposed, would lead to injustice. If debtors had the option of repaying in either gold or silver they could exploit variations in the relative prices of those metals to return their creditors sums of lower real value than those nominated by financial contracts. In addition, Ricardo suggested, adoption of bimetallism would not relax the tight money conditions as Baring expected. The Bank's willingness to issue notes would not be necessarily enhanced by the ability to pay in either gold or silver.

Turning from Baring to Curwen, Ricardo denied that the existing taxation system entailed special disadvantage for the landholder relative to the fundholder. 'Taxes always raised the price of that commodity on which they were laid,' he said, 'and therefore fell on the consumer.'[13] Ricardo also came out against Curwen's call for a reduction of interest, although he did not completely exclude the possibility that such a step might be undertaken.[14]

In conclusion Ricardo commented on the naiveté of the farmers who seemed innocent of the realities of class conflict in contemporary British society. Failure to grasp his model of the distributive process and the role of agricultural protection in it, Ricardo implied, led farmers to misinterpret their own best interests. Protective measures, he believed, offered them no way out of their current difficulties. Such measures merely served to further the interests of a class with which farmers were in direct conflict namely, the landowners. 'With respect to the rents of land', Ricardo observed, 'no interests could be more distinct than those of the owners and occupiers; yet it did happen that the latter were persuaded to petition that House for regulations which might be beneficial to one class, but more injurious to themselves.'

FURTHER CRITICISM OF RICARDO

One of Ricardo's more persistent critics, William Heygate, stressed the fact that depression was quite general.[15] It was not confined to the rural sector and it extended beyond Britain. Economic difficulties were particularly severe, he claimed, in America 'where the principles of the hon. member (Mr. Ricardo) had been pushed to their fullest extent'. In these circumstances, Heygate continued, the passage of the currency bill of 1819 had been a disaster. That bill should have been entitled: 'a bill to add one-third to the national debt; to add, in the same proportion, to all fixed incomes; and to subtract an equal amount from all the resources of productive capital and industry.' Like Baring, Heygate seems to have been impressed by the manner in which deflation had benefited rentiers at the expense of entrepreneurs, whether the latter were engaged in primary or in secondary industry.

At this point Baring re-entered the debate to reply to Ricardo and to again urge the desirability of bimetallism.[16] The fallacy underlying Ricardo's reasoning on the currency, according to Baring, was the use of variations in the price of gold as criteria for measuring degrees of appreciation and depreciation. Such variations afforded no true measure since the price of gold could fluctuate widely over a short period, while commodity prices in general remained unchanged. Judged in terms of commodity prices, the pound sterling was now appreciated by at least twenty-five per cent, as compared with six or seven years before. The reality was far in excess of the percentage of appreciation admitted by Ricardo.

Baring found Ricardo's insistence on the need for a mono-metallic standard to be yet another instance of the weakness of his opponent's methodology when brought to bear on policy issues:

> That one standard of value was a pleasing thing for his hon. friend to fix upon, when discussing these subjects in his closet, was very probable; but for what purpose of practical utility such a standard should be fixed, he, as a practical man, was quite at a loss to imagine; although the establishment of such a standard might be more agreeable to the views of the Royal Society, or other abstract philosophers, who would regulate weights and measures by the vibrations of the pendulum.

Bimetallism, Baring claimed, was sanctioned by business practice, 'in all the great commercial establishments of the world'. Its introduction in the practice of the Bank of England, at this time, would reflate the British economy without a return to a system of inconvertible paper. In reaction to the act of 1819, the Bank had taken the deflationary course of hoarding gold. To counter this, parliament should allow 'the establishment of a double tender [which] would enable the bank to afford such facilities as would materially contribute to relieve the distress of the country.'

Ricardo replied that he 'maintained the advance of the pound sterling with reference to the price of commodities to be only about 4 or 5 per cent.'[17] Further he believed Baring's position to be suspect on a number of grounds. It was not compatible with experience in Russia, Austria, or France. It would 'in a great measure operate against any metallic currency whatever.' Thirdly, the introduction of bimetallism would serve 'to drive gold out of the country'.[18]

GLADSTONE'S POSTSCRIPT

A final reflection on the state of the economy, as illustrated in the petition from Birmingham, came from the prominent tory businessman John Gladstone.[19] He distinguished the failure of effective demand as the source of the continuing distress in the rural sector and in many branches of secondary industry. Agriculture was suffering because of 'the reduction of the wages of labour'. The iron trade and other manufacturing activities were depressed by the loss of wartime demand.

Unlike an increasing number of observers outside parliament who also perceived the same failure, Gladstone did not see a remedy in the stimulation of demand.[20] Rather he looked to elimination of over-production and a gradual increase in domestic prosperity. The parliament could not do anything to aid economic recovery in the short run and he 'deprecated the idea going forth to the public that the House possessed the means of applying an effectual remedy for the distresses.' In this Gladstone was almost certainly expressing the view of many of the influential, non-agriculturalist supporters of the government. Legislative action would avail nothing by way of quick recovery.

A NEW COMMITTEE ON FOREIGN TRADE

Gladstone's sentiments were echoed in the Lords on 21 February by the opposition spokesman, Lansdowne, when he moved successfully for another committee on foreign trade.[21] There was no measure that could bring relief in the short term, Lansdowne believed, but reduction of taxation and, in particular, greater freedom of trade would promote a gradual recovery. The central problem was lack of mobility of capital. Parliament should 'give every facility to capital to dislodge itself, and to break its large masses into divisions which would feed and support different branches of employment.'

The present distribution of capital was sub-optimal, according to Lansdowne, because of the weight of taxation and because trade restrictions tended 'to force trade into channels the most unnatural and unprofitable to the country'. He knew their lordships were in favour of freer trade; 'science had made such progress within those walls, that there was no fear of the exploded doctrine of restriction being maintained in that House.' However he also recognised that particular vested interests could be relied upon to oppose the principle of *laissez-faire* in any given attempt at applying it. The opposition of these interests must be overcome for the sake of 'the unfortunate consumers, who composed nine-tenths of the population'.

After the motion for a committee had been agreed to, Liverpool surveyed the state of the conomy.[22] As in 1820 he quoted the returns on excise to show that 'the comforts of the people could not have very much diminished.' He admitted that there were special difficulties in the rural sector due to the importation of corn from Ireland and because of 'the circumstances which had forced great tracts of waste land into cultivation'. Although the influx from Ireland created problems for the English grower, the Prime Minister thought that this development would be to the ultimate benefit of the Empire as a whole. On the question of freer trade, Liverpool declared himself a supporter of the principle, but recommended caution in undertaking the removal of any existing restrictions.

This survey was far from satisfactory to some of the whig peers. The elderly Lord Erskine argued that the Prime Minister had neglected the basic fact of the redistribution of wealth which had been going on in favour of fundholders at the expense of agriculturalists in particular.[23] The problems of unemployment and low wages had arisen because of this trend. Those who had invested in government stock during the war 'were now to be paid by the industry of the people, and more especially of the agricultural classes, without on their part contributing to the general sacrifice.'

To this Earl Grey added that the burden of payments to public creditors had been greatly enhanced by Peel's currency bill.[24] 'Let them turn and twist it as they would,' he declared, 'the fact was, that we had contracted in depreciated paper an immense debt, which we were unable to pay in our restored currency.' Against the sentiment that 'we must not for a moment look at a breach of public faith', Grey set the maxim: 'Nemo tenetur ad impossibile.'

COUNTRY GENTLEMEN IN REVOLT

On 7 March in the Commons a motion for a committee to enquire into the depressed state of agriculture was carried by a majority of four votes. The motion was moved by Thomas Sherlock Gooch of Suffolk and was seconded by Sir Edward Knatchbull of Kent.[25] Both gentlemen were well aware that their motion was likely to meet with the disapproval of Ricardo and both paid tribute to his status as an authority by requesting that the principles of political economy should not be invoked to stifle the proposal for an enquiry. Gooch asserted the fundamental role of agriculture in English society and he urged the necessity of assisting that sector, 'if we did not wish to degenerate into what our great enemy had called us, a "nation boutiquierre" '.[26] Knatchbull stressed the financial predicament of the farmers and attributed this, in part, to Peel's currency bill. If the less fertile land should go out of cultivation as some advocated, then serious unemployment and loss of capital would result. Among the measures which would assist the struggling agriculturalists, he believed, was retrenchment of public expenditure and, hence, taxation relief.

Other agriculturalists to speak in support of the motion included John Curwen, who repeated his demand for reform of the taxation system so as to include a greater contribution from fundholders.[27] John Bennett and Charles Western emphasised the damage done rural interests by the resumption of cash payments as well as by the continuing heavy taxation.[28] Denis Browne went so far as to argue for a complete prohibition on the importation of corn.[29] He was totally disenchanted by the approach of Ricardo to such policy issues. 'Nothing was more mischievous', Browne charged, 'than the abstract philosophical notions which so much prevailed on all points of political economy.'

RICARDO RESTATES HIS CASE

Some support for the Ricardian view was forthcoming from William Wolryche Whitmore.[30] He desired reduction of taxation and governmental economy, but he had no sympathy for the present degree of protection of agriculture. 'It was no longer politic', he stated, 'to force the cultivation of corn in bad land. The sooner it was put out of cultivation the better.' Ricardo himself joined the debate shortly after this to argue the same case at greater length.[31]

In strict accord with his general principles and previously published views, the only line of action which Ricardo could tolerate was one involving the application of an economic calculus tempered slightly by recognition that the necessary functions of government required financing through taxation. British agriculture must become competitive on a cost basis with agriculture elsewhere. This must mean a reduction in those protective duties which enabled the inefficient segments of domestic rural activity to survive. Whilstever these were permitted to survive there would be farmers in trouble, a sub-optimal distribution of capital throughout the economy, and a failure to maximise consumer welfare. The only duty which should be levied was one which compensated the British farmer for any special disadvantages relative to importers of corn which he might experience because of taxation obligations.[32]

Showing his customary faith in extremely high factor mobility, Ricardo contended that the ill-effects of a reduction of duties were generally grossly exaggerated:

> The prices of corn would be reduced immediately and agriculture might be distressed more than at present. But the labour of this country would be immediately applied to the production of other and more profitable commodities, which might be exchanged for cheap foreign corn if the lands were thrown out of cultivation, through too great a reduction of prices to compensate the production of grain at home.

During the short transition period, Ricardo allowed, there would be some loss of capital. However he was confident that 'the greater part' of the capital now employed in the less efficient rural activities 'would be turned into profitable channels'.

Ricardo denied that the problems of agriculture were attributable to taxation. He also denied that landholders were being treated unjustly relative to fundholders.[33] The plain fact was that too much corn was being produced. England could not grow corn at the same low cost as was possible in a number of other countries.[34]

The speech was rounded off by the usual declaration of optimism concerning the future of the economy, provided sound policies were pursued.[35] Nevertheless Ricardo was apprehensive that if Gooch's motion for a committee was agreed to, there would be increased pressure for an even greater degree of restriction on importation. A majority of members did not share the same apprehension, however, and the motion was successful. At the suggestion of William Dickinson of Somerset, Ricardo was appointed to the committee.

THE COMMITTEE ON AGRICULTURE

After sitting for fourteen weeks the Committee reported to the House on 18 June and, since parliament rose on 11 July, its findings were not debated at any length in this session. Ricardo found himself somewhat isolated in his work with this body, an understandable situation given the strong representation on it of spokesmen for the rural interest. Apart from Gooch and Knatchbull, these included Wodehouse, Holme-Sumner, Western, Althorp, Browne and Curwen.[36] Further, it would seem that his viewpoint received little support from prominent members of the opposition, among whom were Brougham and Baring. Government representatives proved more sympathetic, especially William Huskisson who was responsible for the drafting of the report.[37]

In its ultimate form the report was not a triumph for either Ricardo or the country gentlemen. Most of the latter were sufficiently disaffected that they refused to sign it. The report was, in large measure, a manifesto for free trade and incorporated a number of the arguments which Ricardo had employed in support of the case against protection. At the same time it rejected the contentions that taxation or deflation could account for the special difficulties of the rural as against other sectors of the economy.

On the other hand the report stopped well short of recommending any immediate move to modification of the existing corn laws in the manner desired by Ricardo. Rather it envisaged that there might be an open importation of corn subject to a fixed duty estimated as that necessary to cover the difference between the cost of production in England and the cost of production in countries which were major potential suppliers of grain. This was a far cry from Ricardo's proposal for a countervailing duty which put the local grower and the importer of corn on an equal footing in as much as taxation disadvantages the grower.

The revolt of the agriculturalists had resulted in a compromise document which suggested nothing tangible in relief of their difficulties while it afforded a vehicle for dissemination of some of the leading principles and policies of Ricardianism. Perhaps, on balance, Ricardo could be thought to have gained. The *Glasgow Herald* commented (25 June 1821):

> The labours of the Committee have ended, as was generally expected, in doing nothing. Their cure for the present distress among

farmers is like Sir Abel Handy's plan for extinguishing a fire, "perhaps it will go out of itself." . . . Indeed, the drawers-up of the Report, Mr. Huskisson and Mr. Ricardo, appear fully more anxious to defend their own well-known views in Political Economy than to look after the interests of either landlord or tenant.[38]

10 1821: Payments in Coin Restored

This was the ground *upon which Peel's Bill was passed!* This queer, this 'Change-Alley, this Jew-like notion of the price of gold being the standard. However, this was no *new* notion; it had been harped on by *Oracle Horner* and his Bullion Committee; by *Lord King;* and by a great many others, long before *the Oracle by excellence* (Ricardo) spouted it forth.

Cobbett's Weekly Register
20 October 1821

Baring, Ellice and other critics of Ricardian monetary policy were given renewed opportunities to launch their attacks during a series of debates touched off by a government move to hasten the Bank's resumption of cash payments in terms of gold coin. The bill of 1819 had allowed the Bank this option only from 1 May 1822. However it was now proposed to give the Directors the same choice from 1 May 1821. As well as refining old differences these debates broadened the front of the anti-Ricardian forces by introducing a new analytical strength in the shape of the banker Mathias Attwood.

On 19 March Vansittart asked the House for leave to bring in a bill to effect the desired change in legislation.[1] According to the Chancellor, the alteration was expedient as a counter to the increasing incidence of crimes of forgery. To the extent that coins replaced notes in circulation, the opportunities for forgery would be diminished. Another rationale was that of reversing the trend to contraction of the money supply by hoarding on the part of the Bank. 'The circulation at present was far from being abundant', Vansittart admitted.[2]

BARING MOVES FOR AN ENQUIRY

At the conclusion of Vansittart's speech Baring moved for a Select Committee to consider Peel's currency bill, 'with a view to alleviate the pressure which the due execution of that act is likely to produce upon the several branches of public industry'.[3] He began by stating that he had no objection to the Chancellor's motion, but he believed it would have little effect on the size of the money supply since the Bank would be obliged to withdraw notes from circulation to the extent that it issued gold coin. It was not this particular measure which should be receiving attention, but rather the general principles behind the currency reform in train.

Parliament, said Baring, should discount 'all the idle stories about over production and under consumption and such like trash.' Instead it should reflect that 'no country before presented the continuance of so extraordinary a principle as that of living under a progressive increase of the value of money, and a depression of the productions of the people.' The problem was that the burden of both public and private debt had been increased greatly by the manner in which the legislature had chosen to revert from an era of currency depreciation. One of its main errors was to have accepted the substantial underestimate by Ricardo of the extent to which, previously, the currency had been depreciated.

Ricardo's blunder, he believed, was due to the adoption of the difference between the mint and market prices of gold as the measure of depreciation. In Baring's opinion a far more meaningful index of degrees of inflation was achieved by consideration of changes in commodity prices in general. Further, when these latter were consulted it was apparent that depreciation of the note issue had been much greater during the years of restriction of cash payments than any reference to gold alone would indicate.[4]

The move to restore cash payments and appreciate the currency, Baring continued, had brought commodity prices tumbling from their inflationary heights. The incomes of entrepreneurs were reduced in consequence, but there was not necessarily the same degree of reduction of their outgoings. Private and public debt obligations remained to be discharged at terms established when the currency was of much less value. The upshot was that now 'the industrious were obliged to labour under difficulties, that the drones might live in the greater affluence.'[5]

Baring was not prepared to deny 'the drones' their just due. However he emphasised that they could receive their full legal measure only at considerable expense in terms of the welfare of society at large. An economy would fare better in a period of inflation than in those years when deflation enhanced the position of fixed income earners:

> Of the two operations of raising and lowering the value of the currency, the latter was certainly better than the opposite, because the lowering of the value of the currency was cheating the drones. The person who had anything to sell, found the value of his goods increasing; the man who had to buy, found the value of his money

diminishing. The operation (he was speaking of interest, not of honesty) was advantageous to the country.[6]

Ricardian theory, Baring observed, quite overlooked the link between inflation and economic growth because that theory was wedded to a rigid version of the quantity theory of money. 'The hon. member for Portarlington', he said, 'told them, that the change in the value of the currency immediately had its effect on all commodities. But the effect could not penetrate into all parts of the country, or change habitual expenses.' Among such 'habitual expenses' were certain types of wage payments which tended to be sticky downward. Another instance was that of tithe payments, by which rural producers in particular, were disadvantaged in deflationary periods.[7]

Baring had two positive suggestions for improvement of the monetary system. The first was that parliament should follow Ricardo's advice in making permanent provision for the Bank of England to exchange its notes for bullion rather than coin. The second was 'the establishment of a double standard, namely, of gold and silver'. Against those members of the House who seemed obsessed with achieving a 'pure and perfect' standard as an end in itself, Baring argued that 'nothing should be yielded to the mere coxcombry of desiring a purer standard.' Those who urged the sanctity of an unvarying standard based on gold alone missed the point that 'the establishment of a perfect standard was not so much the *desideratum* as the creation of the means to regulate the price of the currency.'

RICARDO DEFENDS HIS POSITION

In reply Ricardo objected to the charge of 'coxcombry' and repeated his conviction of the superiority of a mono-metallic over a bi-metallic system.[8] Baring's scheme, he was sure, would 'occasion the greatest confusion'. Fluctuations in the relative prices of gold and silver would give rise to 'one of the most variable standards that could possibly be devised'.

Ricardo noted that there had been the criticism 'that if one metal were adopted for a standard of currency, it would be in the power of speculators to raise or lower the standard, and consequently place the Bank in an awkward predicament.' However, he countered this argument with the contention that 'the power which the Bank had of regulating its issues, would always be sufficient to prevent any inconvenience of that kind.' Whether or not other forms of 'inconvenience' might arise from variations of the note issue in response to changes in speculative demand for gold, Ricardo did not say.

He remained unconvinced that the move to resumption had been a significant factor in the depression of economic activity. Rural difficulties, for example, could be shown to have arisen 'from an abundant harvest, from the vast importations from Ireland, which had not taken place formerly, and from the late improvements in agriculture, which, he apprehended, would be felt hereafter more severely.' Baring had greatly exaggerated the potency of what was only a five per cent variation in the currency because of legislative enactment. Ricardo admitted that 'gold might have altered in value.' Yet 'that was an accident against which it was impossible to provide.'[9]

In conclusion Ricardo offered the directors of the Bank of England some advice. 'The rate of interest in the market', he observed, 'had been invariably under 5 per cent since 1819.' Current conditions suggested that it would be sound policy for the Bank, and a considerable aid to businessmen, if that institution reduced its interest rate from the customary five down to four per cent.

THE VIEWS OF PEEL AND ELLICE

Robert Peel spoke next in defence of his Committee's recommend-ations.[10] He rejected Baring's bimetallic scheme as impractical, and also indicated that he was not in favour of Ricardo's plan for a permanent system of payment of notes in bullion rather than coin. Of the two, he found the bullion plan the less objectionable. Nevertheless it could not be preferred to an eventual return to full exchange of notes and coins.

Edward Ellice came to the same conclusion, but on very different grounds from those of Peel.[11] Ellice agreed substantially with the analysis of Baring. The act of 1819 had given rise to 'more injustice than justice' by enhancing the real burden of private and public debt. Financial obligations which had been undertaken when the currency was depreciated by at least thirty per cent must now be met in terms of a much appreciated medium. This debilitating consequence of their recommendations had not been anticipated by the committees of enquiry in 1819, because they had measured depreciation simply with reference to the price of gold. Further, they had not perceived that the Bank's operations during 1818 and 1819 had been such as to bring the market and mint prices of gold in close proximity for a time.

Despite the injustice and 'considering the die was cast by the bill of 1819', Ellice was in favour of Vansittart's motion. He pointed out that in 1819 he had persuaded the Commons to add a clause to Peel's bill which was identical with the present proposal, but that clause had been deleted in the Lords. Swift resumption of payment of notes in coin had been the best course of action then, as now. He had never seen the point of Ricardo's bullion plan, especially as its provision for a graduated return to cash payments ignored the manner in which the Bank must react, given its stated expectations. Events had demonstrated the defects in Ricardo's scheme:

> It was quite clear at that time (1819), under the apprehensions entertained and expressed by the Bank, and while they were not compelled to receive bullion at proportionate rates, to the gradual scale in the bill, that paper would soon become more valuable in the currency than gold, and this was proved by the price of gold having been raised to the mint price, almost before the bill had passed into law.

Ellice added that the partial adoption of the Ricardo plan had led to some 'absurd results'. In Ireland 'the current coin of the realm had been at a depreciation of 3 or 4 per cent.'[12] In England 'individuals had actually taken their gold to the mint to be coined into sovereigns for payment to the Bank, who could not re-issue the money, if it had been demanded, without its passing through the crucible, to be converted into Ricardos.' He concluded that the time had come to put an end to these absurdities. 'The Bank', he said, 'were now in possession of 15 millions uselessly deposited in their vaults.' The country was never in a better position to recommence payments in coin.

When debate concluded Vansittart's request for leave to bring in a bill to effect the necessary changes in the legislation of 1819 was agreed to. Baring's request for a committee of enquiry was rejected. Discussion was resumed on 9 April, with Baring heightening his attack on Ricardian monetary theory and policy. In this he was to be joined by Mathias Attwood, whose views were even further removed from those of Ricardo.

BARING TRIES AGAIN

Despite his earlier disappointment, Baring moved immediately for a new committee of enquiry.[13] He was now convinced that the currency question was '*the* one in which were involved all the distresses experienced by the country and their remedy.' It was imperative for the House to enquire 'whether there was not something bad and diseased at the very root and centre of the existing system of finance.' Since 1819 many businessmen had been ruined and if parliament was in some degree responsible for the damage, then parliament should act to repair it.

Once again Baring complained of the gross underestimate by Ricardo of the degree of currency depreciation which had formerly prevailed. 'Look at the value of all the articles of life', said Baring. There resided the criteria for judging appreciation and depreciation. Baring also renewed his criticism of Ricardo's adherence to the quantity theory, accusing Ricardo of treating the relationship of money and prices as if it were 'a mechanical operation'. Certain prices did not respond immediately to monetary changes, most notably, the price of labour. During a deflationary process money wages were sticky in the short run, since workers associated a given nominal income with a certain consumption pattern to which they had become accustomed.

Baring noted that the behaviour of money wages in a period of deflation had important political implications. The attempt to maintain money wage levels led initially to unemployment and then to lower wages in the long run. This led in turn to social unrest, with workers seeking radical political solutions (such as parliamentary reform) for circumstances that were merely the result of unsound economic legislation. 'It was better', Baring suggested, 'to turn the attention of the labouring classes to the true cause of such a reduction (in wages), than to endeavour to make them profound patriots, by declaiming upon parliamentary reform.'

In conclusion Baring emphasised the evils of the redistribution of income in favour of rentiers which had followed from the manner in which parliament had chosen to return to cash payments. He confessed that, at an earlier stage, he had 'under-rated the inconveniences and difficulties' associated with a return to the former currency standard. Now he saw the question in a different light: 'The true question was whether it would not be more expedient and more just to bring the standard of value to the existing state of things, instead of attempting to bring the existing state of things round to the standard of value.'[14]

THE ENTRY OF MATHIAS ATTWOOD

Attwood seconded the motion for a committee of enquiry.[15] In the opening pasages of his speech he was concerned to show that by resuming cash payments at the old gold standard parliament had severed the connection between the commodity price structure of the British economy and its taxation and debt structures. Instead, the legislature had linked domestic prices to those of Continental nations.

Given European commodity prices and the legally determined price of gold in England, gold could only be attracted and retained when English commodity prices were low and a small volume of money was in circulation. In these circumstances, producer incomes must be low when compared with their levels during the era of restriction of cash payments and high prices. Yet the levels of debt and taxation of the years of inflation were not similarly diminished. The nation had lost the great advantage conferred by restriction, which was 'that it enabled the country to maintain an internal scale of prices, which had a reference to its internal situation, to its taxes and burthens, and did not depend on the scale of prices in other countries.'

Attwood then traced the sequence of alternating prosperity and depression over the war and postwar years. Each period of prosperity, he maintained, was associated with rising prices and increased money supply.

The depression of 1815—16 and the current downturn were due to contraction of that supply.[16] The existing prostration of the economy arose directly from the misguided attempt at 'what is called the restoration of the ancient standard of value, but which has been, in truth, and in fact, and in law, the substitution of another standard for the then existing legal standard of value.' To ascribe the disaster, as did Ricardo, to such factors as abundant harvests or imports of corn from Ireland, was to derive explanations from 'trifling and insignificant operations'.

Ricardo had been quite astray with his prediction in the House in 1819 that there would be 'a variation of 3 per cent in the value of the circulating medium'. The variation had been more in the order of twenty or thirty per cent, and one of the main reasons for Ricardo's underestimate was his neglect of the non-London banks in the monetary system. Country bank issues had been diminished substantially by reduction in the supply of Bank of England paper.

One of the most serious consequences of the parliamentary-induced declines in prices and incomes, Attwood observed, was the creation of class conflict. John Locke was one earlier writer who had shown how these circumstances could lead to different social groups losing their appreciation of their common interest. Thus, farmers and merchants were in contention at present on the issue of free trade versus protection. Again, a plan had been put forward to transfer rural properties to fundholders[17] while, at the same time, there were proposals for 'invading the property of the fundholder'.

It had even been argued, Attwood continued, that the interests of the wage earner were opposed to those of his employer. Some, including William Huskisson and Peel's former tutor Edward Copleston, had contended that a deflationary process which brought losses to employers benefited workers because of lower commodity prices, especially the prices of foodstuffs. But how, asked Attwood, 'in the midst of this diminution in the demand for labour, of this frightful destruction of the funds by which labour is supported, are we to expect to find the condition of the labourer improved? It is contrary to every principle of political economy that has ever been received, to all sense, and to all experience.' The essential unity of employer and employee interests was well depicted in the economic analysis of David Hume. He had shown how both groups prospered from an expansion of the money supply and how both suffered when it was diminished.

Hume's earlier findings were borne out completely by the experience of recent decades, according to Attwood. He went to some lengths to demonstrate that attempts by Liverpool and others to employ excise returns to show that material standards of living had risen in the post-war period, were based on invalid inferences from official statistics. The reality was that workers' standards of living had improved during wartime inflation and had subsequently deteriorated.

Attwood called for reflation of the economy. Legislation was required which would 'give back to the country that standard of value, and that amount of circulation, in which its debts, and taxes, and engagements have been founded, and in which alone they can be discharged.' This would involve the establishment of 'a metallic standard of 5 l.' He admitted that the suspension of cash payments in 1797 had brought injustice for some but parliament must recognise that the act of 1819 had meant even greater injustice for others. If they did not reflate, he warned, they were inviting 'a sudden and a violent catastrophe' which would endanger the survival of the existing social order.

SUPPORT FOR ATTWOOD AND BARING

No other speakers came out in direct support of either bimetallism or a substantial alteration in the price of gold. However there was some sympathy for the analyses underlying these policy proposals. John Berkeley Monck, for example, agreed with Attwood and Baring concerning the inadequacies of Ricardo's understanding of monetary issues.[18] 'Nothing could be more fallacious', said Monck, 'than the argument of the hon. member for Portarlington, as to the difference between the real prices of paper and gold. That hon. member was correct in saying that there was only a difference of 4 or 5 per cent in the price of gold as compared with paper; but then he only viewed one side of the question, and left out of his consideration altogether the depreciation of paper as compared with commodities. The hon. member on a former occasion, had also left out of his view the issues of country banks.'

Hudson Gurney found that Baring's arguments justified his own view that it was necessary to give 'a spring to the nominal prices of all commodities'.[19] To this end he revived a proposal he had first put forward in 1818. Gurney 'had always expected the measure of recurring to a standard which no outstanding contract had been calculated to meet, would produce the distress it had done; and his surprise was, that the distress had not been still greater. In 1818, he had thought the sovereign ought to pass for 21s. — and he thought so still.'

Edward Ellice was satisfied that the prevailing distress was due to Peel's currency bill, and he believed that in 1819, '5 l. 10s. would have been a much fairer standard to adopt than 3 l. 17s. 10d.' Yet now he believed 'it was too late to look back.' Further attempts at adjustment of the standard could bring worse evils than those experienced already. This was not to say, however, that Ellice was confident that the present course would not be accompanied by the class conflict which Attwood feared. The clash between fundholder and landowner was all too apparent. Deflation had effected a 'silent revolution' in the distribution of the ownership of wealth and Ellice 'wished to draw the attention of the House to the effect of this silent revolution on the political relations of the empire.' The resultant wave of unrest, he noted, had come to involve 'the great mass of the population'.

John Irving was in broad agreement with Ellice and he recalled the panic which had arisen in 1819 from the deliberations of the Secret Committees.[21] 'In 1819,' said Irving, 'when the country had arrived at the highest pitch of prosperity by trade, the apprehensions excited by this measure, even before the object of it were known, had the effect of depreciating every commodity at least 20 per cent.' Given that experience, he had some doubts as to the advisability of setting up another committee to reconsider the currency question.

RICARDO IN REPLY

Ricardo disclaimed all responsibility for 'the effect which the present measure might have upon particular classes'. The impact of the act of 1819, he believed, would have been very different if the Bank had followed the advice he had given it at the time. That advice was to commence selling, rather than buying, gold. He also reminded his critics that, given a metallic currency, it was impossible to insulate the currency from the effects of market fluctuations in the price of metals. The act of 1819 had merely entailed a four per cent alteration in the relativity of paper and gold. Nevertheless some members of the House persisted in confusing the variations attributable to legislation with those arising from other factors.[22]

Ricardo admitted that the equilibrium of commodity markets was disturbed in the course of a deflationary process. The existing pattern of demand for commodities was altered by a shift in the distribution of national wealth. Stockholders and landlords, for example, could have different tastes from those of the farming community, and when the effective demands of the first two groups were enhanced at the expense of the third, there could be a glut of certain commodities and an under-supply of others, in terms of demand.

At the same time Ricardo was adamant that the present disequilibrium in the rural sector could not be due to deflation. The demand for corn was not subject to fluctuations depending on the changing relative abilities of various social groups to give effective market expression to their tastes. 'The demand for corn was limited', he affirmed, 'because no man could eat more than a certain quantity of bread.'[23] Thus lower corn prices must be the result of abundant harvests and importation from Ireland. Further reason for doubting that the lower prices stemmed from deflation was provided by the historical fact that 'corn had risen or fallen forty or fifty per cent when no alteration had taken place in the currency.'

When debate ended Baring's motion for a committee was defeated.

Twenty-seven members were in favour of an enquiry. This minority included Henry Grey Bennet, John Bennett, Davis, Gordon, Gurney, Heygate, Irving, Lethbridge, Western, Whitmore, Wodehouse and Thomas Wilson. The opposition to Ricardo's authority as a guide to sound monetary policy had gained ground.[24]

VANSITTART'S MOTION APPROVED

On 13 April the Commons passed the motion for giving the Bank the option of resuming cash payments in coin at the earlier date. The Lords considered the matter on 4 May, but the conclusion was not in doubt. During the Lords debate the Marquis of Lansdowne, for the opposition, welcomed the measure.[25] Lansdowne made a point of stating that he was not convinced by Baring's criticisms of Ricardo. The widespread economic distress could not be attributed to alteration of the price of gold. Lauderdale also approved of the bill, although he revived the question of the desirability of making silver 'a legal tender in payments'.[26] He was also of the opinion that the market price of gold was being maintained at an inappropriately low level.

The Prime Minister was prepared to be agnostic on the question of the ideal form a currency system should assume.[27] Nevertheless the following statement by Liverpool was an accurate reflection of the naive metallism which characterised the thinking of many members in both Houses at this time:

> At critical periods, when a danger of overtrading existed, and a variety of fictitious capital was brought into activity, a paper currency was by far the best calculated to encourage the spirit of the first, and the formation of the latter. Giving, therefore, all its due weight to the argument of economy (of the precious metals in coinage), he apprehended, that where it was wished to establish a fixed and solid system, the preference ought still to be given to a currency composed of the precious metals.

Where this type of sentiment prevailed, the rationales of Ricardo's bullionism or Baring's bimetallism, let alone the broad hints from Attwood concerning the desirability of a managed paper currency, could be perceived dimly, if at all. To the great satisfaction of most of its members, parliament brought the era of restriction of cash payments to an end. The liquidity position of the Bank of England, in terms of gold as against its notes, was confirmed as the pivot for the entire monetary system. The exchange of coin for notes was begun on 8 May.[28]

The new arrangement gave rise to a flurry of activity at the Mint.

During this year it coined nine and a half million sterling in sovereigns plus half a million in silver.[29] This unprecedented output may have helped to boost the flagging circulation of the country, but the position did not improve with respect to Bank of England notes. The Bank did not accept the advice of Ricardo (offered in the foregoing debates) to lower its discount rate and hence its note issue remained limited.[30]

11 1821: Repeal and Reform

It was contended that the interest of the producer ought to be looked to, as well as that of the consumer, in legislative principles. But the fact was, that in attending to the interest of the consumer, protection was at the same time extended to all other classes. The true way of encouraging production was to discover and open facilities to consumption.

David Ricardo
House of Commons, 16 April 1821

In debates on the currency after 1819 Ricardo was almost invariably obliged to go on the defensive. However during the current year parliament was confronted with a number of issues in economic policy which enabled Ricardo to play a more positive role. These included taxation relief, reduction of import duties, repeal of the usury laws and reform of the poor laws. In each of these contentious areas Ricardo pushed ahead with his campaign for minimal legislated direction of economic life.

TAXATION AND THE SINKING FUND

During this session there were motions for abolition or reduction of several specific taxes and discussions of these were generally associated with attacks on the sinking fund, a device which served the nominal end of gradually retiring the national debt. This association was evident with the first of the moves for repeal when, on 6 March, John Maberly of Abingdon was unsuccessful in a bid to lower the duties on inhabited houses and windows. It was also present in the more significant debate on the malt tax later that same month.[1]

On 21 March Western moved for repeal of the 14d per bushel tax which had been imposed on domestically produced malt since 1819.[2] The repeal, he claimed, would be a meaningful first step in aid of both the rural producer and the general consumer. In the course of his speech he questioned the wisdom of maintaining the existing legislation concerning the currency and he protested against the unreality of demands for freer trade while English agriculturalists were obliged to carry such heavy financial burdens as compared with those of their foreign counterparts. 'Gentlemen might as well talk of the abstract rights of man', said Western, 'as of the abstract principles of free trade.'

Ellice supported the proposal for repeal and berated the extravagance of the government.[3] He charged that the government was using the sinking fund to facilitate additional expenditure rather than to retire the debt. Ellice was also critical of the farmers in their opposition to suggestions for repeal of the corn bill of 1815. That measure, he believed, hurt farmers, consumers and export manufacturers alike. He advised agriculturalists to give up all hope of a return to the high prices of the war years. Representatives of the landed interest themselves had put an end to such a hope through their subserviency to the government's monetary policies. Country gentlemen had damaged themselves and their fellows by voting for Peel's bill and by rejecting Baring's suggestion of reflation through bimetallism: 'By the short-sightedness of their own policy they had, in some measure, sacrificed to the monied, the old landed interest of the country, on the independence and prosperity of which our liberties and institutions so mainly depended.'

Lord Folkestone continued on this latter theme and made the most direct assault on the position of the public fundholder to that date in the Commons.[4] He caused considerable commotion in the House with the following statement:

> Suppose the public debt had accumulated to such an amount, that the taxes necessary to pay the interest created such distress among the people, as to require the suspension of our liberties, in order to preserve tranquillity — was not that a case also in which they would be justified in breaking faith with the public creditor?

For the government Huskisson took the line that repeal of the malt tax bore little relevance to the task of relieving current economic difficulties.[5] There had been a substantial fall of prices, he admitted, but members should realise that these had different consequences for the three main classes which constituted English society. Given those consequences the best policies were to keep faith with the public creditor, shift resources out of inefficient avenues of production, and wait.

In his analysis of the impact of falling prices, Huskisson diverged from the Ricardian class classification by distinguishing between wage earners, rentiers and entrepreneurs. There were 'those who obtained their subsistence by their daily labour, second, those who lived upon accumulated and dormant capital; third, those who by their industry and intelligence in the use of their capital gave employment to those who composed the first class.' Wage earners and some rentiers (including the fundholders) had benefited from deflation. 'Merchants, ship-owners, farmers, and those who gave employment to capital' had suffered. Some rentiers too were disadvantaged and these were mainly landowners whose incomes from rentals had decreased.

What could be done for the sufferers? 'The House would be deceiving itself', said Huskisson, 'if it thought that it was in the power of any human legislation to change the course of events like these, which arose from unalterable causes.' At the same time he consoled his listeners with the thought that entrepreneurs and landowners had been especially favoured in the preceding inflationary period. It was also consoling that the fundholders were such deserving folk. They were not idlers (Baring had called them 'drones') but rather 'persons who, after a life of slow gains and patient industry, had confided their earnings to the care of the public honour.'

Despite Huskisson's opposition and that of Castlereagh, the motion for repeal was passed on this first reading by a majority which comprised the whigs, radicals (including Ricardo), and dissident country tories.[6] The bill was taken to a second reading on 3 April, but on this occasion the government was able to muster sufficient support to have the measure thrown out.

Two days later (5 April) John Curwen sponsored an eventually successful motion for repeal of taxation of the use of horses in farming. The motion was supported by Ricardo who followed his usual practice of voting for all proposals for reduction of taxation no matter from which section of the House they originated.[7] His motive in lending his support was that of 'compelling the observance of strict economy in the administration of government'. Ricardo continued that the cause of greater economy was being prejudiced, however, by the government's retention of a sinking fund, which fund he completely rejected in its present form: 'He looked upon the sinking fund to be utterly useless — to be at this moment unproductive of one single good effect — he was quite disposed to abrogate every tax so long as any portion of that fund remained in existence.'[8]

This sweeping condemnation brought an immediate reaction from Baring.[9] Ricardo's outburst he found 'extraordinary and almost absurd'. Baring requested Ricardo to amplify his views on the subject since, as Baring understood it, 'the country would be better able to engage in any contest, or cope with any difficulties with a strong finance than with a strong military or naval establishment.' To abolish the fund would be to undermine the nation's strength by destroying its creditableness: 'To say that a sinking fund ought not to be maintained, was in effect to say that the country should go on borrowing, as long as fools enough could be found to lend their money, and that no security should be offered to the creditor.'[10]

MOVES FOR FREER TRADE

Early in February the Commons had agreed to the appointment of a Select Committee on foreign trade under the chairmanship of Thomas Wallace, who was Vice-President of the Board of Trade and had been Chairman of the Foreign Trade Committee that had reported on the Navigation Laws in 1820.[11] The new committee reported on 9 March, having focused their attention on the question of timber duties. The rationales of this focus were the existence of the Lords report on the same question in the previous year and the imminence of the expiry of the current provisions concerning those duties.

In what is generally regarded as the first practical step towards implementation of the principle of *laissez-faire* in the post-war period the Committee recommended an adjustment of duties such that the per load differential in favour of Canadian as against Baltic timber would be reduced from £3 5s 0d to £2 5s 0d. The report claimed that this would mean an effective differential of £1 10s 0d for the Canadian product, allowing for the greater transport costs involved.[12]

The bill to effect the necessary changes was debated in the Commons on 5 April. As in the areas of monetary policy and public finance Baring and Ricardo were at loggerheads again. Baring declared himself a free trader.[13] Yet the principle of purchasing in the cheapest market could be deviated from 'in cases of urgent necessity'. This was one such case, and for the sake of the British shipping industry retention of some measure of protection was necessary, as the Committee proposed. 'Some sacrifices of the several interests of the public to those of the shipowners was necessary', Baring believed, 'and the only question at issue appeared to be, to what extent this sacrifice should be carried.'[14]

Ricardo was not so ready to sacrifice the interests of the consumers of timber.[15] As far as the principle of *laissez-faire* was concerned, he allowed that 'there were exceptions to be made in cases of very old established arrangements; but this American trade was not one of them.' The pleas entered on behalf of the shipowners in this instance served to exemplify the illogicality of the anti-free trade position. 'It was strange', he remarked 'that inconsistency always marked the progress of monopolists. One set of men now called out for this colonial trade in behalf of the shipping interest, and the very same set of men, if they were spoken to about the West India Dock system would call it partial and oppressive.'

Nothing daunted, Joseph Marryat came back immediately with a strong statement of the protectionist case.[16] Ricardo's abstract theorising denied the traditional link between 'ships, colonies and commerce'. This 'philosopher' proposed that 'we are to sacrifice our ships and colonies, in order that our commerce may go on the better without them.' Marryat did not think that such a policy could stand the test of practical application.

Ricardo's view was in direct conflict with that of Adam Smith, who was in favour of navigation laws which protected a national merchant fleet. The older political economy possessed a sanity lacking in that of the new breed of speculators and philosophers.

The tide was running against Marryat's line of reasoning, however, and the bill eventually passed the Commons. When it came to the Lords there were some for whom it did not go far enough in the direction of freeing trade. One of these was Lauderdale, who saw the continuation of discrimination against Baltic timber as a device to protect the owners of worn-out ships. After the measure had been agreed to, Lauderdale entered a formal protest which described the bill as 'a specimen of our predilections for that illiberal, artificial, and restrictive system of regulation which has long disgraced our commercial codes.'[17]

There was no further legislation based on the work of the committees on foreign trade in this year. Nevertheless they continued that work with recommendations for liberalisation of the China trade (see Chapter 9). Late in the session there was a harbinger of other action when the Lords committee reported on the wine and silk trades.[18] That report envisaged a reduction in the duty on the imports of raw silk and of organzine (a fabric of thrown silk) from France and elsewhere. It also recommended modification of the special arrangements for collective bargaining and arbitration in the London silk industry, despite an uncontested assurance from the silk masters that no change was warranted.[19]

THE USURY LAWS

In his speech on Vansittart's motion for resumption of payments in coin (19 March) Ricardo had touched on the desirability of repealing the usury laws which imposed a ceiling of five per cent interest on loans. Ricardo had thought 'no time more proper for the repeal of those laws than the present, when the rate of interest in the market had been invariably under 5 per cent since 1819.'[20] On 12 April he was given an opportunity to express his views at greater length when a motion for repeal was brought before the House by Onslow.

Arthur Onslow had begun a lengthy crusade against the usury laws in parliament in May 1816. Then, as on the present occasion, he failed to effect their repeal and he persisted without success in 1823, 1824 and 1826. It was not until 1854 that the laws were finally abolished, although progressive relaxation began in 1833 when exemption was granted bills of less than three months' duration discounted by the Bank of England. In this instance Onslow ran into strong opposition from the country gentlemen.[21]

The landed interest feared that by removing the five per cent limit parliament would intensify the trend to diminution of effective ownership and control of national resources by the established rural gentry. Hence various of their representatives made claims such as: 'it would drive many persons to the sale of their estates'; it was 'a bill for more speedily ruining the young nobility and gentry of the country'; or, it 'was calculated to unsettle mortgages, and to persuade lenders that they ought to have obtained better terms'.[22]

Robert Gordon, a London merchant, and one of the few to vote against Peel's currency bill in 1819, opposed repeal on somewhat different grounds.[23] He saw this motion as yet another example of the 'wild and visionary speculations' with which theorists were tempting members of the House. He cautioned his fellows to 'beware of theories from the sad experience of the measure for the resumption of cash payments. This, however, was the age of theories, and nothing was heard of but a recourse to first principles.'

Both Ricardo and Baring argued for repeal. Ricardo expressed his astonishment at the alarm of the country gentlemen and he assured them that 'the lenders of money would not have more power to raise the rate of interest than the lenders (should be 'borrowers') would have to keep it down; and the competition between both would serve to bring it to a reasonable standard.'[24] The usury laws, he added, were 'a dead weight on those wishing to raise money', and were inoperative in that professionals in the money market often found means to evade them. During the war, for example, loans could be made at rates up to fifteen per cent.[25]

Baring made the same observation as that of Ricardo in March, namely that with the market rate below five per cent this was a good time for a repeal.[26] He believed that the rural sector would be benefited thereby. It would have been inappropriate to make the change in 1815 or 1816 when there was a strong demand for money and interest rates were high. Then repeal would have been likely to cause 'alarm and derangement'.

THE POOR LAWS

In the period 1811—21 the rate of growth of population in Britain was slightly more than eighteen per cent, the highest growth rate recorded for any equivalent span of years. Over the earlier portion of the same period there had been substantial inflationary movement. These two trends comprised much of the background to the growing concern with the financial burden of social welfare provisions and with the need for either their abolition or reform. One of the most avid reformers was James Scarlett and on 8 May he requested leave to bring in a bill to alter the Poor Laws in three respects.[27]

Scarlett's bill added up to a close approximation of abolition of the traditional welfare system, given the localised character of much of the existing taxation arrangements. It provided for a limit of future assessments payable by contributors to the poor rate. The limit would be the contribution required in the year to March 1821. Secondly it proposed that no unemployment relief should be given henceforth to any person who was unmarried at the time of the passage of the bill. Thirdly, it sought repeal of the laws of settlement under which justices of the peace could remove paupers from their existing place of residence to their parish of origin. The effect of the settlement laws, said Scarlett, 'was to restrict the free circulation of labour, and to expose the labourer, who, being unable to obtain employment in his own parish, honestly endeavoured to seek it elsewhere, to the penalty of being seized and sent back to a parish where there existed no demand for his labour.'[28]

Scarlett based his case on an appeal to that work-ethic with pseudo-biblical overtones which was currently aiding the acceptance of Ricardian thought in sections of English society. Scarlett declared:

> By the doom of nature man must earn his bread by the sweat of his brow, and nothing could be more injurious to a country than the adoption of a principle in legislation which held out to any considerable portion of the population an exemption from such sentence, and disconnected the ideas of labour and profit. The poor-laws held out to the labourer a prospect of relief, not in old age, not in sickness — but a refuge from the consequences of his own indolence.

Not only did the poor laws, in principle, fly in the face of the reality of Original Sin and discourage a healthy response to that reality, they also encouraged the growth of a pauper population. The poor rates, Scarlett warned the country gentlemen, 'must at no distant period absorb all the land in the kingdom'. The time had come when parliament must act to 'restore habits of industry and provident regulation among the poor'.

Some members, Scarlett recognised, might object to abolition of the laws of settlement on the grounds that 'the fear of removal operated as a check to pauperism.' Yet, he assured the House, pauperism would not increase if his bill was passed. 'The proper check', said Scarlett 'was the fear of poverty.' Scarlett's bill was calculated to make this fear a more real one for future generations of English workers.

At their first reading strong opposition to these proposals came from John Calcraft.[29] He denied that there had been a deterioration in the morale and industry of workers. Further he noted that although the poor rates had increased rapidly from 1776 to 1815, the same period had been one of rapid economic growth. Recent increases in the burden of poor rates he attributed to the prevalence of low wages, lax administration of the existing poor laws, and pressures created by a large national debt. Calcraft also believed that abolition of the law of settlements would 'create litigation, disquiet, and expense, besides other inconveniences which could not be foreseen'.

Further criticism of Scarlett's bill came from Sturges-Bourne, J. B. Monck and John Mansfield of Leicester.[30] Monck found the poor law system objectionable but 'before he abridged the rights of the poor, he must see a repeal of the malt tax, and of the salt tax, and above all, he demanded in their name a repeal of the obnoxious Corn bill.' Mansfield asked what would happen to wage earners in large manufacturing centres suffering a trade depression if parliament agreed to do away with unemployment relief.

Support for the bill was offered by the industrialist George Philips and the lawyer Michael Angelo Taylor.[31] Ricardo too was favourably disposed, although his speech is almost certainly reported most inaccurately and it is not clear whether he was in favour of the entire bill or merely that portion of it which looked to abolition of the laws of settlement.[32] The latter he welcomed as enhancing labour mobility and allowing greater scope for adjustment of supplies of labour to demands in particular markets. This would lead to a greater measure of wage justice and reduce the volume of litigation surrounding the poor laws. He also observed 'if the supply of labour were reduced below the demand, which was the purpose of his hon. and learned friend's measure, that the public debt and taxes would bear exclusively upon the rich, and the poor would be most materially benefitted.'

The reform proposals progressed to a second reading on 24 May and a number of conflicting petitions on the subject were tabled. Scarlett faced a barrage of criticism in the House and Curwen counselled him to withdraw the bill because of 'the generally distressed state of the country'.[33] Sir Robert Wilson characterised the measure as 'the learned member's anti-matrimonial and anti-population scheme', and suggested that, with low agricultural prices and surplus produce, population increase seemed more appropriate than a decrease.[34] Rather than a limit on the poor rates there should be imposition of a ceiling 'upon the dormant capital, which in a great measure contributed to throw the poor out of employ'.

Bennett of Wiltshire and Lord Milton attacked the Malthusian alarmism associated with Scarlett's case.[35] Both of these saw no necessary evil but rather much good deriving from an increasing population. Milton found it absurd that 'it was now proposed to relieve the burthen which pressed on the capital of the country by destroying that population which, although it fed upon that capital, materially contributed to its increase.' Current difficulties were not due to the poor laws but to the transfer of capital to the fundholders whom, like Baring, he designated as 'drones'. Milton allowed, however, that there was merit in a repeal of the settlement laws. 'At present', he acknowledged, 'the poor were in many districts very much in the condition of slaves, attached to the soil.'

When the bill was read a third time on 20 June Calcraft renewed his attack.[36] The growth of secondary industry, he pointed out, had created areas in which the demand for labour was subject to wide, periodic fluctuation. Denial of unemployment relief in those areas during the slack periods must mean 'one of two alternatives — starvation or intestine commotion'. Neither was abolition of the settlement provisions warranted on the grounds of lack of labour mobility. 'The number of hands employed in public works in distant parts' indicated that labour could circulate freely. Further it was not the poor laws which had encouraged population increase in the recent past. Rather the increase was due to 'the high price of labour during the war, and the increased pay given to soldiers'.

The third reading debate was continued on 2 July and at the outset Scarlett announced that he had decided to withdraw the bill, concluding his remarks with a passage from Benjamin Franklin on the deplorable consequences of the English poor laws.[37] Because he also announced his intention to raise these matters again the following year, Hudson Gurney rose to express his absolute distaste for Scarlett's aims and the thinking underlying them.[38] Gurney thundered:

> The learned gentleman's bill went to the reversal of the law of the land, the laws of nature, and the law of God . . . it was an attempt to bring the detestable system of Mr. Malthus to bear upon the legislation of the country — a system which every chapter of sacred history condemns, every page of civil history confutes, and every map of a half-unpeopled world, after a duration of nearly 6,000 years, proves the absurdity of.

The banker repeated Calcraft's prediction of violent social upheaval if welfare provisions were repealed and he found that in the recent past the situation of England had been very like that of the period after the depredations of Henry VIII. In both instances, the poor law system of Elizabeth I had averted 'a rising of the Commons'.

Just as another man of business experience, Marryat, had earlier condemned the 'philosopher' Ricardo on the strategy of trading policy, so Gurney assailed the 'philosopher' Malthus on population and social welfare. Gurney concluded:

> But he hoped and trusted that that House would never be led to legislate on the theories of such philosophers as these; and least of all, to give any countenance to a doctrine which in this country should recognize a right in the rich, to say to the poor, that they had no business to be born; that it was in the order of nature that they should starve; and that whatever might be the abundance of his superfluities, from him they could demand nothing.[39]

12 1822: The Causes of Agricultural Distress

There is a party amongst us distinguished in what is called the *Science* of Political Economy, who wish to substitute the corn of Poland and Russia for our own ... Their reasonings lie so much in abstract terms, their speculations deal so much by the gross, that they have the same insensibility about the sufferings of a people, that a General has respecting the loss of men wearied by his operations ... Political economy is now the fashion; and the Farmers of England are likely, if they do not keep a good look out, to be the victims.

Lord John Russell
Morning Chronicle, 18 January 1822

At the close of the session of 1821 Liverpool's administration had not succeeded in improving its image with either King or country. Still, the Prime Minister was determined to retain power, and he set about strengthening the government's position in the Commons. Peel, who had resigned from Cabinet in 1818, returned as Secretary of State for the Home Department in November. Wellesley was offered and accepted Ireland in December. At the same time a rapprochement was effected with the followers of Lord Grenville who had been operating as a small splinter party independent of whigs and tories.[1]

The advent of the Grenvilles could do nothing but enhance the influence of Ricardianism on the direction of government economic policy. Lord Grenville himself (now in retirement but still very influential) was a great admirer of Ricardo's economics, if not his political philosophy (see Chapter 6). Peel's return to Cabinet also strengthened Ricardo's hand and during the debates of 1822 Peel was to underline his sympathy with aspects of Ricardian thought. Castlereagh too was now prepared to be fulsome in his praise of Ricardo in the House.

The search for political advantage, which was conducive to a Ricardian drift in tory policy, encouraged a simultaneous rejection of Ricardo by leading whigs. The latter set out to exploit and intensify the growing disenchantment of the country gentlemen with the government. In the debates and divisions of 1821 rural members had shown a willingness to defy the ministry, expecially on the subject of taxation. Anti-government sentiment ran high at numerous county meetings across the nation during the first half of the current year. If this sentiment was to further the whig cause, the party could not be seen to condone Ricardo's campaign against agricultural protection or his view that taxation, although an evil, was not especially damaging to rural as against other interests. Lord John Russell made public the party's rejection of Ricardianism in the leading whig newspaper, the *Morning Chronicle*, during January.

There was a growing belief among agriculturalists that Ricardo was *the* enemy. He was seeking their destruction through abolition of the corn laws and through a massive levy on property so as the discharge the national debt. Some of them now perceived that the deflation accompanying the resumption of cash payments was a contributing factor, if not the prime agent, in their present woes. Here too, Ricardo was to blame.[2]

These themes dominated the economic debates of 1822, almost all of which turned around the issue of agricultural distress. In the latter part of the session the focal points were the report of the committee of enquiry into agriculture and the motions on the currency introduced by C. C. Western. At the outset, however, discussions of petitions from rural areas and a motion by Henry Brougham for reduction of taxation, evoked sharp divisions and conflicting analyses.

THE GOVERNMENT POSITION

The initial whig thrust in the Commons came on 11 February when Brougham moved for 'such a reduction of the taxes as may be suited to the change in the value of money, and may afford an immediate relief to the distresses of the Country'.[3] During his speech he attacked those who 'talk in honied accents' of suiting the supply to the demand, and throwing bad land out of cultivation'.[4] In reply Castlereagh (now Marquis of Londonderry) deferred to Ricardo as 'an hon. member of great authority on these subjects' and took the line that relief from taxation was no real cure for the ills besetting the rural sector.[5] It was a 'fallacious hope', he thought, 'that the agriculturalists, or any other great class of the community, could by possibility be withdrawn from the operation of those unseen, but all-powerful causes which necessarily affect and regulate the whole system of our productive industry.'

Relief for the farmer would come, in Londonderry's opinion, 'from the operation of capital, which cannot long remain unproductive. The supply and demand will soon adjust themselves to each other.' Rents would fall, as would the factor costs of farmers, so that 'the remedy for the evil will be found in the unerring laws of political economy. There is the true source of the farmer's hope.'

Continuing in this doctrinaire Ricardian vein, the Marquis instructed the farmer that taxation concessions offered him no real benefits. What the farmer might gain from them 'beyond the ordinary profit of capital would soon be taken from him, either in rent or reduction of the price of his commodity'. The government was not intending to reduce taxes, nor was it disposed 'to lay a sacrilegious hand' on Peel's currency bill of 1819. Nevertheless it was contemplating an advance of £4 million from the Bank on Exchequer Bills. This might aid farmers by increasing the currency circulation and by leading to a reduction in interest payable on mortgages because of a rise in the price of the funds.[6]

Londonderry did not think the loan would be harmful, given the over-caution of the Bank's policy on loans in the recent past and given the influx of gold the country was experiencing. At the same time he made it clear that rural producers could not expect to receive government loans in turn. In general it was most undesirable that governments should lend to individuals. Exceptions might be made occasionally in the case of manufacturers and traders who had 'great tangible property to be pledged'. However there were 'insuperable difficulties' in the way of loans on land and the produce of land.

The next government speaker, William Huskisson, was prepared to be somewhat less doctrinaire and inflexible with respect to rural problems.[7] Huskisson attributed the past distress of manufacturing and the continuing difficulties of agriculture to 'previous over-trading, combined with the altered value of the currency'. Wartime demand and speculative activity had resulted in over supply of some products in the postwar economy. The rural sector had begun to adjust to the postwar circumstances more slowly than manufacturing because agricultural capital was less mobile and had a longer gestation period, and because rural produce could not find overseas market outlets in good seasons.

Whilstever the 1815 corn law bill remained in force, Huskisson continued, it might be reasonable to introduce a government-sponsored stabilisation scheme to counter some of the special difficulties of agriculture. For example a bounty could be offered on the stockpiling of corn in seasons when the market was glutted. He believed the best course was to discontinue the protection of rural industry, but such a scheme provided a second-best solution.

In dealing with the role that currency adjustments might have played in promoting rural difficulties Huskisson distinguished between depreciation of the currency and diminution in the value of money. Depreciation was measured by the relationship of the mint and market prices of gold. Diminution in value was to be judged by reference to commodity prices. During the restriction of cash payments, there had first been a diminution as the note issue increased. Then there had been added a depreciation as gold became scarce. From this he inferred:

> The actual depreciation as it was not the sole cause of the rise of prices ... cannot be taken as the measure of the fall of prices since 1819, unless we could have got rid of the depreciation without recalling into our own use a part of the gold which had been exported, or in any degree diminishing the extent in which credit had become a substitute for actual payments.

Hence remedying the depreciation must have involved a very considerable fall in commodity prices, the fall being intensified by the Bank's accumulating gold and obtaining repayment of its loans to the government. The Bank's apparent willingness to now lend the government £4 million Huskisson construed as an indication that it had been over-zealous in its desire to increase gold stocks. He also criticised the Bank for continuing to maintain its discount rate at a level which was too high in terms of the current need to encourage a greater volume of commercial activity.[8]

Like Londonderry he did not contemplate any revision of Peel's bill. Rather he was prepared to let the prior and subsequent events surrounding that legislation stand as 'a warning never to be forgotten, against any future tampering with the standard value of the currency'. The worst was over, Huskisson believed, and now the economy was making such progress that its 'internal improvements were keeping pace with the growth of its population.' Prominent among the growth factors at work were increasing returns to scale in manufacturing. The prices of products were lowered, he noted, when 'great fixed capitals' were allied with 'the mechanical and chemical improvements which science suggested'. Growth would also be encouraged by the boost to business expectations which would flow indirectly from the proposed loan to the government of £4 million.[9]

When Robert Peel addressed the House a week later (18 February) he explained the special difficulties of agriculture in terms which were somewhat different from those of Huskisson.[10] Referring to the evidence put before the agricultural committee of 1821 by Thomas Tooke, Peel endeavoured to demonstrate that the demand for corn was price-inelastic. Hence excessive supplies must entail substantial falls in market prices. In addition he pointed to the baneful effects on English farmers of imports of corn from Ireland. Peel's conclusion from this analysis was as negative as Londonderry's had been concerning the plight of farmers. 'No measure could be adopted by Parliament', said Peel, 'which could afford immediate relief to that interest.'

In the Lords on 26 February the Prime Minister was almost equally unimpressed by the scope for direct parliamentary action in aid of agriculture.[11] At present in England there was over-production such that the poorer soils could not 'repay the fair profits of the capital expended on them'. The situation had been created by the loss of the wartime demand generated by government expenditures and it was made worse by importation from Ireland. As a corrective Liverpool looked to the operation of 'natural causes' over time: 'On the one hand, the great cheapness of the necessaries of life will increase the consumption of them; and on the other hand, the absence of a sufficient profit to the producer will diminish their production.'

The Prime Minister felt able to give a glowing report as far as the progress of the rest of the economy was concerned, but he indicated that the government did not intend to rest entirely on its laurels. It was seeking economies in public expenditure and would budget for a surplus to enhance the sinking fund. It would also take steps to reduce the higher rates of interest on the national debt.[12] Liverpool also announced that 'finding it impossible to induce the Bank to lower the rate of interest on their discounts, conformably to the expectation which was held out in 1819, his majesty's government resolved on borrowing 4,000,000 l. on exchequer bills from the Bank; with a view of applying that sum in some manner, to the relief of the country.'[13] As yet the government was undecided whether it should lend this money, in turn, to local government or whether it should directly employ the sum to mount public works programmes.

Another line of action under consideration was modification of the corn laws. As these stood there was a complete prohibition of importation until the domestic market price reached a given level. Then free importation prevailed and this threw 'large masses of foreign corn at once into our markets'. Liverpool thought it could be desirable to devise a system where by 'the importation may be regulated by a gradual scale of duties, so as to prevent these sudden and violent fluctuations.'

RICARDO'S POSITION

Ricardo was prominent in the debates of February and March. During these the main objects of his critical attention were the corn laws, the management of the sinking fund and the conduct of the Bank. He was also most anxious to refute the contention that agricultural distress was attributable to excessive taxation and he touched on this question during the debate arising from the King's speech at the opening of parliament on 5 February. Brougham's motion for taxation reduction six days later provided an opportunity for an exposition at greater length.[14]

'A country might be totally without taxes', said Ricardo, 'and yet in the exact situation that England was at present.' The basic problem was 'the abundance of produce now in hand'. A good harvest, the cultivation of poor soils and corn imports from Ireland were contributing factors. The remedy was to have a proportion of the land which was currently under cultivation 'thrown out of tillage'. He did not think that agriculturalists were peculiarly disadvantaged relative to other producers with respect to passing on increased factor costs and he believed that the impact of Peel's currency bill on corn prices was being greatly overstated by its critics.[15]

As a sop to the country gentlemen Londonderry moved on 18 February that the report of the 1821 committee on agricultural distress be referred to another select committee. After debate this was agreed to and the elected members were mainly those who had served on the previous body. Brougham, Huskisson, Wortley, Baring, Curwen, Whitmore and Ricardo were included.

In the accompanying debate Ricardo endeavoured to clear up the misunderstanding which seemed to surround his views on taxation. Ricardo protested that his central concern was the interest of the consumer and hence he was a consistent advocate of tax reduction. Nevertheless he could not admit that taxation was the cause of the distress of agriculturalists, considered as producers. He concluded that he 'always thought that taxes were injurious, but they affected all classes of consumers, and the repeal of any one of them would not be particularly serviceable to the agricultural class.'[16]

Ricardo reaffirmed his opposition to the sinking fund, although he stated that he had no objection to such a fund in principle when it was used to liquidate the public debt. The problem was its misuse. Since the era of Walpole it had served 'only to encourage ministers to engage in new wars by facilitating the contraction of new loans.'[17] Ricardo also reaffirmed the basic thesis of his published works concerning the necessity of a repeal of the corn laws if England was to fully exploit its rich potential for economic growth.

He was not impressed by Huskisson's suggestion of an agricultural price stabilisation scheme. 'Such a system', declared Ricardo, 'was decidedly contrary to every established principle of political economy and common sense.'[18] Neither was he favourably inclined to the proposed £4 million loan from the Bank. This he viewed as a 'hazardous experiment'.

Ricardo was of the opinion that if the Bank had been too eager to accumulate gold in the immediate past there was a real danger now that it might be too ready to part with the metal. The Bank directors 'had not a sufficient degree of talent for the management of so vast a machine as that with which they were intrusted.' These men had bungled the resumption of cash payments by premature action and by unnecessary purchases of gold. Those purchases had driven up the value of gold relative to commodities throughout Europe. The result was that the fall in commodity prices in England had been significantly greater than the five per cent which could have been expected if the implementation of Peel's act had been managed with skill.[19]

On 8 March Ricardo returned to a general criticism of the Bank's policies: 'The directors had convinced him by their conduct that they did not know what they were about.'[20] After 1797 they had issued paper to such an extent as to cause its depreciation. This had meant that 'to recover from that depreciation, the country had found it necessary to undergo a painful process, which had been the cause of a great part of the present distress.' Further they had intensified the deflation by accumulating gold. Given this record he could not trust them to manage successfully the £4 million loan being considered at present. He believed that the loan must result in an outflow of gold from England.

WHIGS ON THE OFFENSIVE

At the outset of the session leading whigs had put great store by a successful showing with Henry Brougham's motion for taxation reduction. The motion was an attempt to win the support of rural representatives who customarily voted with the government, and in this respect it succeeded to some extent. However it failed to gain a majority and Ricardo's influence may have been significant in determining this result.[21]

Brougham argued that the effects of the wartime inflation and of the deflation associated with resumption of cash payments had fallen unequally on the agricultural and non-agricultural sectors.[22] Unlike manufacturers, farmers could not pass on cost increases directly to consumers, nor did they possess the same scope for introducing machinery to compensate for higher input costs. Given such inflexibilities it was more difficult for the agriculturalist to remain viable in a situation where the low money incomes of a period of currency appreciation were coupled with the high money outgoings on borrowings contracted when prices were buoyant and the currency depreciated. To keep them viable the most practical step was taxation relief, assuming the government was disturbed at the prospect of 'a great change of property' and 'the destruction of a class'. Another possible step was a deliberate alteration of the currency standard, but Brougham 'did not say that the country ought to make up its mind easily to such a course.'[23]

In the Lords a fortnight later (26 February) Lansdowne led for the whigs with a repetition of the request for lower taxation.[24] 'The amount of taxation in this country', he declared, 'formed the great obstacle to its recovery from the state of distress in which it was plunged.' Lansdowne showed considerable concern with the problem of lack of effective demand. In his opinion 'the great object to be pursued was, to adopt such measures as would have a tendency to increase and secure consumption.' He rejected the Ricardian solution to current rural difficulties: 'The evil was not to be remedied by taking lands out of cultivation, but by raising the consumption so as to make the produce and the demand meet each other.'[25] Lord Ellenborough argued a similar case and, like Huskisson in the Commons, canvassed the idea of a market stabilisation scheme for corn.[26] 'The present was a period of peculiar difficulty and distress', Ellenborough believed, 'some extraordinary measure, not perhaps justified by the ordinary principles of political economy, should be adopted.'[27]

Some members of the opposition in the Commons sought to stress the role which legislation for cash payments had played in generating rural distress. Ellice was the most prominent of these and he renewed his criticisms of Ricardo as a reliable guide on monetary questions.[28] Ellice was now in complete agreement with Baring that the price of gold was no criterion for judging the state of the currency. Much more meaningful points of reference were 'the debt due to the Bank by the public, and the amount of paper in circulation'. James Scarlett too could not accept Ricardo's analysis.[29] In Scarlett's view 'a great portion of the distress arose from the return to cash payments . . . a superabundance of produce could not of itself have produced it.' It was a fact that with the onset of deflation farmers were obliged to bear an increasingly heavy burden of taxation.

Among the country gentlemen who spoke in support of the opposition's case were John Bennett and Stuart-Wortley.[30] These also emphasised the manner in which alteration of the currency had enhanced the pressure of taxation and Bennett took the rather unusual line of pointing to the regressive nature of the range of commodity taxes which predominated among the revenue sources of the day. Any reform of the taxation system should recognise that those with meagre purchasing power were penalised relative to the rich by the existing arrangements.

ON RICARDO ON THE BANK

Ricardo's accusation that the policies of the Bank of England were to some extent to blame for the problems of the rural sector did not go unremarked. Defending the conduct of the directors of that institution John Pearse, who had been Deputy Governor of the Bank, retorted that he 'preferred the opinion of the proprietors of Bank-stock, who elected them annually, to all the theories of modern philosophers on the subject. Neither theory nor speculation would do for the management of the affairs of the Bank of England.'[31] Hudson Gurney too was prepared to speak up on behalf of the Bank: 'It was only when they (the directors) were interfered with by theorists and speculators that they experienced anything like distress.'[32]

J. B. Monck was inclined to agree with Ricardo that the Bank's actions had given rise to distress, but he did not think that this was due to incompetence in the management of its own affairs.[33] Monck endeavoured to demonstrate that there was a direct conflict between the interest of the Bank and that of the country as a whole. The Bank had been able to do very well for itself, although the country had suffered thereby. The increasing value of Bank stock and the substantial dividends yielded the proprietors were proofs of this contention.

Pascoe Grenfell was of the same mind.[34] Commercial incompetence was not the problem. Rather, his remarks tended to suggest, the problem was permitting a single private enterprise such scope for decisions which profoundly influenced the course of economic policy. Neither Grenfell nor Monck (nor Ricardo at this stage) contended that a solution to problems of incompetence or of conflict of interest might be the formation of a government bank which would assume certain of the functions of the Bank of England.

13 1822: A New Corn Law

The hon. gentleman might, perhaps, think that a manufacturing country could not be so happy as an agricultural country. But he might as well complain of a man's growing old as of such a change in our national condition. Nations grew old as well as individuals; and in proportion as they grew old, populous, and wealthy, must they become manufacturers. If things were allowed to take their own course, we should undoubtedly become a great manufacturing country, but we should remain a great agricultural country also.

David Ricardo
House of Commons, 9 May 1822

On 1 April the Select Committee which had been appointed in February to enquire into the state of agriculture brought in its report. This revealed that the Committee had taken an unfavourable view of suggestions that the government itself might buy and store corn or that it should make loans to local authorities for that purpose. However as a measure of temporary relief it envisaged the possibility of loans to rural producers on the security of corn held in store. The loans could be made whenever the market price of grain was less than 60s. per quarter. The rate of interest would be three per cent, the maximum duration twelve months, and the maximum amount two-thirds of the current market value of the corn.

The major proposal was for an alteration of the corn law of 1815 which absolutely prohibited the importation of foreign wheat when the domestic market price was less that 80s. The Committee recommended that '... after our wheat shall have reached 80s. whenever circumstances, not now to be foressen, may have effected so great a change, a lower price may be assumed for the future import, subject to a duty ... 70s. would not be an improper limit to assign to that price: That a duty from 12s. to 15s. should be imposed upon foreign wheat for home consumption, when the price is from 70s. to 80s. Also, that a duty of 5s. should be imposed upon such wheat, when the price is from 80s. to 85s; after which the duty should be reduced to 1s.'[1]

RICARDO'S FIRST STATEMENT

Ricardo was highly critical of the new report and believed it compared most unfavourably with that of the 1821 committee.[2] The first part of the

earlier document, he stated, was 'well worthy of being placed beside the
bullion report (1810) and the report on the resumption of cash payments
by the Bank.' From it one could deduce the best set of provisions to be
applied to British agriculture. On the basis of the 1821 report he
recommended that 'a duty on importation of foreign grain should be
imposed, equal to the peculiar taxes which fell on the farmer, such as
tythes and a part of the poor-rate; and a drawback of the same amount
should be allowed on exportation.' With such arrangements the British
producer could expect to have a cost structure similar to that of overseas
farmers. He would be able to export in times of domestic abundance and
he would be protected from sudden inundations of cheap foreign grain in
periods of scarcity. English agriculture would be both competitive and
stable.

The latter sections of the 1821 report had proposed protection of the
local grower by means of countervailing duties, i.e., 'duties which should
be equal to the additional expense of growing corn in this country over
other countries.' Ricardo found this most ill-advised, since the cost of
production of corn in England must rise as population expanded and
cultivation was extended to poorer soils. Hence, commitment to a policy
of countervailing duties was commitment to ever increasing food prices
and to an ever increasing degree of protection as the gap widened between
production costs in Britain and other countries.[3]

In the course of this address Ricardo took the opportunity to deny the
now widely held view that agricultural distress was due to the combined
impact of currency appreciation and high levels of taxation. Henry Grey
Bennet rose immediately to protest that Ricardo's case was 'mere words
and sophistry', but Londonderry replied in terms which gave the clearest
demonstration to that time of just how useful a prop Ricardo's reasoning
had become for the administration in its current political stance.[4]
According to the Marquis it was over-production and not taxation which
accounted for the distress. He suggested that Bennet 'might take a lesson
from his friend near him the member for Portarlington, who had shown
how small a portion of that distress now complained of had been thrown
on the suffering individuals by taxation.' Further, although Londonderry
himself was not prepared to give members a detailed explanation of the
phenomenon of over-production, 'if the hon. member for Portarlington
turned his intelligent mind to it, he could make the House understand this
part of the subject.'

THE GOVERNMENT'S POLICY PACKAGE

Londonderry continued his tribute to Ricardian analysis when he brought
forward a series of thirteen resolutions on 29 April.[5] It was by the
operation of market forces rather than legislative action, he contended,

that the rural sector could be set at rights. For substantiation of the validity of his views he referred members to 'the able work which has recently been published by the hon. member for Portarlington (Mr. Ricardo) than whom it is impossible for the House on such questions to have higher authority.'[6] However speaking for the government, Londonderry was not prepared to allow that the time was yet ripe for full implementation of Ricardian policy with respect to the corn laws.

The government decided to support the proposals of the Select Committee by moving for an advance of up to £1 million to rural producers on grain in store. It also agreed with the Committee's plan for alteration of the corn laws. Other measures were the voting of funds for relief in Ireland, conversion of that part of the public debt which related to the Navy five per cents, and stimulation of the money supply. These latter involved the government's proceeding with the £4 million loan from the Bank. Londonderry also moved that the act which gave country banks the right to issue notes for denominations under £5 should be extended to operate until 1833.[7] At the same time he indicated that negotiations were under way with the Bank of England to extend its Charter to 1843 on condition that the Bank consented to a modification of that Charter to permit the wider development of joint stock banking.[8]

In moving the recommendations of the Select Committee on agriculture Londonderry professed himself to be 'the advocate of a free trade, as nearly as circumstances will permit, under such regulated duties, as may protect the country from danger.' He noted that these recommendations differed slightly from those which Ricardo would have preferred. The scale of duties was higher and the Committee's plan retained the principle of absolute exclusion of foreign corn when the local price was below a predetermined level. Yet these differences were justified because of the prevailing glut of corn throughout Europe. It would be a different matter, Londonderry thought 'if the agriculture of the world were in its natural state'. As to the idea of loans on corn in store, he thought it harmless enough but of little use as a corrective for the fundamental problems of agriculture.

William Huskisson was also half hearted in support of the storage loans proposal.[9] He recalled that during the sittings of the Select Committee of the previous year Alexander Baring (who was not in the House for the current debate) had first mooted the idea of the government's buying corn in years of surplus and selling it in times of scarcity. This he disagreed with on principle, although he admitted it could be useful as a device for equating supply and demand whilstever the corn trade was not free. A better means of achieving the same end might be to grant some type of bounty, akin to an export bounty, on stored corn.

Huskisson concluded by moving for the commencement of an approximation of free trade in corn under less restrictive conditions than those allowed for in the Committee's findings. He moved that three months after the price of wheat came to exceed 70s. a quarter at any future date, there should be permanently free entry (although subject to duty), of wheat, rye, barley, oats and other grains, from that time forward. The duty on wheat should be '15s. a quarter, when the price shall not exceed 80s.; and when above that price, 5s.; and above 85s., one shilling.' These resolutions he put forward in direct competition with those which had just been sponsored officially by his leader in the House.

AN ALTERNATIVE PROPOSAL BY RICARDO

Ricardo began by criticising the government's finance and expenditure resolutions.[10] These he saw as 'an attack upon the sinking fund' and as a 'breach of public faith'. He welcomed the intention to ease restrictions on the establishment of new private banks, but he 'solemnly protested against prolonging the charter to the Bank'. Ricardo affirmed: 'The benefit of the paper currency ought to belong to the public. No advantage could ever be derived from the Bank lending money to the public.'[11]

Careless of the praise bestowed on him by Londonderry Ricardo argued that there was 'the most essential difference' between the plan for the protection of agriculture which the Marquis had sponsored and that which Ricardo favoured. Ricardo's own plan involved an initial duty of 20s. per quarter on imported wheat, but this was only because of the extreme pressure of the existing agricultural distress. Again, his plan was conducive to encouraging the price of English corn to attain comparability with the prices of foreign grains, whereas Londonderry's was not. Thirdly, he would do away with the system which exposed the farmers – 'the most distressed class in the country, and the most cruelly used' – to sudden influxes of imported corn when domestic scarcity drove the market price in England above a certain limit. The government proposed to maintain the possibility of such exposure.

Ricardo then moved five resolutions which diverged in a more radical fashion than did those of Huskisson from the Select Committee's recommendations.[12] Under his plan trade in corn would be subject to permanently free importation from that future date at which the price of wheat might exceed 70s. Initially imports would be liable to a duty of 20s. per quarter, but the duty on wheat would be reduced each year by one shilling until it stood at 10s. per quarter. In addition a drawback of 7s. would be allowed on wheat exports. The same arrangements would apply to other types of grain, although the duties and drawbacks would be smaller at each stage.

As reported in *The Times*, Ricardo supported his case for such a substantial departure from the existing protective system with the claim that class conflict would be reduced thereby.[13] Ricardo stated that he 'did not accuse landlords of being hard-hearted or regardless of the situation in which other classes might be placed; but under the system of corn laws which now existed, their interests must be opposed.[14] He was surprised to hear it often repeated in that house, that the landlord had the same interest as all other classes, and to find this declaration loudly cheered as often as it was made.'

These remarks indicate something of Ricardo's frustration at the habitual tendency of the country gentlemen to cling to the view that farmer and landlord were indissolubly linked in a mutuality of interest. They appeared incapable of perceiving his point that the landlord could be benefited while the farmer was 'cruelly used'. Further his comment implies that for Ricardo, a serious conflict of interest was no necessary feature of a future scenario from which the presence of agricultural protection had been eliminated. Serious social conflict (in one of its contemporary dimensions, at least) was no more inevitable than was economic stagnation given the abandonment of past mistakes by the legislature. Just as repeal of the Combination Laws would improve labour-management relations, so repeal of the Corn Laws would create a less divisive situation with respect to landlord and farmer as well as landlord and worker.[15]

THE STORAGE PLAN ABANDONED

On 6 May when Londonderry moved formally that the government be empowered to make loans on grain, John Curwen spoke in favour of the measure.[16] He perceived that it had definite possibilities as a permanent arrangement conducive to more orderly marketing. It need not be regarded as an emergency step. 'A time could scarcely arrive', said Curwen, 'when the demand and the supply would be equal; and in years of abundance the scheme would hold out an important inducement to speculators in grain.'

John Irving was also in favour of the scheme, at least as an expedient in time of distress.[17] He confessed to being the originator of the idea and he assured the House that he 'had not proposed this measure in ignorance of the true principles of political economy.' Thomas Wilson too lent his support.[18] In his view this was 'the only practical measure which had been recommended by the committee'.

However the advocates of the storage plan were in a minority. Several other speakers, including Brougham, came out strongly against it. One of these was its former (albeit reluctant) proponent, Huskisson.[19] The plan was clearly doomed and Londonderry had no hesitation whatsoever in requesting leave to withdraw the unpopular motion.

ATTWOOD ON RICARDIAN THEORY

The highlight of the next day's debate (7 May) was an address by Mathias Attwood. This struck right at the heart of Ricardo's conception of the

British economy as a structure consisting of two sectors, one of which experienced constant or increasing returns while the other was subject to decreasing returns.[20] The speech was by far the most able critique by a member of Ricardo's analysis of the causes of agricultural distress, and it challenged the relevance of any of the plans now before the House as effective counters to that distress. In Attwood's opinion the work of the Select Committee, like that of its predecessors, had merely 'diverted the attention of three successive sessions of parliament from the adoption of any effectual measures of relief or even of effectual enquiry.' He warned the House that it now faced a credibility gap of its own making. There was a widespread belief that those committees had been designed for the purpose of blocking meaningful investigation and action. Because of this, parliament itself 'had probably laid the foundation of great political changes.' The measures which they were considering at present, for example, were 'little better than a mockery of the distress of the agricultural community', since their real aim was to facilitate the importation of foreign grain.

In his attack on Ricardo's diagnosis of agricultural distress, Attwood first pointed to the case of Ireland — 'that country which had exported everything, which had imported nothing'. How could Ricardo possibly account for that case in terms of his theories? 'Instead of finding Ireland relieved by that export of grain, the importation of which had been represented as so destructive to the agriculture of England,' Attwood observed, 'they found Ireland in a condition still more ruinous and deplorable than their own.' If Ricardo was to use abundance of domestic produce which could not be exported as a general explanation for the incidence of distress, then the Irish case did not serve Ricardo's purpose well.

Attwood then quoted from Ricardo's recent pamphlet *On Protection to Agriculture* concerning the inevitable increase in the costs of production of corn which must accompany the attempt to feed an expanding population without recourse to imports of grain. That argument, Attwood charged, turned on the completely fallacious assumption that cultivation was progressively extended from richer to poorer soils as population grew. In reality the reverse held. 'So far from the average quality of land becoming poorer as population and wealth advanced,' said Attwood, 'it became richer.' There was no necessary tendency to declining agricultural productivity, as the events of the Napoleonic war years demonstrated.[21] In that era of rural prosperity land 'produced more corn on an average by the acre, and with less positive labour ... it yielded a greater surplus produce, than at any former period.'

The basic deficiency in Ricardo's postion was due to his abstracting from the variety of factors which conditioned the pattern of land use in practice. Attwood stated:

It was not the best land, which was first cultivated; nor the worst land which was last cultivated. This was determined in a great measure by other circumstances; by the rights of proprietorship, by locality, by enterprize, by the peculiarities of feudal tenure, its remains still existing; by roads, canals, the erection of towns, of manufactories; all those and other obstacles of a similar nature interfered with the calculations of the hon. member.[22]

He added that, by means of pasture improvements, what were once very poor soils could be converted into areas of high yield. It was also true that, over a long period, the average yield from arable land had risen. There was no earlier stage in history, as Ricardo's argument seemed to suppose, when 'the people were cheaply fed from rich soils'.

The history of prices also revealed the invalidity of Ricardo's speculative reasoning. Adam Smith's investigations, for example, had shown that up to the recent war there had been 'no permanent and general rise' in the price of corn in England except for the era of influx of precious metals from the New World. From 1640 (when supplies of new metal began to decline appreciably) until 1794 the price of corn in England had been remarkably stable. Yet according to Ricardo's theory this should not have been the case. Over that century and a half both population and cultivation had undergone expansion. 'No advance in the progress of society, no increase of population', Attwood concluded, 'had ever yet occasioned an advance in the monied price of corn. Nothing but a fall in the value of money, nothing but its increased abundance, had ever produced that effect'.

RICARDO REPLIES

Although his ideas had been the main object of criticism Ricardo paid tribute to Attwood's speech as displaying 'a very considerable degree of talent, much research and great knowledge of the subject upon which he had spoken.'[23] Nevertheless Attwood 'had committed a great many errors', and Ricardo set out to expose these. When he replied on the question of diminishing productivity in agriculture, however, Ricardo's answer did not amount to a direct rebuttal.

Ricardo defended his belief in the dominance of the law of diminishing returns in the rural sector by reference to the intensive margin, i.e., land already under cultivation, as against the extensive margin, i.e., land being brought into cultivation. Attwood's attack had been directed at Ricardo's published statements concerning the latter margin, but Ricardo now tried to shift the weight of his case on to land already in use for grain production. Ricardo argued as if the supposed progression over time to inferior grades of soil was an unimportant feature of his reasoning, although the contemporary reader could well be forgiven for gaining the impression that this feature was crucial.[24] Ricardo stated:

> The hon. gentleman talked of the impossibility of the cultivators of the soil having recourse to land of inferior quality, but the hon. gentleman did not correctly state the argument. It was not that cultivators were always driven by the increase of population to lands of inferior quality, but that from the additional demand for grain, they might be driven to employ on land previously cultivated a second portion of capital, which did [not] produce as much as the first. On a still farther demand a third portion might be employed, which did not produce so much as the second: it was manifestly by the return on the last portion of capital applied, that the cost of production was determined. It was impossible, therefore, that the country should go on increasing its demand for grain without the cost of producing it being increased and causing an increased price.[25]

Ricardo also attempted a brief rejoinder to Attwood's contention that the price of corn had remained stable for a long period. Against Attwood's case from statistics Ricardo was prepared to rely mainly on what, to him, was a self-evident principle:

> In the first 62 years of the last century the average price of the quarter of wheat had been 32s.; but, in the years from 1784 to 1792 it had been 45s. – a very considerable increase on the value of corn. But, he would not rest on any scattered facts what was so evident in principle, as that the extension of cultivation must extend the cost of production of corn.[26]

THE RICARDO PLAN REJECTED

From this point of the debate the tide of opinion began running strongly against Ricardo. Londonderry, who spoke next, was still prepared to pay all due deference to Ricardo's authority and to the principles for which he stood.[27] Nevertheless he explained that his aim was 'to legislate with an even hand between the grower and the consumer', and given the current levels of agricultural prices both at home and abroad, this was not the time for full implementation of the principles which the Ricardo and Huskisson plans were endeavouring to have put into practice.

The conservative Sir Thomas Lethbridge and the radical Sir Francis Burdett were both most enthusiastic about Attwood's speech.[28] Lethbridge also accused the exponents of political economy of acting as servants of a particular class interest opposed to that of rural producers. He trusted that 'the House would not be led away by false speculations, and the abominable theories of political economists.' Burdett could not concur in the wholesale condemnation of economists, but this did not mean that he accepted the Ricardian view that agricultural distress arose from over supply of produce. To hold such a view, he claimed 'was contrary to every principle of political economy'.

After an inconsequential contribution from Frederick Robinson, Ricardo rejoined the debate.[29] Abundance of output, he assured Burdett, could be a source of embarrassment to the rural producer. 'Corn was an article which was necessarily limited in consumption', Ricardo explained, 'and if you went on increasing it in quantity, its aggregate value would be diminished beyond that of a smaller quantity.' Such a diminution would not apply to any intially rare commodity, e.g., superfine cloth, 'until it came within the reach of the purchase of every class in the country'. Further it would never apply in the case of money.

Ricardo concluded by reaffirming the superiority of his proposals for alteration of the corn laws as against the schemes of Londonderry and Huskisson. Londonderry's plan would 'encourage the agriculturist in speculating upon high prices', while Huskisson's would 'make the price of corn in this country habitually 15s. higher than in foreign countries'.

When discussion was resumed the following day the early contributions were decidedly against the Ricardo plan. Lockhart, for example, thought that it would do so much damage to farmers that 'had he not known the amiable disposition of that hon. member (Ricardo) he should be disposed to question his motives.'[30] Lockhart also questioned the assumption that capital displaced from the rural sector could move readily into secondary industry, as Ricardo continued to predict.[31] Gurney, Western and Sir Robert Wilson added their criticisms, the first-named declaring that Attwood's case 'had been unanswered and was unanswerable'.[32]

Some measure of support for Ricardo, however, came from Henry Brougham.[33] As a free trader he approved of Ricardo's plan, except that the duties it envisaged had been set at levels which were too low. They allowed for the special disadvantages of rural producers with respect to tithe and poor rate obligations, but they failed to compensate for the greater burden of indirect taxation which the farmer must bear relative to the manufacturer. The ratio of labour to capital inputs was higher in agriculture than in secondary industry, so the wages bill per unit of value added was higher. Since money wage rates were inflated by the taxation of commodities commonly consumed by workers, it followed that the cost structure of farming must be more influenced than others by such taxation.

Brougham also differed from Ricardo in that he thought much of the present distress was due to excessive taxation, and on 9 May Ricardo opened his address with a reply to Brougham.[34] He agreed that the argument concerning the relative disadvantage of the agriculturalist with respect to indirect taxation would be correct if it could be shown that labour-capital ratios were higher in the rural sector. However he very much doubted this was the case. Brougham seemed to be underestimating 'capital in buildings, in horses, in seed in the ground'. Ricardo added that, in any case, it was unlikely that the duties he proposed were too low since in arriving at a figure of ten shillings per quarter on imported wheat he had assumed that agriculturalists carried the entire weight of the poor rates. In fact manufacturers carried some of that burden.

Ricardo then turned to his optimistic vision of the future of the British economy, the vision which involved the transfer of resources out of agriculture and into manufacturing. There was a certain historical inevitability about that future, he believed, since as economies matured and grew they must tend to emphasise manufacturing. It was up to parliament and its willingness to embrace *laissez-faire*, as to the extent to which England would be allowed to take advantage of that necessary tendency. Parliament could fight against the laws of economic development but the country would be poorer for it. 'There would always be a limit to our greatness,' Ricardo warned, 'while we were growing our own supply of food: but we should always be increasing in wealth and power, whilst we obtained part of it from foreign countries, and devoted our own manufactures to the payment of it.'

When his plan came to the vote, only twenty-five members gave assent to Ricardo's vision of the future economy and his means of achieving it. Brougham, Hume, Philips, Scarlett and Whitmore were among these.[35] Other supporters were radicals — Birch, Beaumont, Davies and Maberly, and liberally-inclined aristocrats — Althorp, Barnard, the brothers George and William Lamb, Sir John Newport and Sir George Robinson.[36] Some of the foregoing and at least ten of the eleven remaining pro-Ricardo voters were men engaged in finance and trade.[37]

CLOSING EXCHANGES

After the defeat of Ricardo's proposals the House passed the original measures introduced by Londonderry. Thirty-six members voted in the negative, among whom were Attwood, Bankes, Curwen, Ellice, Gladstone, Heygate, Lockhart, Monck, Sir Robert Wilson, Alderman Wood and H. G. Bennet. Those who had supported Ricardo, and Ricardo himself, did not oppose the government's motion.

A bill to give effect to Londonderry's measure was finally passed by the Commons on 10 June. During debate on the bill on 13 May Attwood made a last ditch stand against the legislation.[38] He cast doubts on the adequacy and reliability of the information upon which parliament was proceeding. Above all he questioned the wisdom of dismantling the existing corn laws at a time when the rural interest had been nearly destroyed by ill-conceived monetary policies.

This speech drew strong expressions of approval from some sections of the House and Peel felt obliged to reply in defence of the bill of 1819, pointing out that many of those who now applauded Attwood had then been ardent advocates of the return to cash payments.[39] Peel was unmoved by Attwood's 'sarcasm' concerning that bill and he paid public tribute to Ricardo's authority in such matters:

> As he was to share that sarcasm with his hon. friend, the member for Portarlington (if he might be permitted, on account of the respect which he felt for that hon. gentleman's great talents and high character, to use a term which he certainly had no right to use from long intimacy with him), he would only observe that he was willing to share it, so long as he shared it in such company.

George Philips too eulogised Ricardo as 'one of the most original and wisest writers, and one of the soundest thinkers on the subject of political economy.' Philips hoped that Ricardo would go on presenting his plan for alteration in the corn laws each year until parliament accepted it. Joseph Hume also thought it was just a matter of time before the House perceived the wisdom of Ricardo's proposals.[41]

A most singular contribution came from Maxwell of Renfrewshire.[42] Entering the debate on the corn laws for the first time he took the odd position that parliament should approach this question with the welfare of workers as the top priority in mind. 'Let us examine the price of labour in Britain and on the continent', Maxwell suggested, 'and give the farmer indemnity for employing workmen at such prices as may keep the industrious family from privations incompatible with comfort or contentment.'

The arguments for diminution of protection, Maxwell observed, originated with 'the merchant and the monied interest', and he found their case even more unreasonable and contradictory than that of the extreme protectionist faction gathered around Webb Hall. 'Protecting duties must be kept in force', he reasoned, 'where taxation falls upon the necessaries of life in a degree unknown in any other country . . . A good minister would remove the taxes from the necessaries of life, and place them upon property: a wise parliament would sanction a change calculated to give industry a stimulus.' Once the taxation system had been restructured, then there would be scope for reducing the degree of protection of local agriculture.

Maxwell's intervention availed nothing and the government's proposals progressed to the Lords where they were read a third time and passed on 10 July. Lauderdale, although he had emerged latterly as an advocate of free trade, was not prepared to extend the principle to the corn laws.[43] He argued for no change in the existing arrangements and entered a dissentient vote when the bill was passed. As events transpired the alarm of

Lauderdale and the other protectionists at this legislation was not justified. The bill resulted in no effective lowering of prohibitions, since the domestic price of wheat did not rise to eighty shillings until 1828, in which year the act of 1822 was altered. The corn law of 1815 was given a new lease of life, in practice, because of the provision for a reduction in duties only after the eighty shillings level had been attained.

14 1822: The Currency Again

A degree of something like superstitious veneration has been created for what they called a SOUND METALLIC currency at the ANCIENT standard of value; a sort of priesthood is exercised by the learned on this subject, by which, as in the case of religious superstition, unassuming patient men are induced to believe that there are mysteries beyond the reach of common sense, and in like manner, give up the use of their own understanding, thus undergoing the fate of all honest dupes.

Charles Western
Second Address to the Landowners of the United Empire (1822)

Throughout the debates on the new corn law a constantly recurring theme was the attribution of agricultural distress to the operation of Peel's currency bill. In the absence of Baring, Attwood and Ellice were the leading exponents of this view and they received consistent support from Henry Grey Bennet, Lethbridge, Burdett, Gurney and Western. The main thesis was that agriculturalists were being ruined by a combination of high taxation and deflated market prices, the latter arising from resumption of cash payments at the old standard. As a result the government was presiding over a revolution in property ownership, with the traditional landholders facing extinction as a class. Ricardian monetary theory and policy were seen to be aiding and abetting that revolution. A major complaint was that Ricardo persisted in a gross underestimate of the former degree of inflation by continuing to use the price of gold rather than general commodity prices as an index.

Towards the end of the session dissent concerning government policy on the currency was crystallised in consideration of two motions from Western. The first of these was on 11 June when Western urged the necessity for a committee of enquiry into the effects of Peel's bill.[1] He contrasted the present state of the economy with the prosperity of the war years, a prosperity which he now recognised was not 'fictitious' as many had thought. There had been genuine and unprecedented economic growth and genuine expansion of the nation's capital stock. That growth had occurred because of the coincidence of two factors, one of which was monetary. During the war 'a vast increase of credit currency had had the effect of giving a great stimulus to industry, at a period when the produce of that industry could be most advantageously applied.'[2]

In direct imitation of an earlier speech by Attwood, Western then drew the parallel between credit expansion during the war and the economic impact of the opening up of the mines of the New World. Also, following Attwood, he endeavoured to show that corn prices had remained relatively stable over a long period between these monetary events. Western's purpose was to demonstrate that significant fluctuations in the price of corn in England were not related to population expansion, increased cultivation, or importations from Ireland, as Ricardo argued. Those fluctuations were attributable to changes in the money supply, and the low prices which now prevailed had been caused by the contraction associated with the misguided attempt by Peel and others to restore the 'ancient standard of value'.

Western cited David Hume and John Locke as authorities who had stressed the serious social consequences of deflation. He also employed official statistics to show how the real burden of taxation and the poor rates had been increased in the process. The basic problem arose from legislation which had not taken account of the vast changes in the British economy during the twenty-two years of suspension of cash payments. Peel's bill had ignored the commercial contracts, the public debt and the new structure of credit which had been created over the period. Parliamentary enquiry was necessary as a prelude to rectifying the errors of 1819.

INITIAL SUPPORT FOR WESTERN

After a reply from Huskisson deploring the idea of an alteration in anything as sacrosanct as the standard of value, H. G. Bennet and Lord Archibald Hamilton spoke in favour of Western's motion. They were joined by Alderman William Heygate, a consistent opponent of Peel's bill.[3] Heygate was prepared to blame the Bank directors for much of the deflationary pressure, since they had withdrawn small notes from circulation and had reverted to coin rather than bullion payments. The resulting reintroduction of gold coinage had depressed prices because 'gold was liable to be hoarded; and he knew it was so to a considerable extent.' However the Bank directors were not entirely to blame, since they were subject to the confusion stemming from Ricardian theory.

The root cause of the confusion, in Heygate's opinion, was the use of the price of gold as an index of the degree to which a currency might have depreciated. That price was no index, because it was 'regulated by the exchanges, which were governed by the cheapness at which we could manufacture for the foreign markets.'

Hudson Gurney was also in favour of an enquiry.[4] He perceived a lack of historical sense in Ricardo's advice in 1819 that the economy should be diverted from its then inflationary course:

> However injurious the lowering the standard of the coin of a country whilst in circulation might be, there was no country in Europe, or in the civilised world, in which that operation had not repeatedly taken place, and in no instance had it produced convulsion or a general dissolution of the existing state of society. It was the manner in which an over-weighted nation had generally relieved itself with the least shock, the least distress, and the least injustice of any.

Gurney thought that the chief problem arising from the legislation of 1819 was its destruction of the basis for rational planning by entrepreneurs. The parliament had 'most mistakenly coined to an historical standard which no outstanding contract had been calculated to meet, and which falsified every man's reckonings.'

RICARDO SHIFTS HIS GROUND

Under the pressure of events and, perhaps, in response to the arguments of Attwood and others, there were some perceptible changes of emphasis in Ricardo's position when he joined this debate.[5] He now allowed that while contraction of the note issue would eventually turn the foreign exchanges in favour of England, induce an inflow of gold and permit an expansion of the supply of coinage, 'there might be an interval during which the country might sustain great inconvenience from undue reduction of the Bank circulation.' That interval was created by the lag betweeen the withdrawal of paper and the minting of gold. 'While all these operations were going on,' Ricardo admitted, 'the currency would be at a very low level, the prices of commodities would fall, and great distress would be suffered. − Something of this kind had, in fact, happened.'

Continuing in this vein, Ricardo now portrayed his attitude to Peel's bill as one of interest in an 'experiment'.[6] The point of the 'experiment' was to see 'whether a bank could not be carried on with advantage to the general interests of the country, upon the principles of not being called upon to pay their notes in coin, but in bullion.' The experiment had failed, not because it was wrong in conception, but because, in practice, the Bank had made 'unnecessary purchases of gold which had led to so many unpleasant consequences'. The directors were in control of a 'difficult machine' and were incapable of operating it according to the right principles.

Ricardo found himself ill-used on this issue, both within and without parliament. For example, Heygate had just made it a point of criticism that he (Ricardo) continued to use the price of gold as an index of depreciation.[7] Yet Heygate's criticism turned on a misunderstanding of what Ricardo meant by 'depreciation'. Ricardo distinguished between 'depreciation' and 'diminution of value' of a currency, whereas Heygate identified the two. Ricardo had never claimed that the price of gold was a measure of the value of a currency.

When a country was on a gold standard, Ricardo explained, commodity prices could be influenced by changes in the value of gold and by depreciation or appreciation of the paper currency in terms of the standard. A legislature was powerless to control the influences arising out of variations in gold itself; however it had some command over the paper-gold relationship. Parliament had exercised the latter power in 1819 and this had induced a fall of about five per cent in commodity prices. The greater observed fall in commodity prices (and hence, increase in the value of money) was not due to the correction of the former depreciation of the currency but to changes in the value of gold over which there was no control.

Ricardo felt himself to be 'as it were put upon his trial' in this debate. Only a year and four months before he had referred to '1819, when the plan which he had the honour to recommend was adopted by the House'.[8] However he now informed that same House that 'his plan had not been adopted, and yet to it was referred the consequences which were distinct from it; and he was held responsible for the plan that had been adopted, which was not his, but was essentially different from it.' The essential differences were that parliament had given the Bank the option of accelerating the return to payments in coin as against bullion and that the Bank had not taken his advice to sell rather than buy gold.

The basic problem was that the legislature had bestowed extensive powers on a group of incompetent merchants, the directors of the Bank. 'Quantity', declared Ricardo, 'regulated the value of everything. This was true of corn, of currency, and of every other commodity, and more, perhaps, of currency, than of anything else. Whoever, then, possessed the power of regulating the quantity of money, could always govern its value.'[9]

Turning to his parliamentary critics, Ricardo expressed his agnosticism concernings changes in the value of money. 'By comparing money with its standard,' he observed, 'we had certain means of judging its depreciation.' However he knew 'of none by which we were able to ascertain with certainty alterations in real or absolute value'. John Locke and Adam Smith, for example, were mistaken in the belief that the average price of corn could be employed for this purpose. Since precise measurement was impossible, Ricardo strongly implied, then the question of changes in the value of money was not worth pursuing in a policy context.[10]

In conclusion Ricardo urged the wisdom of allowing Peel's act to remain untouched, despite its deficiencies in practice. Ricardo now undertook the incredible about-face of basing his case for retention on the importance of the very variable from which he had been only too ready to abstract in 1819 namely, the state of business confidence. 'The measure of 1819', he announced, 'was chiefly pernicious to the country, on account of the unfounded alarms which it created in some men's minds, and the vague fears that other people felt lest something should occur, the nature of which they could not themselves define.' Parliament should avoid even the suggestion of further change, which suggestion could touch off another crisis of confidence.[11]

ATTWOOD'S MAJOR STATEMENT

The most powerful case for enquiry was made in the outstanding speech by Mathias Attwood.[12] He was intent on showing that governmental action, sanctioned by parliament, had been responsible for economic depression and therefore, in all justice, parliamentary action should be undertaken to repair the damage. Attwood employed a deal of empirical material to attack the present stance of the ministry, the currency act of 1819, the Bullion Report of 1810 and Ricardian theory. He began by illustrating the 'absurdities' which parliament had been led to perpetrate under the influence of the 'ill-omened philosophy' of Ricardo:

> Sums of money have been voted out of the taxes to export the people by whose means or consumption the taxes were paid. These unhappy and redundant multitudes; the best strength of the country, if the wisdom of the government were equal to the resources of the people; we purposed to carry to distant shores . . .[13] But the distress of the labouring classes operating through a lessened consumption of agricultural produce, and aided by the poverty of the farmer and corn dealer, had scarcely produced an excessive supply in the markets, but we adjusted our theory to that state of things also. As we had too many people at one time, we had too much land at another. And our remedies corresponded. They were first to export the population, and next to abandon the soil; and to absurdities like these we have been driven.

After this indictment Attwood employed the evidence of Thomas Tooke before the committee on agriculture in 1821 to show that there had been a general fall of prices, a fall which was injurious to secondary as well as primary industry. The very generality of the fall indicated that it was not due to over-production in agriculture but rather to a contraction of the money supply. Further the government was deeply implicated in the contraction. Between November 1817 and May 1822 there had been a reduction of twenty-five per cent in the circulation of Bank notes. The reduction had commenced before prices began to fall and before Peel's bill was enacted. The main factor involved had been the decision to repay government debts to the Bank.[14]

In authoritative fashion Attwood detailed how, since 1815, substantial and sudden alternations of the volume of government debt with the Bank had led to the generation of a sequence of depression, boom and depression again. Seen against this background he now recognised that the much-vaunted Committees on resumption, with their much-discussed adoption of the Ricardo plan, were only significant as part of a political exercise. 'The Committee of 1819', said Attwood, 'had this effect and object, at least, and that only; that it committed the political opponents of the administration to the support of a measure, of the effects of which its authors were at least doubtful.' The prior decision to repay the Bank was the crucial decision in terms of economic impact.

Having shown the House how Ricardo had been used and the opposition compromised by the government, Attwood allowed that most members at the time had acted out of ignorance rather than bad faith. That ignorance extended back at least as far as the Bullion Committee of 1810 whose recommendations, if they had been adopted 'would have delivered this country, bound, and incapable of resistance and amidst every description of internal disorder, calamity and distress to the conditions of the foreign enemy.' One manifestation of that ignorance in 1819 had been the tendency to discount as 'over-traders' those business-men who had been already ruined by the financial manipulations of the ministry. Members had then spoken 'as though it were not the character of traders at all times to trade to the full extent of their power and their means — as though our commercial eminence itself were not founded on that character.'

The House had also been led astray by Ricardo who 'denies that prices will fall except in proportion to the reduction in money.' This dictum was falsified by the evidence now to hand. Ricardo's prediction had been incorrect because taxes had not been reduced as Bank of England issues declined. Further, he had failed to take account of the fact that country bank issues and all forms of paper credit must be diminished when their Bank note base was reduced.[15] Attwood also noted that in the course of deflation, hoarding of money had been a common phenomenon.

The outstanding error of Peel's committee in 1819 was to accept Ricardo's view that paper was depreciated by only four or five per cent at that time, since that was the existing margin between the mint and market prices of gold. In reality paper had been depreciated by between twenty and thirty per cent as compared with gold, but an infusion of £7 millions of gold into the market by the Bank had just then masked the real extent of the depreciation.[16] This demonstrated the folly of using the price of one commodity, gold, instead of the general price level as a guide in this matter.

The correct policy would have been to prevent the Bank from selling bullion, oblige it to return its note circulation to its wartime level and, then, observe the rise in the market price of gold. That price established, it should have been confirmed by legislation as the future standard for a return to cash payments. A fixed metallic standard could have been thus restored without inflicting such widespread misery.

Concerning that misery Attwood was particularly disturbed to note that government spokesmen, including Peel and Huskisson, had claimed that the deflationary pressure had injured employers while it benefited their workmen. He utterly rejected the implication of inherent class conflict which such claims carried. The plain evidence was that entrepreneur and wage earner suffered together. Both had been sacrificed for the 'miserable object' of return to an obsolete currency standard. The pressing need now was to relieve their sufferings by reflation of the economy.[17]

PEEL ATTEMPTS A REPLY

Peel opened with the supercilious comment that he would avoid 'entering into those abstruse topics in which the hon. member who had just sat down had indulged, and which were hardly fit to be debated in an assembly like the present.'[18] Nevertheless even he was willing to give some ground in the face of Attwood's onslaught. Resumption of cash payments, he admitted, may have 'tended, in some degree' to depress the rural sector, although Continental agriculture was in difficulties like its English counterpart. His Bill may have worsened the position of the domestic industry 'first, to the extent of the actual difference between depreciated paper and the ancient standard of value; and next, to the extent of that additional value, which a variety of events might have given money itself.'

Despite this he was completely opposed to any change in the currency arrangements. Enquiry into the possibility of change would invite public derangement and confusion. Deliberate inflation would be a serious breach of faith with the public creditor. In addition, he noted, the nation was by no means as distressed as Attwood claimed. Poor rate payments had decreased, excise revenue was up, and there was a new buoyancy in a number of manufacturing centres.[19]

Against Attwood's contention that employer and employee had suffered alike because of inflation, Peel was adamant that this was not the case. Also, Peel was sufficiently wedded to the wage-profit conflict thesis to deny that wage earners had prospered during the wartime inflation:

> The natural result of a return to a metallic currency must be a diminution in the profits of the master, and an increase in those of the men. The reverse had been the effect of our continued paper system;

the speculations and, in some instances, the gains of the masters had risen; but the workman's wages had been low, and his comforts inconsiderable.[20]

WESTERN'S MOTION LOST

For the opposition Burdett and Brougham were in favour of enquiry. The former was now convinced that agricultural distress could not be explained, at this stage, by transition to peace, or by foreign importations, or by local over-production. The state of the currency seemed the only explanation left.[21] Like Ricardo he had reached the conclusion that the Bank directors should not be left in control of the note issue. Burdett was even more explicit than Ricardo that the time had come for the government to assume that function. He agreed with Ricardo that a free trade in corn was highly desirable, but he did not share the same fears concerning the harm that might flow from establishment of a new committee of enquiry on the currency. Further, he objected that Ricardo persisted in ignoring the fact that in this period of deflation, entrepreneurs were suffering the injustice of being required to meet financial obligations under contracts written when the value of the currency was much lower. To go on supporting Peel's act was to condone the continuation of a most substantial amount of social and personal injustice.[22]

Brougham could not accept the Ricardian view that rural difficulties were due to over-cultivation.[23] He could not see that 'with an increase of population within the last 30 years, in the proportion of 3 to 2, and without any extraordinary application of machinery in its cultivation, such a circumstance could arise. How this assertion could be supported, under such circumstances, was to him a mystery which he was not able to solve.' If there was over-cultivation he would expect the prices of rural produce to be lower than in the years immediately preceding the war, but this was not the case.

Brougham also rejected Peel's assessment of the current state of well-being of the populace. Excise figures, to which Peel had referred, were no guide to the condition of living standards and the fall in the cost of the poor rates was nominal only. In commodity terms that cost had increased. Attwood had been much more accurate in his assessment of the situation and, despite the different complexion of his politics Brougham paid tribute to the tory banker:

The hon. member for Callington (Mr. Attwood) had brought to bear upon this question a degree of practical knowledge, logical acuteness and, he might add, eloquence, which had rarely been combined on such a topic . . . it was almost impossible for any person interested in the subject, not to listen to him with attention and respect — nay, with admiration.[24]

When a vote was taken on Western's motion at 3 a.m. only thirty were in favour of an enquiry. The majority gave their assent to a proposition, brought forward as an amendment by Huskisson, 'that this House will not alter the standard of gold or silver, in fineness, weight, or denomination.' In the minority, apart from those mentioned above as supporting Western, were John Bennett, the bankers Denison and Thompson, Moore, Monck and Wodehouse.

WESTERN TRIES AGAIN

On 10 July Western moved a series of eighteen resolutions relating to the currency and the state of the nation.[25] These resolutions pointed to the unemployment and violence that were rife in rural England and to the unrest and starvation which prevailed in Ireland. The position of the farmer, faced with falling prices and an increasing real burden of taxation, was contrasted with that of the public creditor who had gained substantially in real terms. Western's final resolution requested consideration of either currency reform or a reduction of taxation together with revision of financial contracts between individuals. Such measures were urgent so that 'justice may, as far as possible, be administered to all, and the country saved from a revolution of property, and also from a pressure of taxation beyond the ability of the people to sustain.' In speaking to these resolutions Western, although he was a confirmed protectionist, declared that reflation of the economy was worth purchasing at the expense of abrogation of the corn laws, should that prove necessary.

Ricardo was on his feet immediately to give a point-by-point refutation of Western's case.[26] Distress was a fact, he agreed, but it could not be imputed solely to Peel's bill. The main problem was 'the abundance of the quantity of produce'. Certainly the real burden of taxation had been increased by deflation, but this could not explain the peculiar difficulties of the agriculturalist, since all classes in the community had been affected to the same extent. Again there was no doubt that deflation had involved an increase in the real value of the farmer's mortgages and other debts. This was no injustice to the farmer, however, because it merely compensated for the benefits he had derived from the decreasing value of those obligations in the preceding years of inflation.

Western ascribed the distress of Ireland to the act of 1819, but it was clearly due to the failure of the potato crop in that country. Ricardo refused to accept that it was contradictory on his part to attribute the Irish problem to under-supply of food and the English problem to over-supply. In Ireland wages were determined by the price of potatoes, whereas in England they were dependent on the price of corn. It could not be expected that Irish wages would be sufficiently high to enable labourers there to purchase corn when potatoes were in short supply.[27]

ATTWOOD AGAINST PEEL AND RICARDO

Attwood rehearsed his leading arguments of the debate on the earlier motion by Western and then moved on to attack aspects of Peel's speech of a month before.[28] Wage earners, he insisted, had not been benefited by the deflation in recent years. Rather they had been 'necessarily, finally, and irretrievably, deteriorated, degraded and depressed.' In the short run falling commodity prices had brought unemployment. In longer run money wage rates had followed prices downward, employment was restored, but still workers were worse off than they had been before 1819. The problem was that with their reduced money wages they were obliged to meet the wartime taxes levied directly on commodities which were significant elements of their consumption pattern.

Whereas Ricardo thought that money wages would rise and fall with the purchase price (including the margin of taxation) of the subsistence of labour, Attwood suggested that the money rewards of labour would alter with the money value of output. Changes in the latter were linked, in turn, to movements in the supply of money. 'Ultimately and permanently', Attwood declared, 'the wages of labour rose or fell with the price of property, of commodities, and provisions; they adjusted themselves to the alteration in the value of money, whatever that alteration might be.' Given Attwood's theory, there was no necessary reason why an unchanging level of commodity taxation (falling directly on goods habitually consumed by workers) must be met by employers in terms of a higher wages bill than would be the case if taxation were reduced. For the Ricardians, however, the subsistence theory of real wages supplied a necessary reason. Most workers could not be penalised by commodity taxation in the manner described by Attwood.

Attwood also assailed Peel's view that the poor rates had fallen. He produced calculations to show that measured in real terms they had risen in recent years. By contrast pauperism had declined during the years of inflation, and these facts gave the lie to Peel's claim that, unlike employers, workers had not benefited in the inflationary process. Wage earners and profit earners prospered and suffered together.[29] The facts also gave the lie to the charge that the poor law system was bad for the morale of the workers. The evils which were said to stem from that system were the outcome of the combination of deflation and commodity taxation which forced labourers into pauperism.[30]

Finally Attwood took up the question of the Irish misery. The suffering there was far too extensive to be explained by the partial failure of the potato crop, as Ricardo and others believed. Parliament itself was largely responsible for the situation in Ireland, since it arose out of the very act which Attwood sought to change. 'It sprang,' he said, 'from that scarcity of money which they themselves effected.'[31]

Attwood explained that the problem in Ireland was lack of effective demand and he referred members to the writings of Thomas Malthus in 1815 for substantiation of his case.[32] Then, as now, food was readily available, but demand was not forthcoming because of 'a total want of employment'. In the Irish case there was no dearth but 'the people died without the means of purchase'. Behind the failure of demand and the unemployment stood a contraction of the money supply engendered by Peel's bill of 1819.

In Ireland, 'protected by no poor-laws, where there was little surplus capital, and little trade', neither tenants nor landlords had any defence against strong deflationary pressures. The predominantly agricultural economy had collapsed as the market prices of produce fell to increasingly low levels. The result was a sequence of events — unemployment, social violence, military repression and now 'a scene of famine and despair'.[33]

THE MOTION FAILS

Peel professed to be unmoved by Attwood's analysis. The potato, not parliament, was the cause of Ireland's misery.[34] Alderman Heygate, however, agreed that a major factor in the distress was 'the violent reduction of the circulation, occasioned by the premature act of 1819'.[35] He thought there had been other factors also at work including 'the cessation of the war demand'.

After Burdett had spoken in favour of an enquiry, debate concluded. Once again the dissidents were disappointed. The House adjourned at 4 a.m. with Western's resolutions rejected, apparently without division.

REVIEW

There is a persistent myth that Ricardianism was the creed of a burgeoning urban middle class. This myth is sponsored mainly by social historians who try to press the realities of the early nineteenth century into some type of Marxian evolutionary mould. Yet the political status of Ricardianism by the end of the session of 1822 casts doubt on the validity of the Marxian interpretation. By continuing to employ the idea of 'the capitalist' as an analytical category such interpretations miss the point that Ricardianism had become a most useful tool supporting the interest of the rentier. This was a conservative interest which included the wealthier land-owning aristocrats but took little cognisance of the needs of the entrepreneur, whether or not that entrepreneur was a progressive farmer like Curwen, a ship owner like Marryat, an international financier like Baring, or a fur trader like Ellice.

The point being made is well illustrated in respect of Irish policy, as

Professor Collison Black has observed:

> It may appear strange that the proposals of the economists accorded
> so well with the interests of the landlords, when traditionally the
> economists have been depicted as the champions of the urban middle
> class against the old landed aristocracy; but it should be remembered
> that the economists' quarrel was not with the landlords as landlords,
> but as protectionists. Tories and the older Whigs might look askance at
> political economy with its Radical associations, but in regard to the
> fundamentals of Irish policy its recommendations accorded with their
> own preconceptions.[36]

Ricardo also served the interest of the rentier well with his views on the
need to keep faith with the fundholder and on the desirability of
preserving the traditional mint price of gold. His analysis of the incidence
of taxation, although not intended to be such, was of great assistance to
Liverpool's rentier-oriented administration. His emphasis on the opposition of wages and profits could be used by Peel, Huskisson and others to
counter any suggestion that wage earners and entrepreneurs constituted a
common interest group, members of which were disadvantaged alike by
the government's predisposition to cater for the 'drones', as Baring called
non-enterprising holders of wealth.

By 1822 Ricardo had so lost faith in the abilities of prominent
businessmen that he was prepared to turn over control of the note issue to
ministers. Not only the behaviour of the Bank directors but the (to him)
irrational and inexplicable fears which had beset the business community
because of a 'minor' currency adjustment in 1819, were indications that
many entrepreneurs did not understand their own best, or the nation's,
interests. Again, some of their leading representatives in parliament, such
as John Gladstone, would not only vote against Ricardo's proposals for
modification of the corn laws, but would even oppose the milder
modifications introduced by the ministry. Others had earlier expressed
doubts, and positive opposition at times, concerning other moves to freer
trade. This latter was to re-emerge as a theme in debates of the next year.

15 1823: Government Finances and Freer Trade

> But my best canto, save one on astronomy,
>   Will turn upon 'political economy.'
> *That* is your present theme for popularity:
>   Now that the public hedge hath scarce a stake,
> It grows an act of patriotic charity,
>   To shew the people the best way to break.
> *My plan* (but I, if but for singularity,
>   Reserve it) will be very sure to take.
> Meantime, read all the national-debt sinkers,
>   And tell me what you think of your great thinkers.

> Lord Byron
> *Don Juan*, Canto XII (1823)

As the year opened the signs of a definite revival of the economy were becoming more evident. Manufacturing employment continued to expand, wages rose, expectations improved and new capital developments were undertaken in the industrial towns. After December 1822 corn prices began to rise and at harvests the yield from agriculture was once again abundant. By mid-year it was possible to believe that at last the long-awaited era of continuing post-war prosperity might have actually dawned. There was a notable decline of popular agitation in rural areas for parliamentary action.[1]

With the revival, political economy (virtually identified with Ricardianism) moved closer to the apogee of its fashionable acceptance among those with political power but little first-hand knowledge of business life. One of the more fortunate results of the trend was the entry of Lord Byron, via his 'English Cantos', as an acute observer of the foibles of economic policy and its makers. Less fortunate was the new, strident tone which emerged in some of Ricardo's parliamentary statements on issues debated during the year. On questions such as the continuance of the sinking fund and legislation for marine apprenticeships he felt free to adopt a doctrinaire stance more befitting one of his minor disciples.

Within government circles the Ricardian cause may have suffered a severe setback in August 1822. Londonderry, who had been openly sympathetic with some of Ricardo's analyses and policies, committed suicide.[2] This opened the way for the re-entry into Cabinet of George Canning who had not figured to any marked degree in economic controversy in parliament over the previous four years.[3] Canning was installed at the Foreign Office and as leader in the Commons and from this point he began to exercise an increasingly important political role.[4] His elevation was accompanied by Robert Peel's assumption of management responsibilities for the business of the Commons.

Another alteration was the retirement of Vansittart as Chancellor of the Exchequer. Vansittart moved into the Lords and was succeeded by Frederick 'Prosperity' Robinson. Although Robinson had been President of the Board of Trade since 1818, there was little in his parliamentary record to suggest that he would make a capable or decisive Chancellor. Considerably more promising in that respect was William Huskisson, who replaced Robinson at the Board of Trade.[5] Thomas Wallace, formerly Vice-president of the Board of Trade, was promoted to Master of the Mint. Wellesley-Pole, the former Master, was retired to the Lords.[6]

Outside parliament there were a number of new developments that were to prove significant in terms of the future course of social thought in England. John Stuart Mill and some other younger men enhanced the viability of the Benthamite movement by the formation of a group they called the 'Utilitarians'. The ranks of the Ricardians within the Political Economy Club were strengthened for a time by the advent of Ricardo's disciple from the North, J. R. McCulloch.[7] At the same time, at Trinity College, Cambridge, a prominent element in the future opposition to Ricardianism was beginning to fuse. There, J. F. D. Maurice, later a key figure in Christian Socialism, was setting the views of Coleridge against those of Bentham.[8] Also of importance was the foundation, first in Glasgow and then in London, of Mechanics' Institutes, a form of educational venture that was soon to be duplicated in major industrial centres throughout the country.

APPLAUSE FOR PROSPERITY ROBINSON

A series of budget resolutions was presented by Robinson on 21 February.[9] These envisaged the achievement of a surplus of £7 million of which £5 million would be employed to reduce the national debt. Further there would be some reductions in taxation. Because of anticipated increases in excise duties, Robinson proposed to decrease or abolish taxes on windows, the employment of servants, and the use of horses and carriages. When these measures were announced (it is recorded in the *Annual Register* for 1823, p. 180) there were 'demonstrations of applause more loud and more general than perhaps ever before greeted the opening of a ministerial statement of finance.'[10]

Ricardo was extraordinarily expansive.[11] He expressed his delight at 'the plain, sound, practical, and excellent speech' he had just heard. Ricardo continued that 'the science of political economy had never before had so able an expositor as it had now found in that House.'[12] Yet there was one problem. Robinson had miscalculated in that there would be only £3 million, and not £5 million, available for reduction of the debt.

The main thrust of Ricardo's speech was aimed at a long-standing goal — swift abolition of the national debt and of the sinking fund which was thought necessary to service it. As on previous occasions, Ricardo offered to 'contribute any proportion of his own property, for the attainment of this great end, if others would do the same.' He added the observation that 'taxes raised in order to pay off debt, ought to be looked upon in a very different light, from those that were raised for the immediate services of the state. The one, we might be considered as paying to ourselves; the other was for ever lost to us.'[13]

The aspect of the sinking fund which Ricardo most disliked was its supposed relationship to preparedness for war. The government justified the fund as a system of debt repayment. However it also related the device to an obligation to be ready to undertake military expenditures. 'There was something mysterious', said Ricardo, in the concept of using the one means of satisfying both ends.

Alexander Baring could not understand Ricardo's anxiety to do away with the fund by a direct levy on wealth.[14] Nevertheless he concurred in the compliments to the Chancellor and in the fact that Robinson had miscalculated as Ricardo suggested. Other speakers were rather less complimentary.[15] Lord Folkestone regretted the lack of reference to agricultural distress in Robinson's speech. H. G. Bennet was disappointed that the misery arising from currency adjustments had not been acknowledged. Lord Milton believed that the rural situation demanded far greater taxation relief than the Chancellor was proposing.

RICARDO VERSUS BARING ON THE SINKING FUND

The clash between Baring and Ricardo was renewed on 28 February in debate on a motion from Captain Maberly which sought to do away with the sinking fund by means of a change in the conditions under which the land tax could be purchased and redeemed. Ricardo commented that Maberly's scheme, although it had merit, was no substitute for a true sinking fund.[16] He went on to explain how, in recent years, Vansittart had systematically despoiled that fund while claiming to maintain it as a means of reducing the public debt. This had been done despite the fact that the commissioners responsible for administering the fund had 'most conscientiously and perfectly discharged their duties'.[17] Ricardo fully expected that Robinson or some future Chancellor would be tempted to act in the same way as had Vansittart whilstever the fund remained in existence.

Baring was not impressed by Maberly's plan and he lampooned Ricardo as wishing to do away with the fund by a levy on wealth so as to prevent some Cabinet Minister from doing the same thing.[18] In Baring's opinion Ricardo's scheme for abolishing the national debt was impractical. Further it was useful to maintain a sinking fund so that loans could be more readily raised in time of sudden national emergencies. Such a fund enhanced the creditableness of any government. Baring referred to experience and opinion in France, America and Russia as supporting his contention.

Huskisson flatly rejected Ricardo's plan.[19] 'Much as he admired the general reasonings and great talent of the hon. member for Portarlington', Huskisson could not agree with him here. On the other hand he expressed great admiration for Baring's attitude: 'Coming, as that opinion did, from an individual of the hon. gentleman's knowledge and experience, it would have more weight in the country, and tend more to the maintenance of the public credit, than if it had preceeded from almost any other person in the House.'

Despite this rebuff, Ricardo protested even more vehemently when a bill to establish a new sinking fund was introduced on 6 March. The praise of Robinson just two weeks before gave way to bitter condemnation of the ministry and of the parliament itself.[20] Ricardo stated that he 'did not think the national purse safe in the hands of ministers. It was too great a temptation to entrust them with.' Further on in his speech he declared that he 'could be quite easy in recommending the measure of a sinking fund, if they had a different kind of parliament — one that moved in more direct sympathy with the people. He confessed his fear of the present parliament, and its disposition to ministerial compliance.' There was an unusual sarcasm in his comment on Baring: 'His hon. friend, with his enlarged views, wished for a sinking fund, not to pay off the debt, but to furnish ministers with the means of going to war, in cases of extremity.'

Ricardo told the House that failure to discharge the debt was akin to 'sleeping on a volcano'. Standing at £800 million, that debt had serious social implications.[21] It gave ministers greater opportunities to dispense patronage. The taxation it demanded created 'heart-burnings' throughout the community. Further, the customs and excise system which helped support it gave rise to immoral activities such as smuggling and to 'a most unnatural state' in the economy. It was for these reasons that he urged parliament to adopt his plan to decrease the debt without delay.

Baring replied that, in this matter, Ricardo, despite his intellectual capabilities had 'over-reached himself, and lost sight of man, and of all practical conclusions.'[22] Baring stated:

To begin with the plan of paying off a part of the debt, by a new disposition of the property of the country, he must be allowed to say, that it was the plan of a man who might calculate well and read deeply, but who had not studied mankind. It was ingenious in theory, and obvious enough; but not very sound for practice.

The plan would entail the transfer of at least a third of the current property of landholders to the fundholders. Country gentlemen could never be expected to consent to this.

Further criticism of Ricardo was forthcoming when debate continued on 11 March. Some of this emanated from quarters in which Ricardo had found support on most other issues in previous years. 'Many plans had been devised to pay off, by one great effort, the national debt,' observed Pascoe Grenfell, 'and the crotchet of his hon. friend (Mr. Ricardo) for accomplishing that great object by a general contribution from all the property of the country, was the wildest of them all.'[23] Sir Henry Parnell, while he agreed with Ricardo on the subject of the old sinking fund, 'could not agree with him in his conclusion, that there ought not be any new sinking fund.'[24] Parnell put forward his own plan for a fund which could not be abused by ministers. This could be effected 'through the medium of long annuities, determinable in a fixed number of years'.

When Robinson's bill for the establishment of a new sinking fund arrangement was brought in for a third reading on 14 March, William Whitmore also came out against Ricardo's abolitionist zeal.[25] Like Baring, he thought 'a sinking fund essential for the preservation of the credit of this country'. He was in favour of the Chancellor's motion, but H. G. Bennet, Hume, Hamilton and Ricardo contended that Parnell's plan should be given a trial.[26] Both Baring and Ellice were quite unconvinced that the Chancellor had £5 million at his disposal for the purposes of the fund, but they were in favour of his proposal in principle.[27] Despite these reservations the House found Robinson's measures to be a signal advance on the existing arrangements and it duly gave its assent to the bill.

MOVES FOR FREER TRADE

The beginnings of a drift towards *laissez-faire* had been evident in 1821 with the reduction in the degree of protection given Canadian as against Baltic timber. This had continued in 1822 with the modification of the corn law of 1815, and with some other measures which, although significant as part of the trend, evoked little debate. These included partial amendments to the long-standing Navigation Laws which gave preference to British shipping. The important change in those Laws was to henceforth allow a European ship to transport goods to Britain from the port of origin of the ship concerned. When the relevant bill was read a third time in the Commons (4 June 1822) Ricardo had occasion to praise the efforts of Thomas Wallace, then Vice-President of the Board of Trade, in pressing this matter. Ricardo was critical of George Canning, however, for having stressed the beneficial effects which protecting duties might have on certain industries.[28]

Associated developments during 1822 were the Colonial Trade Bill and the West Indian and American Trade Bill. These liberalised intercourse between the colonies and non-British territories, but still hedged the trade about so as to protect British home manufacturing and shipping interests.[29] The colonies then (and to some extent, the shipping industry) were the first to begin to feel the brunt of the effect of the mounting sympathy for free trade. The campaign moved a little closer to home in 1823, but the remote colonials were still a prime target for applications of the new philosophy which it is doubtful most of them espoused.[30]

FREER TRADE IN CORN

William Whitmore was particularly active in the cause of greater liberalisation. On 3 March he introduced a petition requesting equalisation of the duties which favoured imports of West Indian sugar as against those from the East Indies.[31] This led to debate later in the session and he prefaced this move in favour of the East Indies interest with the tactical ploy of reviving the question of the corn laws just one week beforehand.

On 26 February Whitmore requested leave to bring in a bill to amend the corn laws.[32] He advocated a progressive reduction in the stipulated level at which the market price must stand before corn could be imported. The appropriate level, he thought, was sixty shillings per quarter rather than the existing eighty shillings. The move was justified, according to Whitmore, because the higher prohibiting price encouraged instability in the rural sector. In years of good harvests, it led to over-production and low prices for domestic grain which in turn led to under-production and famine prices in years when the seasons were unfavourable.

John Curwen rose to combat Whitmore's case and stated that he wished to see 'every acre of land that could be made available, under cultivation'.[33] The problems of agriculture, he believed, arose mainly from lack of effective demand, which demand could be stimulated by remission of commodity taxes which fell directly on the poor.[34] The government could compensate for the remissions by taxation of the incomes of fundholders and by economies in its expenditure. John Bennett was also in favour of lighter taxation of low income earners and he put forward national-sufficiency in food grains as a sound policy goal sanctioned by the authority of both Smith and Malthus.[35]

Huskisson could not agree with the two progressive farmers, but he allowed that the present was not the time for changing the corn laws.[36] At the moment there was wide disagreement among experts concerning current land values and the prospects of farming enterprises. It may be true, as Whitmore contended, that existing legislation promoted rural instability but, since this represented no immediate threat, the law was best left as it stood. In the future it might well be changed to permit 'a regular and moderate importation'.

Once again Ricardo found himself at odds with Huskisson.[37] Why wait to amend the corn laws at a time when the evils forcast by Whitmore were besetting agriculture? He was in favour of an affirmative vote now on Whitmore's reforms. Ricardo added that he would like to go further than this through the establishment of the system of protection he had advocated the previous year. His system had the advantage of doing away altogether with a fixed price beyond which imports were totally prohibited. This step would create the conditions for the stability which Whitmore sought.

Attwood came back immediately at Ricardo with the contention that price fluctuations arose from monetary causes and not from the corn laws.[38] He also noted that those who adopted the 'whimsical theory' of the Ricardians concerning the link between high grain prices and high production costs on infertile land could not explain how consumers were well able to meet the high prices of the war years. Effective demand then was more than adequate because of 'the cheap money of the Restriction act.' Attwood concluded by denouncing 'the blind activity . . . with which those who advocated the introduction of foreign grain supported their object; and the supineness of those, on the other hand, who desired to maintain, in their own markets, a preference for the productions of their own agriculture.'

THE SUGAR DUTIES

Whitmore's motion on the corn laws failed but on 22 May he followed up the petition on East and West Indies sugar duties with a request for a select committee to investigate the possibility of altering the arrangements concerning those duties.[39] The motion was opposed by two West Indies merchants, Charles Ellis and Keith Douglas, who argued that any reduction in the degree of advantage given that region's sugar would constitute a breach of 'the colonial compact' upon which the development of the industry was based.[40] Both also forecast economic ruin in the West Indies if the advantage was revoked.

Ricardo retorted that all duties in colonial trade injured both England and the colonies concerned.[41] 'If any compact existed by which the industry, either of the colonies or of the mother country, was rendered less productive, ' said Ricardo, 'the sooner it was got rid of the better.' He produced one of his leading articles of faith to calm fears concerning the ruin that would follow if West Indies sugar proved uncompetitive in free market conditions: 'The capital now employed in the production of sugar would, under such circumstances, be converted to the growth of a more beneficial, because a more remunerating commodity.' Ricardo also observed that if sugar could be produced more cheaply in the East Indies, then that must prove to be the decisive influence on the world price of the commodity in the long run. Cost of production, not the relationship of supply to demand, was the factor which in all instances regulated price.[42]

In opposition to Whitmore and Ricardo, Joseph Marryat affirmed that there could be justifiable exceptions to the *laissez-faire* principle. Among these were 'considerations of our colonial trade, and the advancement of our naval power'.[43] Marryat complained of the damage that could be done by acting in terms of Ricardian dogmatics: 'The advocates of that school would make everything bend to their application. As in the bed of Procrustes, they would lop the limb that was too long, or stretch those that were to short to fit the abstract principle.'

Most members of the House, including Huskisson (who found Ricardo's approach in this matter too abstract), were not willing to consign the West Indian planters to a procrustean fate. Whitmore's motion for an enquiry was lost by 161 votes to 34.

WALLACE'S WAREHOUSING BILL

Early in the session (12 February) Thomas Wallace moved to revive the committee on foreign trade which had been at work the previous year. One of the first fruits of this exercise emerged on 21 March when Wallace introduced a bill which would permit foreign goods to be deposited in British warehouses and exported free of duty.[44] During a brief debate both Marryat and Ricardo expressed their approval of the measure. The bill then passed its first reading, although Stuart-Wortley had some doubts about its effect on the wool merchants of Leeds.

At the second reading stage (24 March) Robert Peel and others felt that the new arrangement might create some difficulties for the Irish linen trade. If this was so there were grounds for treating that trade as a special case.[45] This view prevailed and when the bill was passed (21 April) Wallace explained that 'the state of Ireland made it desirable that no irritation, however erroneous the grounds of it might be, should be added to the causes of the present disturbances. It was desirable, therefore, to replace that trade upon the same footing of exemptions as before.'[46] With this exception, then, Wallace was able to take a considerable step towards his goal of 'making this country the general depot, the great emporium of the commerce of the world.'[47]

RECIPROCITY OF DUTIES

A most significant departure from the Navigation Laws was initiated by Huskisson on 6 June. Those laws sought to give preference to British shipping by levying higher duties on imports conveyed in the ships of other nations. Now, Huskisson moved for the power to declare by Order in Council that where other countries reciprocated, foreign ships would be permitted to transport goods to Britain subject to the same level of duty as in British vessels.[48] The President of the Board of Trade indicated his guiding philosophy in this matter as follows: 'It was high time, in the improved state of the civilization of the world, to establish more liberal principles; and show, that commerce was not the end, but the means of diffusing comfort and enjoyment among the nations embarked in its pursuit.'

Some supporting remarks by the former Vice-President, Wallace, underlined the manner in which the progress of *laissez-faire* was now bound up with the beginnings of a rise of a new wave of top public servants. Wallace observed that 'in the course of his official experience, he had found, that on every occasion when the shipowners had come forward to oppose a public measure originating with the government, they were universally wrong.'[49] The expertise of the politician-bureaucrat could now be used to counter the conventional counsels of the business practitioner, and that expertise was informed, in part, by the true principles of political economy. Men like Huskisson and Wallace could employ their 'official expertise', however, to provide for a more satisfactory application of those principles than could a detached, speculative thinker like Ricardo.

Ricardo congratulated Huskisson on this move which, in practice, would have the effect of increasing the discretionary powers of the civil service.[50] Then, Joseph Marryat who had been so vociferous in his condemnation of the decision to alter the timber duties in 1821, also commended the bill.[51] In what seemed a major change of tack, the shipowner announced an adjustment to the new winds of *laissez-faire*. Marryat declared:

> It was the duty of this country to act upon liberal principles, and to give way in some instances, in order to preserve the commercial interests of Europe, and of this country in particular.[52]

When the bill was read a third time (4 July) the mover was the new Vice-President of the Board of Trade, Charles Grant, and the legislation came under attack from merchants with interests in the Indian and West Indies trades, one of whom was Alexander Robertson.[53] The latter claimed that this measure was a virtual repeal of the Navigation Laws and he deeply regretted that Adam Smith's arguments in favour of those laws 'should be opposed, with any chance of success, by a new set of political economists whose principles he considered decidedly erroneous'.

Ricardo, Hume and Huskisson made brief contributions in favour of repeal and Wallace replied to criticism at greater length. He argued that a navigation law policy had outlived its usefulness now that British naval power was clearly superior to its former 'continental rival' (presumably the Dutch). Most of the House accepted this view and the bill was passed with only fifteen votes in opposition.[54] The dissidents were merchants and bankers.

The success of this legislation was a clear indication that, in periods when business was buoyant, the new political economy of Liverpool's administrators could hope to prevail politically. Provided the measures in question appeared to threaten the interests of only a particular section of the business community the spokesmen for other sections would not oppose them. One by one particular sectional interests could be divested of the legislative protection to which they clung. At the same time the ground was being prepared for the regulation of the framework of business life by professional public servants who challenged the dominant role of powerful business interests operating directly within and around the legislature.[55] Further, this trend may have led to the encouragement of a greater degree of concentration of ownership and control in some sectors of industry (as, for example, in the case of Scottish linen manufacturing). If so, such encouragement complemented the transfer of property from small landholders to fundholders which the government had fostered by its earlier policies.

16 1823: Political Economy and the Workers

Gentlemen ought, however, to inculcate this truth on the minds of the working classes — that the value of labour, like the value of other things, depended on the relative proportion of supply and demand. If the supply of labour were greater than could be employed, then the people must be miserable . . . But the people had the remedy in their own hands. A little forethought, a little prudence (which probably they would exert, if they were not made such machines of by the poor-laws), a little of that caution which the better educated felt it necessary to use, would enable them to improve their situation.

David Ricardo
House of Commons, 30 May 1823

Labour issues regained some prominence in the debates of this year. There were moves to amend the Combination Laws and to alter the regulations governing the employment and conditions of some workers in both the shipping and silk industries. The issue of the impact of machinery on employment opportunities was also canvassed. Throughout these discussions, Ricardo and his followers insisted on treating labour as a 'thing' and sought to have labour relations dealt with simply as exercises in the application of the principle of free trade. In the case of the Merchant Vessels Apprenticeship Bill, Ricardo took this approach to such extremes of doctrinaire intransigence that he eventually found himself in a minority of one.

THE COMBINATION LAWS

On 3 March Peter Moore requested leave to bring in a bill to amend the laws against combinations of workmen.[1] He envisaged legislation which would legalise trade unions and permit the establishment of a type of wages board system. He stated that he had three objects in view: 'First, to bring back a great number of eminent artificers from the continent; secondly, to effect a better distribution of the profits of labour between the employers and the employed; and thirdly, to facilitate the means of recovering debts and deciding suits between artificers and their employers.'

The motion was seconded by John Maxwell.[2] 'It was needless to comment upon a law', said Maxwell, 'which bound the employed, and left the employer free as air; and which gave protection to wealth and power, by withdrawing it from poverty and weakness.' At this both Huskisson and Peel counselled that time should be allowed before the matter was considered and the issue was raised again on 27 May.

Edward Littleton presented a petition from the coal and iron masters of Dudley against Moore's proposed legislation.[3] Moore replied that his bill would benefit employers in that it would assure adequate wages for workers and thus reduce the burden of the poor rates.[4] He indicated that under its provisions wages would be determined by collective bargaining supplemented by recourse to arbitration in case of unresolved disputes. The bill, he believed, was of great historic significance. If a select committee was appointed on the issue and rejected his proposals he would let the matter rest. Nevertheless, he 'would never give up the fact that he (Mr. Peter Moore) was the person who had brought forward such a measure.'

Stuart-Wortley and Huskisson approved of the principle of doing away with the old laws, but they were doubtful concerning the new industrial relations regulations which Moore envisaged.[5] Huskisson thought that those new laws would 'control, embarrass, and perplex the regulations of any trade or manufacture'. George Philips too complained that the bill 'contained a number of restrictions between workmen and employers which would be injurious to both parties'.[6] Huskisson suggested no further action in this session and there the matter lapsed temporarily.[7]

MACHINERY AND THE WEAVERS

Manchester cotton weavers petitioned against the introduction of machinery in their industry and the issue was brought to the attention of parliament by Huskisson on 25 April.[8] This provoked little debate. Huskisson 'expressed his dissent from the opinion of the petitioners [and] ... saw no immediate means of affording them relief.' Peel asserted that the weavers were now living in 'comparative comfort', and Philips denied that the weavers could be harmed by the use of machinery. 'As far as regarded the rate of profit at present obtained', Philips observed, 'the men were in general better off than their masters.' Maxwell took a rather different view and suggested that there should be a reduction in the taxation of wage earners so that they could better compete with machines for employment opportunities.

A somewhat more extensive debate was touched off on 30 May when Attwood presented a similar petition from the weavers of Stockport.[9] Attwood noted that the petitioners requested the establishment of a minimum wage and complained of loss of employment because of the introduction of machinery. Such requests, he knew, were not likely to be received with favour by the House, but he believed that members should pay attention to them. Attwood continued:

> When they (the weavers) complained of the means of subsistence being taken from them, in consequence of improvements of machinery, and applied to the House for compensation, they raised a question of great extent and difficulty, and which was not to be met by the common assertion, denied by no man, nor denied by the petitioners, that all such improvements were beneficial to the wealth and interests of the community at large.

In contrast, Philips contended that there was no real problem in the case of the weavers.[10] Their wages might be low, but so was the price of food. The introduction of machinery was in the interests of workers, since wages were highest where machinery was most extensively employed. Further, they would only be harmed by fixing a minimum wage, because this would give rise to unemployment. The best course was to leave labour markets perfectly free. 'The sale and purchase of labour', Philips concluded, 'ought to be as unrestrained as the sale and purchase of any other commodity.'

John Curwen, who in 1819 had suggested the establishment of minimum wages for agricultural workers (see Chapter 2) came out against the proposal in this instance.[11] On the machinery question, Henry Grey Bennet recommended that the weavers should read a publication by William Cobbett. This would show them their errors.[12]

Ricardo then entered the debate and, to the surprise of Philips (and presumably many other members) he announced that he had certain reservations concerning Cobbett's pamphlet and the introduction of machinery.[13] There was a new dimension to add to the conflict of employer-employee interests. 'It was evident', he said, 'that the extensive use of machinery, by throwing a large portion of labour into the market, while, on the other hand, there might not be a corresponding increase of demand for it, must, in some degree, operate prejudicially to the working classes.'[14]

Philips protested and reiterated that 'the wages of the artisan were more liberal where machinery was used than where it was not used.' Ricardo replied that this fact did not touch his argument. His point was 'not that the use of machinery was prejudicial to persons employed in one particular manufacture, but to the working classes generally. It was the means of throwing additional labour into the market, and thus the demand for labour, generally, was diminished.'

Ricardo saw a way around this problem. One could not expect employers to refrain from introducing the cost savings which machinery bestowed: 'The question was, — if they gave up a system which enabled them to undersell in the foreign market, would other nations refrain from pursuing it? Certainly not. They were therefore bound, for their own interest, to continue it.' However, workers themselves could remedy the situation by restricting the supply of labour through a lessening of the working-class birth rate. 'A little forethought, a little prudence . . . a little of that caution which the better educated felt it necessary to use', declared Ricardo, 'would enable them to improve their situation.' If workers would only calculate the reproduction of their kind in terms of market logic as was done in the production of other commodities, Ricardo implied, all might yet be well.[15]

A rather different prescription was offered by Maxwell who brought forward a petition from Middlesex similar to that of the Stockport weavers.[16] Maxwell stressed the desirability of maintaining the level of effective demand in the economy: 'If wages were higher the working-classes would be able to consume a greater quantity of produce of every kind; and they must all acknowledge, that to devise a mode by which the consumption of produce would be extended, was a great desideratum.'[17]

On this ground as well as on those of reducing crime and maintaining the nation's taxable capacity, Maxwell urged that workers 'be protected as much as possible from the effects of machinery'.

THE MERCHANT VESSELS APPRENTICESHIP BILL

The lengths to which Ricardo was prepared to go in contending that the laws of market logic should be made to impress themselves on the life of the community were illustrated vividly by his role in the debates on new marine apprenticeship arrangements. On 13 March the House went into committee to consider a proposal by Huskisson that 'every merchant vessel in every trade should have an equal number of apprentices in proportion to her tonnage.'[18] Huskisson also recommended that apprentices should not be liable to be impressed under the age of twenty-one and that shipowners should be given the right to recover wages paid in advance to seamen who deserted but subsequently returned to England. Both Hume and Ricardo expressed reservations concerning these measures, the latter professing to see in them an attempt to lower the wages of seamen.

When a report on the bill was brought up on 24 March Ricardo moved an amendment that would have the effect of deleting the provision for definite numbers of apprentices to be employed.[19] 'It was a maxim', said Ricardo, 'that no person ought to be controlled in his own arrangements, unless such control was rendered necessary by paramount political circumstances.' He continued that the bill could not lead to an increased supply of skilled seamen, as its advocates supposed:

> So long as there was employment for seamen, there would be encouragement enough for them; and when there was not, those who were now here, would resort to foreign countries for employ. The only effect of the bill would be, to reduce the wages of seamen; and that alone would render it objectionable.

Huskisson could not accept this simplistic approach to the problems of skilled labour supply and he contended that vital national interests were clearly involved.[20] 'It had been the uniform policy of parliament', Huskisson pointed out, 'to maintain the maritime greatness and strength of this country . . . The bill would [afford] the best means of education to a race of skilful pilots and seamen.' In support of Huskisson an exasperated Joseph Marryat quoted Napoleon at Ricardo:

> Buonaparte had once said, that if he had a throne of adamant, he believed the political economists would grind it to powder. In like manner, the political economists in this country were ready to grind the navy and shipping interests to powder, rather than abandon their favourite theories.[21]

Hume retorted that the measure 'was about as useful and politic as a statute of one of the Edwards for the better stuffing of feather-beds.'[22] In all apparent seriousness he claimed that 'if the bill were to pass into a law, the effect would be to man the whole of the merchant ships with apprentices.'

Ricardo insisted on dividing the House on this issue and mustered six votes for his amendment. The hard-core doctrinaires on this occasion included Whitmore, Grenfell and H. G. Bennet.

Despite this rebuff Ricardo persisted when the bill was read a third time on 18 April.[23] Ricardo moved an amendment which would involve rejection of the legislation as a whole. He opposed the measure 'as imposing injurious restrictions on a particular trade, and interfering with the private rights of the individuals connected with that trade.' Huskisson, he believed, had not shown that shipping was a special case or that the bill would be helpful to seamen.

In reply Huskisson stated that 'the measure had given universal satisfaction to the ship-owners, and he believed that there was scarcely a man in the House, except the hon. member (Mr. Ricardo) who was not satisfied of its utility.'[24] No member rose to refute Huskisson's belief and Ricardo was forced to withdraw his amendment. The original bill was then passed.[25]

THE IGNORANT WORKERS OF SPITALFIELDS

During the following month Ricardo and Huskisson found themselves in agreement on a campaign to destroy the industrial relations system of the silk industry at Spitalfields in London. That system had been established in the eighteenth century by legislation designed to encourage the growth of the industry in that locale and a number of its features resembled those associated today with employer-employee relations under an industrial award or union contract. The Spitalfields Act allowed for wage determinations to be made in cases of dispute by magistrates of London, Westminster, Middlesex or the Tower. There were regulations concerning rates to be paid on various qualities of work, manning scales for machine work, protection of hand work against competition from machine production, entry of apprentices, and limitations on those who could be employed as journeymen. In addition the Act sanctioned collective bargaining and debarred employers in the London area from investing their capital in similar enterprises elsewhere in Britain.

On 9 May Thomas Wilson presented a petition from the London silk manufacturers requesting repeal of the Act.[26] Ricardo immediately welcomed the move and expressed his astonishment that such archaic legislation could still be in force.[27] Wallace and Huskisson were also in favour of repeal and the latter undertook to bring in a bill to that effect. Edward Ellice, however, suggested that the matter should not be rushed and that all interested parties should be given time to petition parliament.[28]

Events moved swiftly. On 12 May Thomas Fowell Buxton, the member for Weymouth, asked for a committee of enquiry on the subject.[29] Huskisson was not prepared to be so diverted, however, and he replied that nothing would be gained by a committee. 'From all he had been able to learn', Huskisson assured the House, 'he felt convinced that the trade would be much more flourishing than it was at present, if the restrictions in question were totally removed.'

Huskisson's assurance was made to appear extremely hollow when, on 21 May, Alderman Heygate, now Lord Mayor of London, introduced a petition against repeal from the weavers of Sudbury. This was supported by another, presented by Buxton, from 11,000 journeymen silk weavers of London and Middlesex.[30] Nothing daunted, Hume charged that the thousands of signatories were acting out of ignorance of the true principles of political economy.[31] 'They did not understand the operation of those principles to their own advantage or disadvantage', said Hume. This combination of arrogance and naivete drew an immediate retort from Buxton.[32] 'The petitioners', he replied, 'did not pretend to understand political economy — a science, the principles of which appeared to change every two or three years. All they demanded was to be heard.'

This latter comment stung Ricardo, who assured Buxton that 'the principles of true political economy never changed; and those who did not understand that science had better say nothing about it, but endeavour to give good reasons, if they could find any, for supporting the existing act.'[33] Confident that he was reasoning in terms of eternal verities, Ricardo went on that it was impossible for him to offer bad advice to workers: 'He most assuredly would not utter a word that could be injurious to the manufacturing classes: all his sympathies were in their favour: he considered them as a most valuable part of the population, and what he said was intended for their benefit.' From this Ricardo concluded that as he saw no good reason for continuing the Spitalfields Act there was no good reason for delaying its repeal.

Huskisson also would brook no delay.[34] In contrast with Ricardo he did not base his authority in this matter on command of unchangeable truths but rather on the expertise he had acquired as a public servant. Huskisson informed the House that the Spitalfields regulations had been the subject of review and discussion for some years now at the Board of Trade. Those discussions had indicated that repeal was required. In addition there was a growing urgency in this matter since the London silk industry was likely to be ruined because of an increasing competitive disadvantage relative to manufacture of silk elsewhere in England.

Among the absurd features of the Act, in Huskisson's opinion, was the provision for arbitration. When, as at present, there was a dispute between masters and journeymen concerning the prices for work, a magistrate would be called in. This person would be obliged to arbitrate in ignorance of the real state of affairs. Huskisson was obviously disturbed at such an abrogation of the logic of market forces, but Buxton hurried to assure him that this had rarely occurred. Buxton had it on good authority that workmen had only twice applied to the magistrates during the life of the Act.[35]

Speakers in favour of delaying repeal and appointing an investigating committee were Baring, Maxwell, Milton, Spring Rice, Calcraft and Ellice. Even George Philips, although he was an advocate of repeal, stated that he believed the issue should not be rushed since he 'was desirous that the necessity of the repeal should be manifested to the workmen themselves.'[36] Ellice made the point that workers in general throughout Britain were subject to restrictions under the Combination Act and the act forbidding the emigration of artisans.[37] He thought that it would be appropriate to repeal these acts if the Spitalfields legislation was to go.

HUSKISSON PRESSES ON

Some factor beyond the call of duty or his apprehension of the requirements of sound economic policy seems to have been driving

Huskisson on to demolish the Spitalfields system quickly, despite opposition within both the Commons and the Cabinet. Accordingly on 9 June the report of a bill for repeal was put before the House. Two lawyers were then admitted to the bar of the House to speak against the bill on behalf of the silk workers. When they had withdrawn Buxton moved immediately for referral of the legislation to a select committee.

Buxton argued that passage of the bill must pauperise the workers concerned.[38] They would be sacrificed on the altar of the current vogue for worship of the new principles of political economy. Arrangements that had proved satisfactory for fifty years were to be abolished for the sake of an intellectual novelty that was likely to prove ephemeral. He asked members to consider the history of economic thought over those fifty years. At the outset mercantilist principles had been widely accepted, but these had come to be overturned by Adam Smith. More recently there were those who would accept Ricardo's view that Smith was in error in a number of respects. Clearly there was no stability in the conception of what 'the soundest principles of political economy' might prove to be. There was no guarantee that 'some future system of political economy would not overturn the system of his hon. friend (Ricardo)'.

Despite the demonstrable fluctuations in economic thought and opinion parliament was being asked to legislate as if Ricardian doctrines were immutable. They were being asked to do away with a system which had admirable features. Buxton illustrated this latter by contrasting silk weaving in London and Coventry. So marked was the superiority of living standards and community morals in London that as recently as 1818 a parliamentary committee had recommended an extension of the Spital-fields act to cover the industry in Coventry.

Huskisson, Ricardo and Philips were against delay and urged immediate repeal. Huskisson contended that this would be in the best interests of the workers since the existing system was conducive to relatively high wages, the transfer of silk manufacture to other centres, and hence unemploy-ment for the London weavers.[39] Ricardo took up this point.[40] 'If these acts were repealed', he predicted, 'no doubt the number of weavers employed in London would be greater than at present. They might not, indeed, receive such high wages; but it was improper that those wages should be artificially kept up by the interference of a magistrate.'

Ricardo could not or would not understand Buxton's point concerning the mutability of economic thought. 'The words "political economy" ', said Ricardo, 'had, of late, become terms of ridicule and reproach. They were used as a substitute for an argument, and had been so used by the hon. member for Weymouth.' At the same time, he was firm that no amount of argument would change his mind on the Spitalfields question. He was 'as anxious for inquiry as any member, in cases where it was at all necessary; but, admitting all that the opponents of this bill stated they could prove, it would not change his opinion.'[41]

Speaking in favour of delay Ellice rebuked those who declared the workers ignorant. 'The artisans in the metropolis', said Ellice, 'were by no means the unthinking uneducated people the right hon. gentleman [Huskisson] imagined them to be.'[42] He wished to see more evidence put before the house on this particular issue. Peter Moore was of a similar mind and Henry Bright also urged enquiry.[43] 'Ought the House to refuse it', asked Bright, 'merely because some persons talked largely about the principles of political economy?'

This last point was refuted in a brief by revealing speech by the new Vice-President of the Board of Trade, Charles Grant.[44] The repeal, he emphasised, was not a mere exercise in applied Ricardian doctrine, but rather a considered move by professional public servants acting on accumulated data. Secondly, the data had been supplied exclusively by the Spitalfields employers:

> It had been said that his right hon. friend [Huskisson], in submitting the present bill, had founded it on principles of political science, and not on any practical effects as to the manufacture in Spitalfields. Now, he could assure the House, that in the repeated communications which his right hon. friend had with the master manufacturers, he had grounded his arguments for the repeal of these acts on facts alone.

Buxton's motion for an enquiry was lost by the slim margin of eight votes and Huskisson hurried his bill on to a third reading just two days later (11 June). Heygate, Moore, Bright and George Byng, the member for Middlesex, protested at the haste and at the sufferings which the weavers were bound to experience. They were joined by Hudson Gurney who commended the blend of collective bargaining and arbitration established at Spitalfields.[45] 'Something of the sort took place in all trades,' he contended: 'Make what combination laws you may, the necessity of an understanding between the parties will always abrogate them in practice.'

Ricardo and Hume, on the other hand, were now more confident than ever that the workers would benefit by the change.[46] Ricardo believed that under the existing arrangements the incomes of weavers were lower than they would otherwise be, although their rates of wages appeared high. Again, in periods of brisk activity, wages would not rise to the extent possible in a free market, because of the intervention of the magistrates. The volume of work available to the London weavers would be expanded by the repeal and their wages would not decline since rates were at present as high in the silk industry elsewhere in the nation as in London.

In response to a request by Ellice, Huskisson undertook to agree to the appointment of a committee to consider abolition of the Combination Laws and the statues prohibiting the emigration of skilled workers, if the House supported him in the present instance.[47] This underaking may have helped carry the day. Forty members voted against repeal, but the bill passed with a majority of thirteen in favour.

RESISTANCE IN THE LORDS

When the bill came to the Lords, that House showed a willingness to take serious account of the views of a group of workers, provided the latter observed the proper parliamentary forms and eschewed violent agitation. For some of the peers at least, those views could not be discounted simply on the authority of public service opinion and the zeal of the political economists. This fact was evident from the outset when Liverpool moved for a select committee to consider the question of repeal on 16 June.[48] In marked contrast to Huskisson, the Prime Minister asked that the petitions of the silk weavers should be given a fair hearing.

None of the peers opposed the establishment of a committee but Lord Ellenborough argued that there was no good reason to seek change in this area.[49] Why alter existing arrangements when an industry was prospering? The only answer he could find was that an attempt was being made 'to gratify the theoretical views of political economists'. Ellenborough was prepared to distinguish between the industrial relations provisions of the Act and those which restricted the employment of capital by Spitalfields masters to London and Middlesex within ten miles of the Royal Exchange. He approved of the industrial relations regulations which he thought should not be judged in the light of free trade doctrine. These he looked on 'more as a measure of policy than of trade'. However the restriction on the use of capital was a different matter and he believed that the journeymen weavers had no objection to repeal of that aspect of the Act.

The Lords returned to debate on the issue on 16 July after a committee report. Lord Bexley (Vansittart) moved for the third reading of the bill of repeal, claiming that the committee had favoured the step despite the continued opposition of the weavers to 'any relaxation of what they called their charter'.[50] Passage of the legislation was resisted by the Earl of Harrowby, who was convinced that 'the residence of a large manufacturing body in the metropolis was *prima facie* a great evil.'[51] His worry was that repeal would destroy the cottage industry character of London silk production and introduce a factory system. This would mean that 'thousands of weavers who now lived with their families would be taken away from them, and stowed into enormous buildings, where their excellent moral habits would be destroyed, while half a dozen great manufacturers would amass large fortunes.'

Harrowby was prepared to defend a system of wage determination which set a statutory minimum to rates of payment. This was not harmful, as the political economists claimed, since it made for better adjustment of supply to the state of demand. In the absence of a minimum, low wage levels induced by slack demand would lead weavers to try to increase output 'the effect of which would so inundate the market as to obstruct the return of a large demand.'[52]

Liverpool replied that there was no evidence to suggest that the factory system was demoralising.[53] Further, there was the fact that an earlier Lords committee — Lansdowne's committee on foreign trade in 1821 — had recommended the measure now before the House. Whatever were the wishes of the workers concerning the bill, he was confident that 'it was for their interests that it should pass.'

The Lord Chancellor then cautioned gradualism in alteration of such long-standing laws and the Earl of Rosslyn suggested that the bill might be amended to permit employers to invest their capital wherever they wished, whilst the existing industrial relations system was retained.[54] Overnight Rosslyn's compromise was accepted and, much to the satisfaction of Ellenborough and Harrowby, the bill was passed in the amended form the next day (17 July).[55] Harrowby added the footnote that he 'trusted the workmen would be sensible that to the uncommon prudence and propriety of their conduct, what had taken place was attributable.' Well-behaved workers with a case, it would seem, could look to the Lords for protection against employers anxious to use the legislature for personal financial gain.

EPILOGUE

In the Commons the next day (18 July) Huskisson announced that the bill had been so altered by the Lords that he would not proceed with the legislation.[56] Apparently the fact that the masters of Spitalfields were enabled to freely employ their capital in any region did not satisfy the purpose for which he had promoted repeal with such determination.[57] Other members made brief expressions of pleasure or regret at this outcome and Canning was content with the ambiguous statement that he trusted the Lords would devise a better measure in the next session.[58]

When the news was announced in London, weavers declared three days of public celebration. Yet their rejoicing was somewhat premature. In the following year at the instigation of Lauderdale, and with little debate, the Spitalfields Act was removed from the statute books.

17 1823: Equitable Adjustment of Contracts

I have seen small poets, and great prosers, and
   Interminable — *not eternal* — speakers
I have seen the funds at war with house and land
   I have seen the country gentlemen turn squeakers, —
I have seen the people ridden o'er like sand
   By slaves on horseback — I have seen malt liquors
Exchanged for 'thin potations' by John Bull —
   I have seen John half detect himself a fool. —

Lord Byron
Don Juan, Canto XI (1823)

Although the prices of agricultural produce began to rise during this session of parliament they were extremely low at the commencement of the year. In December 1822 the price of wheat was thirty-nine shillings per quarter, as against fifty-three shillings in December 1819. As a result, the 'squeakings' of the country gentlemen rose to a crescendo in late 1822 and early 1823 with a series of county meetings which attracted very large numbers of small landowners and farmers.[1] At these meetings resolutions were passed concerning the need for parliamentary reform, taxation reduction, government economy and 'the equitable adjustment of contracts'.

The campaign for equitable adjustment reflected the growing realisation that the holders of public securities and other non-agriculturalist rentiers had gained by the deflation of recent years, whilst the fortunes of the rural sector had slumped. To redress the balance, it was proposed that contracts should be revised to reduce the real burden of financial outgoings on those who could not or would not give up their involvement in the land. William Cobbett was prominent in this campaign as were a number of parliamentarians including H. G. Bennet and Edmund Wodehouse.[2]

THE EARLY DEMANDS FOR ADJUSTMENT

The independent and forthright Lord Stanhope moved to the attack almost immediately after the King's Address on 4 February.[3] 'The public annuitants', he claimed, 'now receive twice as much in the produce of the earth as they did in 1819, and nearly twice as much as they then did in other commodities.' This, he charged,was 'a most nefarious fraud practised on the nation', 'an act of public robbery', and 'the most systematic spoliation which ever yet disgraced a government or desolated a country.' The Lords ought go so far as to refuse Supply until the government had acted to right the wrongs involved.

There were similar sentiments expressed in the Commons, initially by Lethbridge on 14 February.[4] He protested at the lack of government action on agricultural distress and was supported in this by Curwen. As Curwen analysed the situation, the problem was lack of effective demand and this could be remedied, in part, by obliging 'the funded interest' to at once meet fifty per cent of the cost of the poor rates.[5] The merchant Alexander Robertson was also convinced that the same 'interest' should be curbed for the sake of non-rural entrepreneurs.[6] During the war the government had borrowed heavily 'on ruinous terms'. This meant that now society was 'completely in the hands of a great monied body in that metropolis [London], who could, at their pleasure, keep the interest of money at as high a rate as they chose.' Whereas Ricardo (like Smith before him) thought that the money rate of interest was governed by the rate of profit, Robertson complained that the link between the two rates no longer held. 'The system of credit which had been adopted in this country for many years', he believed, 'was one great cause of the evils the people were now labouring under.'

Ricardo entered the controversy on 26 February in response to a petition from Surrey requesting equitable adjustment of all money contracts. He could not accept that, with the alternation of inflation and deflation, there was any injustice which required adjustment.[7] The fundholder was merely receiving his just due.[8]

Ricardo also rejected any suggestion that his plan for resumption which parliament had adopted in 1819 had anything to do with the subsequent problems of rural producers. To this end, he referred members to the analysis of a Bank of England director, Samuel Turner. According to a recently published pamphlet by Turner:

As to the operations of the Bank, Mr. Peel's bill remained a dead letter. It had neither accelerated nor retarded payment in specie; except by the payment of ten millions of exchequer bills to the Bank, which enabled it to expend that amount in the purchase of bullion. Taking into consideration the rule by which the bank directors generally admitted they regulated their issues, namely, the application for discounts, and coupling with that the low rate of interest of money, the circulation would have been the same, and consequently the distress of agriculture as great, even if that bill had never passed.[9]

CRITICISM OF RICARDO

Against Ricardo's defence of the rentier Wodehouse set the very substantial authority of Henry Thornton.[10] In the debate on the Bullion Report in 1811 that outstanding monetary theorist had argued that when a currency remained depreciated for a decade or more, it would be most unjust to restore the previous standard of value.[11] J. B. Monck then questioned the relevance of Ricardo's use of Mushet's calculations, seeing that they did not account for the fact that deflation had disadvantaged debtors 'in perpetuity'.[12] He added that it was not just a question of justice between debtor and creditor but 'heirs at law, mortgagers, and others who made contracts under very different circumstances . . . if the House did not interfere, must be stripped of their property, and consigned to absolute ruin.'

Ricardo's contention that agricultural distress was unrelated to the decision to resume cash payments was greeted with astonishment by H. G. Bennet.[13] Robert Peel also bridled at the suggestion that his bill of 1819 was irrelevant in shaping subsequent events.[14] 'How was it possible to suppose', asked Peel, 'that, after the long derangement which had taken place in the currency, its value could be restored by the bill of 1819, without partial pressure and inconvenience? It was no solid objection to this measure that such pressure was proved to exist. It was a consequence that could not be avoided.' Peel stood by his bill despite the 'pressure and inconvenience', because it was based on prior undertakings by parliament to restore the currency standard after peace had been established.

Lord Folkestone charged that Ricardo had seriously underestimated the extent to which the currency had been depreciated in 1819 before the plan for resumption.[15] Mushet's tables which Ricardo invoked in the present dispute were subject to the very same objection. To this Ricardo replied that he had originally estimated the depreciation as five per cent but he knew now that it was ten per cent due to the machinations of the Bank that he had not anticipated.[16] 'If the measure of which he approved had been acted on', said Ricardo, 'the depreciation would have been but 5 per cent; because it would have been measured by the price of gold.' Frankly puzzled, Folkestone retorted that he 'had supposed the hon. member to have been arguing with reference to Mr. Peel's bill; but now he discovered that his argument rested on a measure which existed only in his own imagination.'[17]

A MOTION FOR AN ENQUIRY

On 11 June the House considered a motion for an examination of the effects which alterations in the value of the currency had had on money contracts and other financial arrangements since 1793. The main protagonists were Western and Wodehouse and the Commons debated the matter over two days' sitting. Discussion traversed the ground of Western's two motions on the currency in 1822 and of the above controversy concerning equitable adjustment. In the end only twenty-seven members voted for an enquiry, but the debate enabled prominent participants in prior clashes to restate their positions in detail. Some new arguments were raised by both defenders and attackers of the monetary *status quo*.

Western repeated all of his earlier criticisms and, in the course of recommending corn price movements as the best measures of inflation and deflation, he now charged that Ricardo's adherence in parliament to the price of gold as the best measure was inconsistent with his published views.[18] He quoted from Ricardo's pamphlet *On Protection to Agriculture:*

> When two commodities vary, it is impossible to be certain whether one has risen or the other fallen. There are no means of even approximating to the knowledge of this fact, but by a careful comparison of the value of the two commodities during their variation, with the value of many other commodities.[19]

In the light of this, said Western, it was astonishing that Ricardo had not brought the value of other commodities, like corn, into his reckoning when he was considering the relativities of paper and gold. By ignoring other commodities, he had grossly underestimated the degree of inflation existing prior to resumption of cash payments.

Wodehouse stated that he had great admiration for Ricardo's talents and character, but 'to believe that he had a clear perception on the subject of money, was utterly impossible.'[20] Against the Ricardian view Wodehouse cited the authority of both David Hume and Henry Thornton. He also quoted Francis Horner, John Locke and the former Lord Liverpool in support of the contention that corn prices offered the best means of judging variations in the value of a currency. Among contemporary authors, he singled out Henry James of Birmingham who, in Wodehouse's opinion, had convincingly demonstrated the fallacies in Copleston's writings on money.[21] The problem was that parliament was continuing to ignore authoritative observations on currency matters, just as Alexander Baring had been ignored in 1819. Parliament had ignored Baring despite the belief that he 'was supposed to have had opportunites of judging of this question, beyond any individual that could named.'

The main government spokesmen against the need for an enquiry were

Peel and Huskisson. The former could not see how such an investigation could be justified with the economy showing such obvious signs of increasing prosperity.[22] He put the demand for a committee down to an aberration of the national character: 'The English were, on all public questions, apt to be too desponding. The English were great Hypochondriacs with regard to their own country.' To set up a committee would be a blow to public confidence. To endeavour to adjust contracts, as Western and others demanded, was beyond the bounds of practicability. Further, Peel indicated, his fundamental agreement with the Ricardian perception of the problems of agriculture remained unshaken.

Huskisson also argued 'the utter impracticability of adjusting contracts made over a space of some thirty years'.[23] He doubted very much that there had been the massive transfer of property from landholders because of deflation as the advocates of adjustment claimed. Certain land speculations had failed, but that was all. There ought to be no going back on the decision of 1819, although he was prepared to allow that parliament had erred in as much as 'the substitution of silver for gold as a standard might, and perhaps ought to have taken place in 1819.'[24]

RICARDO AGAINST A COMMITTEE

Ricardo delivered a lengthy speech over which he had taken considerable pains.[25] In it he did not deny that prices had fallen because of a decreased money supply or that the value of money had increased. His main differences with Western concerned 'the degree in which the value of our currency had been increased, and the degree in which prices generally had been diminished by the bill (called Mr. Peel's Bill) of 1819'. Ricardo also explained that his object in supporting that legislation had been to prevent 'the caprice or interest of a company of merchants' from generating fluctuations in the value of the currency. His idea had been that of protecting the standard from the injudicious exercise of the type of power over it which restriction of cash payments had bestowed on the Bank of England.[26] He added that 'he had cared little, comparatively, what the standard established was', so long as it was a fixed one.

During this speech Ricardo remained firm that, although inflation and deflation might redistribute the wealth of the nation, these processes 'could have no effect at all upon the powers of a country'. Huskisson was chided for differing from Ricardo on this question. Ricardo also protested his complete impartiality in his original advocacy of Peel's bill. He owned no 'funded property' and because of the variety of his assets it was difficult to determine whether he had gained or lost overall by the deflation of recent years.

After an extensive attack on Western's arguments Ricardo concluded this, his last major speech on the currency, as he had concluded his first major speech in 1819. He exuded optimism:

> The difficulties of the measure of 1819 were now got over. The
> people were reconciled to it. Agriculture, he believed, would soon be
> in the same flourishing condition as the other interests of the country.
> If they were not, it would only be on account of the mischievous corn
> law, which would always be a bar to its prosperity.

BARING ON RICARDO

Baring was also opposed to an enquiry.[27] 'Time was everything', he
declared, and although great injustice had followed currency adjustment,
this was the wrong time to try to make amends. Only further injustice
would follow the establishment of a committee now because of the impact
of such a step on the state of expectations. Still, he thought the present
debate useful, if only for the fact it would help save parliament from
'preserving any deceitful landmarks, to puzzle and lead astray posterity'.
Baring then proceeded to attempt to tear down a number of the 'deceitful
landmarks' which he believed Ricardo had erected. Ricardo had 'asserted
opinions which held extremely cheap any statement, that the alteration in
the currency had produced the distress which had been complained of.
Posterity would assuredly be more acute than he was, if they understood
perfectly what his hon. friend meant.'

Posterity would find that Ricardo appeared to have little sympathy for
those 'numerous families [which] had been reduced to beggary, without
perceiving the invisible hand which had struck them down.' Even where
Ricardo did admit some measure of distress 'it was accompanied by so
much of argument on the other side, and so little of feeling for those who
had suffered, that it absolutely went for nothing. Indeed, his hon. friend
appeared to be ignorant, that this tampering with the currency had been
the great cause of the distress which had been experienced.'

Baring then pointed to a characteristic of Ricardo's reasoning that was
prophetic of the epistemology of much of the economics of the
mid-twentieth century. Ricardo frequently argued as if the immeasurable
was non-existent and his approach to the questions of inflation and
deflation was vitiated by this methodological weakness. 'As to the
question of depreciation', observed Baring, 'if it could not be brought,
like Mr. Mushet's calculations, to a table, his hon. friend would not admit
it to exist at all.' Ricardo's obsession with the relativity of paper and gold
to the exclusion of other considerations was a prominent manifestation of
this. That obsession blinded him to the fact that 'there had been a
depreciation of the precious metals themselves, in consequence of the issue
of paper, when they came to turn out all the gold and silver from England

into the market of the world.' Ricardo insisted on employing as a measure a relativity that was not relevant to the analysis of the problems at hand.

ATTWOOD ON RICARDO

Attwood attempted to reinforce Baring's rejection of Ricardo as an authority on monetary matters.[28] Like Baring, he found that Ricardo was reasoning in terms of fallacious measures of depreciation and appreciation of the currency. Because of the suspension of cash payments, he argued, the precious metals 'were no standard: their value had been altered by the very circumstance of their having been disused as a standard.' This fact, Attwood claimed, had been perceived by Francis Horner of the Bullion Committee, who had subsequently repudiated that Committee's published view that bullion price was the measure of change in the value of a currency. After 1810 Horner had settled on corn as the best measure, since he recognised that bullion 'rose or fell in an inconvertible paper, from the same causes as any other commodity advanced or declined; and was capable of affording no better a criterion than any other commodity of the value of paper.'

Malthus was also invoked as favouring the view that changes in the value of money were to be judged by movements of commodity prices in general, and of agricultural produce in particular. Further, Attwood contended that in a work written during the short-lived attempt to return to the old currency standard in 1815 (*The grounds of an opinion on the policy of restricting the importation of foreign corn*) Malthus had correctly anticipated the damaging effects on entrepreneurs of Peel's bill. Malthus had understood that the holders of government stock would benefit at the expense of 'the industrious classes of society, and the landlords' in a deflation.[29]

Attwood then set out to refute Ricardo's view that low agricultural prices were due to an excessive supply of produce stemming from over cultivation. He believed that the low prices were due to a 'destruction of agricultural capital' allied to a failure of effective demand. Both factors were the result of deflation engendered by parliamentary action. To understand this, one had to look at the mechanisms behind the equation of demand and supply in markets.

Parliament was to blame then, and parliament should remedy the injustice and distress through sanctioning the adjustment of contracts. He added that it would be sound policy to assist entrepreneurship by monetisation of silver. Attwood noted that when Baring had made a similar proposal it had been rejected as an unprecedented step, but this was not true. Before 1793 silver had been a standard for the currency together with gold, and before the eighteenth century it had been the sole standard.

THE CASE OF IRELAND

Another speaker to reject the Ricardian explanation of agricultural distress was Henry Grey Bennet.[30] He too introduced the problem of effective demand, as it was illustrated by the condition of Ireland, that country which had been 'beggared, robbed, and stripped by a legal enactment'. Bennet stated: 'It was a humbug to say, that in England the calamity we now suffered had been caused by over-production, and in Ireland, that the same distress was caused by a dearth. The evil had one common source, namely, engagements, contracts, debts, made in one currency, payments called for and enforced in another.' In both countries only fixed income earners had escaped damage from the destruction wrought by Peel's bill.

In Ireland Bennet pointed out 'there was famine without a dearth; people perishing of hunger, and no deficiency of food; farmers destroyed for want of a market; people starved for want of the means of purchase.' The origin of this misery was the legislation of 1819. It had created a situation in which 'the demand for old rents with the new prices, or paper rents with metallic payments, had been the cause of the seizure of all the property belonging to the smaller cultivators in Ireland.' The general failure of demand was the result of the cumulative effects flowing from that seizure of property.

Once again, the Irish case could be cited as a major challenge to the universal applicability of Ricardian principles. Unfortunately, there was no opportunity for Ricardo to reply to Bennet in this debate, but he was able to make some remarks concerning Ireland eleven days later (23 June) when Robert Wilmot-Horton requested a vote for £15,000 to help assist the settlement of 500 Irish emigrants in Canada. Ricardo was in agreement with the project 'by way of experiment', but he could not consent to any large grants hereafter. His belief was that captial would flow in to create employment in Ireland if only security of property could be guaranteed there.[31]

It is notable that this 'security' theme is dominant in the report of a parliamentary committee on Ireland of which Ricardo was a member and which reported on 16 July, three days before this session of parliament ended.[32] The report found that unemployment was due to lack of capital engendered by the disturbed state of the country. Yet public order could not be restored until the populace found employment. The solution was for government to intervene directly to create employment through public agencies so that eventually there would be the degree of security which would attract private capital.[33]

WESTERN'S MOTION IS LOST

As in the case of the controversy on the Spitalfields Act Ricardo was again a member of a majority in favour of gagging further discussion of a significant policy issue. On 12 June the move for a committee was defeated. Apart from those mentioned above as speaking in favour of an investigation, the minority included a number of Ricardo's opponents over the previous four sessions. Among these were Brougham, the labour sympathisers Maxwell and Moore, the merchants Ellice, Gordon and Wood, plus Folkestone, J. P. Grant, John Bennett and Monck.

REVIEW

In mid-July, near the end of the session, Ricardo returned home to Gatcomb and died there on 11 September. Some six weeks before his death he received Trower's comments on the legislative year. Trower wrote:

> In looking back upon the proceedings of Parliament, during the last Sessions, I think it impossible not to feel gratified, upon the whole, at the course of their proceedings. It is obvious that a more enlightened spirit, a spirit better suited to the temper of the times has influenced their decisions, than has been evinced on former occasions ... A new course of proceedings has been marked out; much has been done, still more has been promised; and the spirit in which this promise has been made, affords a sufficient security for its future performance.[34]

This was a fair assessment and the hope that it contained was borne out to some extent in legislation over the remainder of the decade. Nevertheless, the great bulk of what Ricardo had hoped to achieve by way of reform of public policy remained unaccomplished. His one clear moment of triumph, the passage of Peel's Bill, had quickly turned into a hollow victory and at the time he received Trower's letter he was at work on his plan for a National Bank. Most prophetically, that plan anticipated a transfer of power from businessmen and cabinet ministers to the forerunners of the professional public servants who were to do so much in the Benthamite cause in decades to come.[35]

Also on the negative side was the increasingly articulate opposition which Ricardo had aroused, notably within the business community. Thus James Mill wrote to McCulloch (10 January 1824): 'You can have little notion of the dread of publicity which hangs over many of us; and of the aversion to Political Economy which yet here is almost universal.'[36] Just how the Ricardian legacy of principle and policy was able to cope with its parliamentary critics over the remainder of the decade, despite widespread aversion, is an issue which must be left to another volume.[37]

Notes

CHAPTER 1

1 On the post-war years to 1819, consult R. J. White, *Waterloo to Peterloo* (Harmondsworth: Penguin, 1968).

2 A relevant study is Oliver MacDonagh, *A Pattern of Government Growth, 1800–60* (London: MacGibbon & Kee, 1961).

3 The definitive collection of his works, together with a wealth of biographical information, is Piero Sraffa (in collaboration with M. H. Dobb), *The Works and Correspondence of David Ricardo*, I–X (Cambridge: Cambridge University Press, 1953–5).

4 Concerning the link between Ricardo's thought and the appearance of a new style of civil servant, see S. E. Finer, *The Life and Times of Sir Edwin Chadwick* (London: Methuen, 1952), esp. 19–27.

5 Cf. ibid, 21–2. Belief in the existence of a 'middle class' was a characteristic of the thought of James Mill, in particular. On Mill and Ricardo, see T. W. Hutchison, 'James Mill and the Political Education of Ricardo', *Cambridge Journal*, 3, 2 (1953).

6 See, e.g., Elie Halévy, *The Growth of Philosophic Radicalism* (London: Faber, 1952) 340–2.

7 F. W. Fetter, 'The Rise and Decline of Ricardian Economics', *History of Political Economy*, I, 1 (spring 1969) 72.

8 Cf. J. A. Schumpeter, *History of Economic Analysis* (N.Y.: Oxford University Press, 1954) 471–2.

9 Alexander Baring, in *Hansard*, n.s. 8 (1823), col. 508. The serious nature of this defect also came to be recognised by J. S. Mill. For a critique of the methodology of his predecessors by Mill see his 'Miss Martineau's Summary of Political Economy', *Monthly Repository*, May 1834, in *Collected Works*, IV.

10 Henry Lord Brougham, *Historical Sketches of Statesmen Who Flourished in the Time of George III*, Second Series (London: Knight, 1839) 189. This approach of Ricardo's was greatly facilitated by what Professor Hutchison has so aptly termed Ricardo's 'monistic' conception of the objectives of economic policy. T. W. Hutchison, *Positive Economics and Policy Objectives* (London: Allen & Unwin, 1964) 134–6.

11 Quoted in Ralph W. Hidy, *The House of Baring in American Trade and Finance: English Merchant Bankers at Work, 1763–1861* (Cambridge, Mass.: Harvard University Press, 1949) 48.

12 Mark Blaug, *Ricardian Economics* (New Haven: Yale University Press, 1958) 150. This is not to say that Ricardo's ideas did not remain a considerable force in the formulation of economic policy after 1830. Consult A. W. Coats, 'The Role of Authority in the Development of British Economics', *The Journal of Law and Economics*, VII (October 1964) 88–95.

13 '. . . the dismantlement of the old techniques of economic control had been proceeding steadily since 1815. Here the clue to action was the consideration of highly specific problems, with the discussion of general rights or principle

186   *Notes*

kept to minimum.' S. G. Checkland, *The Rise of Industrial Society in England, 1815–1885* (London: Longmans, 1964) 342. See also O. MacDonagh, 'The Nineteenth Century Revolution in Government: a Reappraisal', *The Historical Journal*, I (1958) 52–67.

14   A. Briggs, *The Age of Improvement* (London: Longmans, 1959) 201.

15   For a more comprehensive account, consult M. Blaug, op. cit. Four more recent studies of relevance are: T. Sowell, *Classical Eeonomics Reconsidered* (Princeton University Press, 1974); D. P. O'Brien, *The Classical Economists* (Oxford, 1975); R. V. Eagly, *The Structure of Classical Economic Theory* (Oxford, 1974); M. J. Gootzeit, *David Ricardo* (Columbia, 1975). See also A. W. Coats (ed.), *The Classical Economists and Economic Policy* (London: Methuen, 1971). D. P. O'Brien, *J. R. McCulloch, a Study in Classical Economics* (London: Allen & Unwin, 1970) offers numerous important insights. See also, Donald Winch (ed), *James Mill, Selected Economic Writings* (Edinburgh and London: Oliver & Boyd, 1966).

16   It was in this context that the Ricardians used the law of comparative advantage, one contribution that was little remarked by immediate contemporaries but came to be recognised later as a significant innovation.

17   See P. Sraffa op. cit., VIII, 350–1 and 369.

18   See, e.g., *Edinburgh Review*, Jan 1824, XXXIX, 320–1.

19   On the politics of reform, consult John Cannon, *Parliamentary Reform, 1640–1832* (Cambridge University Press, 1973).

20   Arthur J. Taylor, *Laissez-faire and State Intervention in Nineteenth-century Britain* (London: Macmillan, 1972) 36.

21   P. Sraffa, op. cit., I, 152.

22   P. Sraffa, op. cit., IX, 287. However in the third edition of his *Principles* (Chapter 31, 'On Machinery') Ricardo argued that the position of wage-earners could be improved temporarily by such expenditure. See, P. Sraffa, op. cit., I, 393–4.

23   D. Winch, op. cit., 234. Mill was writing during the period when the population of England and Wales was later estimated to have increased from 9 millions in 1801 to just under 14 millions by 1831.

24   Op. cit., 242.

25   Cf. Mark Blaug, op. cit., 69–71. The manner in which revision could upset the simple model is explored in P. D. Groenewegen, 'Three Notes on Ricardo's Theory of Value and Distribution', *Australian Economic Papers*, 11, 18 (June 1972) 53–64.

26   D. P. O'Brien, op. cit., 355, notes that McCulloch 'frequently regarded capital in the context of the determination of wages as pre-accumulated wage goods.' See also P. Sraffa, ibid., 95–6.

27   D. Winch, op. cit., 251. See also P. Sraffa, ibid., 150.

28   O. St Clair, *A Key to Ricardo* (London, 1957) 120

29   D Winch, op. cit., 230.

30   Op. cit., 246.

31   T. De Quincey, *The Logic of Political Economy* (Edinburgh and London: 1844) 203, 204.

32   J.R. McCulloch, 'Political Economy', *Supplement to the Encyclopaedia Britannica* (1824) VI, 313–9, and D. Winch, op. cit., 262–3.

33   P. Sraffa, op. cit., IV, 16.

34   Consult, for example, ibid., 21: 'The general profits of stock depend wholly on the profits of the last portion of capital employed on the land: . . .' However, it should be noted that, as Piero Sraffa observed (op. cit., I, xxxi), Ricardo enunciated this principle in his *Essay on Profits* (1815) but did not repeat it in his *Principles of Political Economy* (1817). On this issue see S. Hollander,

'Ricardo's Analysis of the Profit Rate, 1813–15', *Economica*, n.s. 40 (August 1973) 260–82. See also, ibid., 42 (May, 1975), 182–202.

35 In McCulloch's writings the Ricardian case against the Corn Laws was posed mainly in terms of their encouragement of wide fluctuations in the prices of agricultural products. See D. P. O'Brien, op. cit., 378–83.

36 See P. Sraffa, op. cit., IV, 37.

37 It was allowed that improvements 'are ultimately of immense advantage to landlords' since 'they give a great stimulus to population, and at the same time enable us to cultivate poorer lands, with less labour.' Consult op. cit., 1, 81. See also op. cit., IV, 41.

38 *Edinburgh Review*, XLVI (June 1827) 33. Ricardo was of the same mind. See P. Sraffa, op. cit., IX, 192–3.

39 P. Sraffa, op. cit., III, 65n.

40 Op. cit., IV, 66–7.

41 See, e.g., J. R. McCulloch, *The Principles of Political Economy* (Edinburgh and London: 1849) 217.

42 P. Sraffa, op. cit., I, 363–4.

43 J. A. Schumpeter, op. cit., 329.

44 W. Stark (ed.), *Jeremy Bentham's Economic Writings*, 1 (London: 1952) 121–90.

45 D. Hume, 'Of Money', *Economic Writings*, ed. E. Rotwein, (London: 1955) 38.

46 D. Winch, op. cit., 294. See also P. Sraffa, op. cit., III, 120–2 and IV, 36–7 for Ricardo's rejection of the validity of Hume's view.

47 M. Dobb, *Theories of Value and Distribution Since Adam Smith* (Cambridge University Press, 1973) 66–7. In contrast with Smith's analysis the new 'mathematical' precision also implied that economists could make clear-cut distinctions between statements of a positive, and statements of a normative nature. On this see T. W. Hutchison, op. cit., 24–6.

48 P. Sraffa, op. cit., VII, 120.

49 On the nature and significance of Ricardo's methodology consult N. B. De Marchi, 'The Empirical Content and Longevity of Ricardian Economics', *Economica*, 37 (August 1970) 257–76.

50 P. Sraffa, op. cit., 1, 11.

51 Ibid, 36.

52 Ibid, 46.

53 D. Winch, op. cit., 191.

54 D. P. O'Brien, op. cit., 126.

55 See P. Sraffa, ibid, xlix.

56 Ibid.

57 Cf. M. Blaug, op. cit., 21–2.

58 Cf. P. V. Mini, *Philosophy and Economics* (Gainesville, 1974) 89–95.

CHAPTER 2

1 The reasons for the non-viability of the Whigs are detailed in Austin Mitchell, *The Whigs in Opposition, 1815–1830* (Oxford: Clarendon Press, 1967).

2 On Sharp (1759–1835), see Lloyd Sanders, *The Holland House Circle* (New York and London: Bloom, 1969).

3 Concerning Ricardo's entry into Parliament, see P. Sraffa, op. cit., V, xiii-xix, and VIII, 17–9.

4 These statistics are derived from Gerrit P. Judd IV, *Members of Parliament, 1734–1832* (New Haven: Yale University Press, 1955).

5 Some remarks of Walter Bagehot help explain the situation: 'The House was

188   *Notes*

composed mainly of men trained in two great schools, on a peculiar mode of education, with no great real knowledge of the classics, but with many lines of Virgil and Horace lingering in fading memories, contrasting oddly with the sums and business with which they were brought side by side.' W. Bagehot, *Collected Works*, 3 (London: The Economist, 1968) 268.

6   Hansard, 39 (1819) col. 17.

7   Ibid, 25–8. Lansdowne, formerly Lord Henry Petty (1780–1863), had entered the Commons in 1802. Educated at Edinburgh, where he was lectured by Dugald Stewart, and at Cambridge, Petty had been Chancellor of the Exchequer in Lord Grenville's coalition cabinet in 1806. The young Chancellor went into opposition with his fellow whigs when Grenville's ministry collapsed in 1807. He entered the Lords in 1809 and subsequently took a leading role as a moderate whig, both in and out of office.

8   Ibid., 28–33. Robert Banks Jenkinson (1770–1828), the second Earl of Liverpool and formerly Lord Hawkesbury, had become Prime Minister in 1812. An Oxford graduate, he joined the Commons in 1790 and the Lords in 1803. Before becoming Prime Minister, he had been at the Mint, the Foreign Office and the Home Office, and was Secretary of State for War and the Colonies, 1809–12. His administration was to last for fifteen years. Consult W. R. Brock, *Lord Liverpool and Liberal Toryism, 1820 to 1827* (London: Cass, 1967) and J. E. Cookson, *Lord Liverpool's Administration: The Crucial Years, 1815–22* (Scottish Academic Press, 1975).

9   Hansard, op. cit., 33–5. James Maitland, eighth Earl of Lauderdale (1759–1839), pursued a chequered political career. He was educated at Edinburgh and Glasgow (where John Millar was a strong influence), sat in the Commons, 1780–9, and entered the Lords in 1806. To 1821 (after which his views began to take on a distinctly tory character) he was the leading Scottish whig in opposition. He published extensively on political economy and outstanding among his writings are *An Inquiry into the Nature and Origin of Public Wealth* (1804, 2nd ed. 1819) and *Three Letters to the Duke of Wellington* (1829). Certain similarities between his thought and that of John Maynard Keynes have attracted the attention of historians of economic thought in recent decades. See, e.g., Thomas Sowell, *Say's Law* (Princeton University Press, 1972) and Morton Paglin, *Malthus and Lauderdale: the Anti-Ricardian Tradition* (New York: Kelley, 1961). On some of his earliest writings see H. F. Thomson, 'Lauderdale's Early Pamphlets on Public Finance (1796–1799)', *History of Political Economy* 2, 2 (Fall 1970) 344–80.

10   Hansard, op. cit., 25.

11   Ibid, 339–48.

12   Ibid, 652–4. In 1818 Sir Robert Peel (the elder), 1750–1830, who himself had been a major industrialist in cotton, had introduced legislation on this subject. It had passed the Commons. However it had been withdrawn in the Lords after trenchant criticism by Lauderdale. Thomas Malthus had come out in favour of the proposal in his *Essay on Population* (5th ed., London, 1817) 282.

13   Hansard, ibid, 655–6.

14   Ibid, 899–901. This measure had been introduced in the Commons during 1818 by Henry Grey Bennet (1777–1836) the member for Shrewsbury.

15   Ibid, 901–2.

16   Hansard, 40 (1819) 1130–3.

17   E. Halévy, *The Liberal Awakening, 1815–1830* (London: Benn, 1961) 46.

18   Bourne (1769–1845), who had been a Treasury official, 1804–9, and was a commissioner for Indian affairs, 1814–22, was in the Commons from 1798 to 1831. He had experienced some success with minor amendments to the Poor Laws during the session of 1818.

19 Hansard, 39 (1819) 402–8. Curwen (1756–1828), a Cumberland farmer, was a quite outstanding figure among the agriculturalists of his day. He actively promoted the causes of scientific farming and improvement of the lot of the labourer in his own business undertakings, through bodies such as the Workington Agricultural Society, and by publications. Indicative of his· concerns is *Hints on the Economy of Feeding Stock and Bettering the Condition of the Poor* (London: Crosby, 1808) 364 pp. Among the notable features of this work is its un-Malthusian emphasis on the scope for population expansion and for increased productivity in rural industry. In parliament Curwen was member for Carlisle and, later for Cumberland from 1786 to 1828. He twice refused a peerage.

20 Hansard, op. cit., 1157–8.

21 Cf. F. W. Fetter (op. cit., 73): '... whether it was the Malthus of the first edition or the Malthus of the second edition on whom Ricardo drew cannot be answered unequivocally ... Ricardo's formal model of income distribution was based on population behaviour of Malthus's first edition of the *Essay*; but much of what Ricardo said, when not constrained by the rigors of his model, robbed Malthus's ideas on population of their perpetual poverty note and would allow for the "lower orders of society" enjoying the comforts of today's American suburbanite.'

22 Hansard ibid, 1158–9.

23 Hansard, 40 (1819) 465–9.

24 It seems likely that Curwen, representing Carlisle, was moved by the current of industrial unrest in that area. Throughout May of 1819 workers there were protesting against a substantial reduction of wages. Again it is notable that among the current writers on political economy there was some support for Curwen's position on the need for 'legislative interference'. See, e.g., the anonymous *Enquiry into the Consequences of the Present Depreciated Value of Human Labour* (London, 1819), in which the author attributes the existing difficulties to a failure of effective demand which can be remedied only by government action to raise wages.

25 Hansard, ibid., 470–1. The social bias inherent in Ricardo's, and most other forms of Malthusianism both then and now, was shrewdly observed by the powerful journalist William Cobbett (*Cobbett's Weekly Political Register*, 11 September 1819): 'Mr. Ricardo from the Change, is *afraid* that this regulation (Bourne's) will be an encouragement for the labouring people *to go on breeding*, as he says they are *too apt* to do! I wonder whether any plan, bullion or other has suggested itself to the mind of this great statesman to check the population amongst the loan and scrip gentry? None of the declaimers against an increase of population ever think of this.'

26 Ibid., 472. Later in the session during a brief debate on emigration (Hansard, 40, cols 1549–51), Hume declared that it might be advisable to forcibly transport the unemployed poor to the colonies. Hume (1777–1855) was an Edinburgh surgeon who, after a tour in the employ of the East India Company, was able to enter parliament initially in 1812. As a devotee of the teachings of Jeremy Bentham and James Mill, he eventually became the major spokesman for the radical viewpoint in the Commons. His obsession with the minutiae of governmental expenditure earned him a certain degree of respect from some comtemporaries. During Ricardo's term in parliament Hume was (with the possible exception of George Philips) the most consistent supporter of the policies advocated by Ricardo. The latter reciprocated. As Edwin Cannan observed: 'Ricardo's name is constantly to be found in the short lists of the tiny bands which Joseph Hume carried with him into the lobby after inflicting his dreary collections of figures upon the House' (*Economic Journal*, 4 (1894)

417). Ricardo's friend Hutches Trower, amused at Hume's antics, described him as 'a compleat Ferret' (P. Sraffa, op. cit., VIII, 202). However, Ricardo replied to Trower that Hume was 'a most useful member of parliament' (ibid., 210). A speech of Ricardo's in tribute to Hume at a public gathering in the latter's honour is reproduced in P. Sraffa, op. cit., V, 471—4.

27   Hansard, ibid., 1126—7. Charles William Wentworth Fitzwilliam (1796—1857), Viscount Milton and 3rd Earl Fitzwilliam, was a prominent whig. He sat in the Commons, 1806—33, mainly as representative for Yorkshire.

28   Ibid., 1125.

29   Ibid., 1127. For a comprehensive treatment of the debate on the poor laws, both inside and outside parliament at this time, see J. R. Poynter, *Society and Pauperism: English Ideas on Poor Relief, 1795—1834* (Melbourne University Press, 1969).

30   Hansard, ibid., 1514.

31   Hansard, 39 (1819) 402—8.

32   Hansard, 40 (1819) 1019. Parliament had abolished the wartime income tax in 1816, partly on the grounds of its 'inquisitorial' nature. Mansfield seems to have hoped that a property tax would not be open to the same objection. His desire to substitute the latter for commodity taxation was very possibly motivated to some extent by existing conditions in Leicester. Some 3000 weavers were on strike there at this time. Concerning the abolition of the income tax and the serious long term consequences of that step for fiscal policy, see Sydney Buxton, *Finance and Politics; an Historical Study, 1783—1885* I (London: Murray, 1888) 12—5. For biographical information on Mansfield, consult C. J. Billson, *Leicester Memoirs* (Leicester, 1924) and R. W. Greaves, *The Corporation of Leicester, 1689—1836* (Oxford, 1939). John Mansfield (1778—1841) was a former mayor. of Leicester and represented that constituency in the Commons, 1818—26. He was a member of a local banking firm which had evolved from a family drapery business in the 1780s.

33   Hansard, ibid., 1022—4. For a thorough study of this aspect of Ricardian thought consult Carl S. Shoup, *Ricardo on Taxation* (N.Y.: Columbia University Press, 1960). Professor Shoup states (p. 247): 'The passages on taxation in the speeches [of Ricardo] are remarkable in their consistency with the doctrines already advanced in the *Principles*. They do not add to the theory appreciably . . . Ricardian tax doctrine was set down, in all its essentials, in October and November of 1816.'

34   This was Ricardo's first reference in parliament to a particular policy stance that was soon to permanently jeopardise his status and influence in the House.

35   Hansard, ibid., 1213—14. Russell (1792—1878), who had studied at Edinburgh under John Playfair, first entered the Commons for Tavistock in 1813. His liberal views were very much in evidence from 1817 when he strongly opposed the repressive measures brought down by the government to quell the unrest in that year. In December 1819 he made his first major speech on parliamentary reform, and thereafter continued to be a dominant figure in the reform movement. In 1846 he became prime minister for a period of nearly five years, and returned to that office briefly in 1865. See Spencer Walpole, *The Life of Lord John Russell*, 2 vols (N.Y.: Greenwood Press, 1968).

36   Hansard, ibid, 1214—16.

37   Ibid., 1219—20. The rate of tax on malt was increased that year.

38   Ibid, 1220.

39   Hansard, 39 (1819) 402—8. As a wartime measure the Act 'to prevent unlawful combinations of workmen' was hurried through parliament in twenty-four hours during 1799. The following year it was reaffirmed with some amendments. Under its provisions overt collective bargaining was declared illegal.

40   Hansard, 40 (1819) 337—9. Peter Moore (1753—1828) was a vicar's son who

made his fortune while in service with the East India Company. At a cost of
some £25,000 he entered parliament for Coventry in 1803 and retained the seat
until 1824. He was prominent in the more radical segment of the whig party,
and his concern with industrial labour issues was evident as early as 1814 when
he provided strong opposition to an attempt to emasculate the laws concerning
apprenticeship. As a reputable nabob, he was active in the promotion of several
public undertakings and a number of private business ventures during his time
in parliament. The failure of some of the latter eventually forced him to flee the
country.

41 Ibid. 339—41. Frederick John Robinson, afterwards Viscount Goderich and
Earl of Ripon (1782—1859), had joined the cabinet as President of the Board of
Trade in 1818. After graduation from Cambridge he had entered Lincoln's Inn,
and gained a seat in parliament in 1806. In 1815, as Vice-President of the Board
of Trade, he had introduced the Corn Law Bill which absolutely prohibited the
entry of foreign wheat into England until the average domestic market price
reached eighty shillings per quarter. He was promoted from the Board to
Chancellor of the Exchequer in January 1823, and for a brief period after the
death of George Canning in August 1827 he was Prime Minister. For detail,
consult Wilbur D. Jones, *Prosperity Robinson: the life of Viscount Goderich,
1782—1859* (London: Macmillan, 1967).

42 Hansard, ibid., 346—7. Philips, later Sir George Philips (1766—1847), was one
of the few active industrialists then seated in the House. He had extensive
interests in Lancashire cotton manufacturing and represented first Steyning and
then Wotton Bassett, 1818—30. Sympathetic to the whig cause, he was one of
the strongest exponents of the Ricardian creed in parliamentary debate during
the period covered by this study. Historians intent on portraying Ricardian
political economy as the economics of nascent capitalism could find in Philips
an excellent exemplar for their position.

43 Outside parliament the outstanding Baptist preacher, Robert Hall, called for
the establishment of a minimum wage in his *An appeal to the public on the
subject of the Framework Knitters' Fund* (1819). See also his *A reply to the
objections advanced by Cobbett against the Framework Knitters' Friendly
Society* (1821).

44 Hansard, op. cit., 1290—2. The document was signed by 'a number of
journeymen tradesmen, and mechanics of London and Westminster'.

45 Ibid. 'Free labour' for Ellice did not necessarily mean complete absence of
labour legislation. Hence, earlier he had supported Moore's proposals concerning the wages of silk weavers (see above). In that instance he argued (ibid., 342)
that government intervention could not be said to be mischievous when 'both
the master manufacturers and those employed by them, were unanimous in
their wish for legislative interference.'

46 Ricardo to McCulloch, 4 December 1820. P. Sraffa, op. cit., VII, 316. There is
the strong suggestion here that trade unions will wither away in a regime of
genuinely free competition and personal liberty. In his *Memorandum Book*
(1818—19) Jeremy Bentham wrote: 'Oppression well exemplified by anti-
combination and anti-emigration laws. Anti-combination acts prevent men
from earning subsistence at home; anti-emigration acts from earning it abroad:
both join in driving men into the poor-house and suborning suicide.' *Works* (ed.
J. Bowring) 10 (N.Y.: Russell and Russell, 1962) 509.

CHAPTER 3

1 On the events and economic literature of the period of suspension of cash
payments see Frank W. Fetter, *Development of British Monetary Orthodoxy,
1797-1875* (Cambridge, Mass.: Harvard University Press, 1965), Chs 2 and 3.

Consult also Jacob Viner, *Studies in the Theory of International Trade* (London: Allen and Unwin, 1955), Ch. 3.

2　Grenfell (1761-1838) was a businessman with extensive interests in copper and tin. He had built a considerable reputation as a critic of the slave trade and of the Bank. In the Commons 1802–26, he was regarded as extremely knowledgeable in financial matters.

3　Hansard, Vol. 39 (1819) cols 108–11.

4　According to the official figures on an initial capital of £11.6 million, there was a net gain to the Bank (dividends plus capital value) in the nineteen years from 1797 of over £29 million.

5　Ibid., 149–51.

6　Ibid., 151–3. Wellesley-Pole (1763–1845), later 3rd Earl of Mornington, had first entered parliament in 1790 and represented Queens County, 1801–21. He had been Chief Secretary for Ireland, 1809–12, succeeding his brother, the future Duke of Wellington, in that post.

7　Ibid,, 154–6.

8　The pamphlet in question was *A Letter to the Right Hon. Robert Peel... on the pernicious effects of a variable standard of value, especially as it regards the condition of the lower orders and of the poor laws.* By one of his Constituents, (London and Oxford, 1819). The author was Edward Copleston, the former tutor of Peel at Christ Church and later Bishop of Llandaff. This pamphlet went into three editions during 1819, and Elie Halévy comments (op. cit., 54): 'The pamphlet was a sign that if he [Peel] declared in favour of the [monetary] doctrine of Horner and Ricardo, Oxford would not disavow him.'

9　Hansard, op. cit., 153–4. Wilson was a London alderman and businessman who represented London 1818–26.

10　Ibid., 188–90 and 212–13. A similar petition arrived from Bristol on 3 February. S. G. Checkland writes 'The trade of Liverpool and Manchester lived by the discounting of bills of exchange. There was a strong opinion in Liverpool led by the radical-Whigs that was hostile to the gold standard system' (S. G. Checkland, *The Gladstones* (Cambridge University Press, 1971) 110). See also T. S. Ashton, 'The Bill of Exchange and Private Banks in Lancashire, 1790–1830,' in T. S. Ashton and R. S. Sayers, *Papers in English Monetary History* (Oxford, 1953), and L. S. Pressnell, *Country Banking in the Industrial Revolution* (Oxford: Clarendon Press, 1956) 170–80.

11　The government was worried and uncertain on the question. William Huskisson wrote to his wife (23 January 1819): 'Between ourselves the Govt. are very much embarrassed what to do, and will not, I apprehend, have the best of it ... Yesterday he (Liverpool) said if Tierney were to beat us, it would be fatal, if not to the whole Govt. at least to the Treasury.' Quoted in C. R. Fay, *Huskisson and His Age* (London: Longmans, 1951) 196.

12　Hansard, op. cit., 213–29. Tierney (1761–1830), the son of a wealthy merchant, was a Cambridge graduate who later studied law. In the Commons from 1789, he gained a considerable reputation as a debater and considerable notoriety after a duel with Pitt in 1798. He was Treasurer of the Navy in 1802, President of the Board of Control for the Affairs of India in 1806 and a leading force in opposition, 1817–21. For detail see H. K. Olphin, *George Tierney* (London, 1934).

13　That committee, which was chaired by Francis Horner, included Tierney, William Huskisson, Alexander Baring and the great monetary theorist Henry Thornton. Ricardo's published views had some impact on its deliberations and its report recommended a return to the principle of cash payments on demand by the holder of Bank notes.

14　Hansard, op. cit., 229–36. On 20 January the Committee of the Treasury of the Bank of England had resolved in favour of the idea of a parliamentary enquiry rather than face the possibility of an over-hasty return to cash payments.

15   Ibid., 240—9. Robert Stewart (1769—1822), Viscount Castlereagh and later 2nd Marquis of Londonderry, was Secretary of State for Foreign Affairs as well as leader of the House. In the Commons from 1794, he quickly achieved a prominence among the tories which was maintained to his death. He committed suicide in 1822. See C. J. Bartlett, *Castlereagh* (London: Macmillan, 1966).

16   Hansard, op. cit., 253—67. Canning (1770—1827), an Oxford graduate, entered the Commons as a tory in 1794 despite earlier close associations with the whigs. He was Foreign Minister in 1807, but resigned from the Cabinet after a duel with Castlereagh in 1809. In 1816 he became President of the Board of Control for the affairs of India, and he returned to the Cabinet as Foreign Minister in 1822 when Castlereagh died. He was appointed Prime Minister in April 1827, and died the following August. A recent study is Wendy Hinde, *George Canning* (London: Collins, 1973).

17   The volume of pamphlets on the resumption issue published in this year far outstripped those dealing with a perennial like the poor laws or with factory legislation. Something in the order of seventy pamphlets (most of which urged the dangers of resumption) appeared. These included a third edition of Ricardo's *Proposals for an Economical and Secure Currency* (first published in 1816) and the second edition of William Huskisson's *The Question Concerning the Depreciation of our Currency Stated and Examined* (first published in 1810). Other contributors of some note in terms of the history of economic analysis included Thomas Attwood, Sir William Congreve, Lord Lauderdale, John Rooke, Sir John Sinclair, Robert Torrens, Samuel Turner, John Weyland and John Wheatley.

18   During the currency debates of 1811 Canning had opposed the resumption of cash payments (a policy recommended by the Bullion Committee) as a step that was most untimely in a war economy. Also during that year he was co-author (with George Ellis) of 'Tracts on the Report of the Bullion Committee', *Quarterly Review*, V, IX (February 1811) 242—62.

19   Hansard, op. cit., 267—8. Manning (1763—1835), the father of Cardinal Henry Edward Manning, was in the Commons 1794—1830.

20   Ibid., 268—9. William, later Sir William, Heygate (1782—1844) was a banker. He became Lord Mayor of London in 1822 and represented Sudbury in the Commons 1818—26. One of the more perceptive developments of the theme of Heygate's speech, which is to be found in the pamphlet literature of the day, was Walter Hall's *A View of Our Late and of Our Future Currency* (1819).

21   Hansard, op. cit., 269—75. The reference to 'Jew brokers' was almost certainly a jibe at the activities on behalf of the Treasury of Nathan Meyer Rothschild.

22   Tierney continued with attempts to bring down the ministry until mid-May. His failures in this respect greatly weakened the cohesion of the whigs and contributed to a new political prominence for radical members, including Ricardo. See A. Aspinall, *Lord Brougham and the Whig Party* (Manchester University Press, 1927) 94—6.

23   Ibid., 277—8. Ellice (1781—1863) was a graduate of Marischal College, Aberdeen, and of St Andrews. Known as 'the Bear', he amassed a fortune in the Canadian fur trade and continued to hold extensive interests in both trade and land in that country as well as the United States. He was first elected for Coventry, with Peter Moore, in 1818. Initially a radical whig, he was closely associated with Sir Francis Burdett and was instrumental in securing the passage of the first reform bill. In 1836 he helped found and was first chairman

of the Reform Club. When he entered the Cabinet as Secretary of War in Lord Grey's government of 1833 he was the first practising merchant to achieve such a political status. He had also been Parliamentary Secretary of the Treasury, 1830–2.

24   Ibid., 380–3.

CHAPTER 4

1   For contemporary comment as to the most knowledgeable and active members of these committees see P. Sraffa, op. cit., V, 353–4.

2   A bullion payment scheme had been suggested by Ricardo as early as 1811 in the Appendix to his pamphlet *The High Price of Bullion a Proof of the Depreciation of Bank Notes* (London: 1809; 4th edition 1811). It was given a more extensive treatment in his *Proposals for an Economical and Secure Currency* (1816). Also, in 1811 Ricardo had outlined the proposal for graduated reduction of the price of gold in a private letter to George Tierney. See P. Sraffa, op. cit., VI, 67.

3   House of Commons, *Reports from the Secret Committee on the Expediency of The Bank Resuming Cash Payments, Ordered by the House of Commons to be Printed, 5 April and 6 May 1819, Minutes of Evidence*, pp. 133–42 and 227–32. Ricardo's evidence is reproduced in P. Sraffa, op. cit., V, 371–415. Mr Sraffa adopts a numbering system for Ricardo's answers to questions by the Commons' Committee as well as the numbering system used in the Lords report. These numbers are referred to in what follows. It should be noted that Ricardo's avenues of influence on these committees were not confined to formal evidence and publication of pamphlets. On 28 February he wrote to Hutches Trower: 'The inquiry into the state of our currency, and exchanges, is proceeding in both houses very satisfactorily. I have had many conversations with several of the Committees of both Houses – with Lord Grenville, Marquis of Lansdown, Lord King, Mr Huskisson, Mr F. Lewis, Mr Grenfell and others.' P. Sraffa, op. cit., VIII, 19.

4   On this point see also the evidence of Alexander Baring, House of Commons, op. cit., 192.

5   A contemporary pamphleteer, John Rooke, in his *A supplement to the remarks on the nature and operation of money* (1819) 15, observed that Ricardo appeared to lack 'any conception of the effects produced upon public wealth by an expanding, or a contracting currency.'

6   House of Lords, *Reports respecting the Bank of England resuming Cash payments: viz. The First and Second Reports by the Lords' Committee appointed a Secret Committee to enquire into the State of the Bank of England, with respect to the Expediency of the Resumption of Cash Payments ... Communicated by The Lords, 12th May 1819. Ordered, by the House of Commons, to be Printed, 12 May 1819, Minutes of Evidence*, 184–93 and 196–204. Ricardo's evidence is reprinted in P. Sraffa, op. cit., V, 416–57.

7   The diarist J. L. Mallet noted at this time: 'Ricardo does not think that the distress will be so great but in this he differs from all other commercial men.' Quoted in ibid., 353.

8   Cf. Lord Lauderdale, *Further Considerations on the State of the Currency* (1813), esp. 96–7.

9   This exchange (see especially Questions 73–76) not only indicates the considerable gulf between the ideas of these two economists, but also provides an unique glimpse of Ricardo's mode of reasoning 'on his feet' when pressed on general theoretical issues in dialogue.

10   The effect had been remarked on some years before in Henry Thornton, *An*

Enquiry into the Nature and Effects of the Paper Credit of Great Britain (1802), 263.

11 Jacob Viner has commented (op. cit., 198) that Ricardo's approach 'rests on concepts of "supply" and "demand" too physical and an implicit assumption of price and money-cost flexibility too unrealistic to serve adequately the purposes of analysis of short-run disturbances in a monetary economy.' Again, F. W. Fetter (op. cit., 90–1) writes of 'the doctrinaire nature of Ricardo's approach, and his lack of concern with the problems of price adjustment . . . he virtually ignored the complications that might follow from a further reduction of commodity prices due to other causes being added to the price reduction he anticipated from the reduction in the price of gold.'

12 For this evidence see House of Commons, op. cit., 249–52, and House of Lords, op. cit., 85–90 and 91–8.

13 'There are six great powers in Europe,' said the Duc De Richelieu, 'England, France, Russia, Austria, Prussia and Baring brothers.' Alexander Baring (1774–1848) was in command of the last named 'power' for eighteen years. Throughout that period he was a dominant figure in the world of international finance. For a time he was also a director of the Bank of England. Baring was a member of the Commons 1806–35. At first he supported the whig cause, but after 1831 he allied himself with the tories. He served as President of the Board of Trade and Master of the Mint during Peel's administration of 1834. In 1835 he was gazetted Baron Ashburton, taking the first of the seven peerages that were to be conferred on members of the Baring family over the space of sixty-six years. In 1842 he was appointed special ambassador to the U.S.A. and concluded the 'Ashburton Treaty' to settle the frontiers of that country and Canada. Later, he opposed the Bank Charter Act of 1844 and published *The Financial and Commercial Crisis Considered* (London: Murray, 1847). He also wrote *Inquiry into . . . the Orders in Council* (3rd ed., 1808).

14 House of Lords, op. cit., 132. See also House of Commons, op. cit., 191.

15 House of Lords, op. cit., 110.

16 Ibid., 128. See also House of Commons, op. cit., 195. Here Baring appears to have in mind the phenomenon that later came to be termed 'forced saving'. Increased money supply leads to increased commodity prices without a corresponding rise in factor prices. Rentiers' real consumption is thereby diminished, although they continue to make the same money expenditures. Hence there are 'savings' which the entrepreneur can invest to expand production.

17 House of Lords, op. cit., 127–8 and 131.

18 Baring may not have been entirely disinterested in making this last point. At the conference at Aix-la-Chapelle in 1818 the British government had undertaken to lend assistance to the French government in its public borrowing. Now Baring was busy raising very large sums for the French through the firm of which he was principal (Baring Brothers) and J. L. Mallet wrote in his diary (2 March 1819): 'Narrower means of credits, a closer system of discounts, a return to a sound currency in this great commercial country, could not fail affecting all Europe for a time; and it is *for a time*, and for that *very time*, that Baring wants facilities of every kind.' Quoted in P. Sraffa, ibid., 352. At one point in his evidence before the Commons committee (203) Baring admitted that resumption would interfere with the French loan negotiations.

19 House of Commons, op. cit., 180 and 195.

20 House of Lords, op. cit., 101.

21 Ibid., 102 and House of Commons, op. cit., 180–1, 195 and 198.

22 Ibid., 198. For the Bank's own views at this time see the resolution of the Court of Directors, 25 March 1819, in ibid., 262–4.

23   House of Lords, op. cit., 134. See also House of Commons, op. cit., 186.
24   Ibid., 184. See also House of Lords, op. cit., 134.
25   House of Commons, op. cit., 186. To this observation he added (189): '. . . the quotations of the price of bullion are, from want of competition, arbitrary; but further, the price of gold seems also to depend a good deal upon the price that the Bank may at particular periods chuse to give for it.'
26   Ibid.
27   Ibid, 193.
28   House of Lords, op. cit., 136. Before the Commons Committee (op. cit., 184), he argued that the existing note issue was not excessive (as Ricardo claimed) when considered in terms of the economy's present needs.
29   House of Commons, op. cit., 194.
30   Ibid.
31   House of Lords, op. cit., 137.
32   House of Commons, op. cit., 200.
33   House of Lords, op. cit., 132. See also House of Commons, op. cit., 191. In 1816 Baring had argued that cash payments could be more easily resumed in terms of silver rather than gold. Hansard, 34 (1816) col. 964.
34   F. W. Fetter, op. cit., 86.
35   Hansard, 39 (1819) cols 1398—401. At this stage Peel (1788—1850) had been in the Commons ten years and, two years before had gained the prestigious position of Member for Oxford University. On this phase of Peel's career see Norman Gash, *Mr Secretary Peel: the Life of Sir Robert Peel to 1830* (London: 1961). A general study is George Kitson Clark, *Peel and the Conservative Party* (London: Cass, 1964).
36   Hansard, ibid., 1401—4 and 1406—8.
37   Ibid., 1404—6.
38   Ibid., 1408—9.
39   The Lords gave their assent the next day, 6 April, after little debate. See ibid., 1420—2.
40   Ibid., 1414—5. Gurney (1775—1864) was associated with the country banking establishment of the same name at Norwich. He had inherited a fortune from his father and represented first Shaftesbury and then Newtown, 1812—32. It is not entirely clear from Hansard whether it was he or his relative Richard Hanbury Gurney (1784—1854) who spoke. The latter had just been elected to the House for Norwich. However Hudson Gurney's involvement in this issue is attested by his tendering evidence to the Lords Committee (as mentioned above).
41   This warning from a member closely associated with banking helps bear out the observation by F. W. Fetter (op cit., 99): 'Opposition in 1819 to resumption at par was much stronger outside Parliament than inside, where politics gave a misleading picture of unanimity.'
42   The diarist Mallet noted: 'The Committee of the Lords was unanimous with the exception of Lord Lauderdale who stuck to his own theory; the Committee of the Commons unanimous with the exception of Tierney and Mr Manning. Tierney from factious motives, and ignorance of the question: Manning as a Bank Director of the old school.' Quoted in P. Sraffa, ibid., 365.
43   These bars came to be known as *Ricardoes*. In practice, they remained mere curiosities since after the passage of the bill for resumption, the market price of gold fell below £4.1s.0d. per ounce. This feature of the Ricardo plan proved quite redundant, as Alexander Baring had expected. On the *Ricardoes*, see F. W. Fetter, op. cit., 91—2 and 97—9; P. Sraffa, ibid., 368—70; and J. Bonar, 'Ricardo's Ingot Plan', *Economic Journal*, XXXIII (September 1923) 281—304.
44   Hansard, 40 (1819) cols 215—17.
45   P. Sraffa, op. cit., VIII, 26—7.

CHAPTER 5

1   Hansard, 40 (1819) cols 597—600. The petition was drawn up at a meeting in May at the London Tavern. Sir Robert Peel (the elder) was in the chair and Robert Torrens was one of the speakers. Torrens criticised Ricardo's views in a pamphlet, *A comparative estimate of the effects which a continuance and a removal of the restrictions upon cash payments are respectively calculated to produce; with strictures on Mr. Ricardo's proposal for obtaining a secure and economical currency* (London, 1819). For a full-length study of Torrens see Lionel Robbins, *Robert Torrens and the Evolution of Classical Economics* (London: Macmillan, 1958).

2   Hansard, op. cit., 600—4.

3   Ibid., 605—6.

4   Ibid., 606—8. The Mint regulations to which Lauderdale referred were those which officially demonetised silver by act of parliament in 1816. (See *Hansard*, 34 (1816) 912ff. and 946ff.) Gold was declared the sole standard of value, and silver coins merely 'counters'. Silver was made legal tender only for transactions involving sums less than two guineas. A pound of silver was to be coined into 66 shillings, including a margin of four shillings to cover costs. The new silver coinage was issued in March 1817. These arrangements had called forth a strong protest from Lauderdale (ibid., 1235—9). For further detail consult F. W. Fetter, op. cit., 64—7, and Sir John Craig, *The Mint* (Cambridge University Press, 1953) 284—8.

5   Hansard, op. cit., 610—28.

6   See, e.g., Ephraim Gompertz, *A Theoretic Discourse on the Nature and Property of Money* (London: Richardson, 1820).

7   In his diary J. L. Mallet noted that, at a dinner held at Ricardo's London residence on 6 March, 'Everyone [is] full of Mr Baring's evidence before the Lords' Committee.' Those present took the general tenor of Baring's evidence to be against resumption. Mallet also observed that 'Ricardo looks very blank.' Quoted in P. Sraffa, op. cit., VIII, 18.

8   Hansard, op. cit., 628—40. Lauderdale also entered a Protest on this legislation in the Journals of the House of Lords. Throughout his parliamentary career Lauderdale lodged eighty-six such Protests on various species of legislation.

9   These remarks were almost certainly occasioned by the interchange between Ricardo and Lauderdale on effective demand, capital and credit in the Lords committee on 24 March (see Chapter 4). Ricardo had little time for Lauderdale as a theorist and in a letter to McCulloch (3 January 1819) described Lauderdale's position on the currency as 'very absurd'. (See P. Sraffa, ibid. 3.) Lauderdale published his views in *The Letters of Daniel Hardcastle to the Editor of 'The Times' Journal, on the subject of the Bank Restriction, the Regulations of the Mint, ec., With Notes and Additions* (London, 1819).

10 Hansard, op. cit., 640—3. In 1811 King had gained considerable notoriety by sending a letter to his tenants in which he announced that he would no longer accept payment of rent in bank notes at their nominal value. He wished to be paid in coin or in paper money equivalent to the gold-value of the rent. King defended his action in parliament (Hansard, 20 (1811) 790 ff).

11 Criticism of the 'over-trader' in parliament was usually an ex-post condemnation of an individual who was accorded the widest approval ex-ante. Many members do not seem to have realised that they approved of a socio-economic order which must involve entrepreneurial failure as well as success. In this they were assisted by the Ricardian view of capital and labour as extremely mobile factors that the entrepreneur could readily switch from employment to employment as old avenues of profit closed and new ones opened.

12 Hansard, 40 (1819) 645—55.

13   P. Sraffa, ibid., 32.
14   Hansard, op. cit., 672—4. The petition was a direct outcome of the meeting at the London Tavern, as noted above. Although Peel had made his fortune in cotton, he had formed a banking firm in 1790 and could thus claim some authority in matters of finance. On his activities as an entrepreneur, see S. D. Chapman, 'The Peels in the Early English Cotton Industry', *Business History*, XI (1969).
15   Hansard, ibid., 676—702.
16   This reversal was to prove typical of Peel's political behaviour. 'From a certain peculiarity of intellect and fortune,' writes Walter Bagehot, 'he was never in advance of his time. Of almost all the great measures with which his name is associated, he attained great eminence as an opponent before he attained even greater eminence as their advocate . . . So soon as these same measures, by the progress of time, the striving of understanding, the conversion of receptive minds, became the property of second-class intellects, Sir Robert Peel became possessed of them also.' W. Bagehot, op. cit., 245.
17   Peel's view was supported by Wellesley-Pole but was attacked by John Peter Grant of Great Grimsby (Hansard, op. cit., 705—23).
18   Ibid., 702—5.
19   Ibid., 723—36. By this time the Whigs had suffered a clear political defeat on an issue in which they had expected to gain a great deal. Austin Mitchell (op. cit., 124) comments: 'Currency, which Tierney had used as an issue to attack the government in February, soon boomeranged. Being on the committee curtailed Tierney's power to speak out when the extension of the suspension was agreed to in April, and neither he nor (Earl) Grey fully approved of the payments resumption finally agreed.'
20   Hansard, ibid., 736—40. Vansittart (1766—1851) was the son of a governor of Bengal. After graduation from Oxford he trained as a lawyer and first entered the Commons in 1796. In 1801 he was appointed Joint Secretary of the Treasury, an event which *Spirit of the Public Journals* (1802, 206) greeted as follows:

> 'If blocks can from danger deliver,
> *Two* places are safe from the French:
> The *first* is the mouth of a river,
> The *second* the *Treasury Bench*.'

However, having built a considerable reputation for financial expertise, Vansittart became Chancellor of the Exchequer in May 1812. He remained Chancellor until December 1822 by which time he had become widely unpopular, especially because of the continuation of some of the wartime taxation measures. There was also considerable distrust of his budgetary practices. In March 1823 he moved to the Lords as the first Baron Bexley.
21   In the debates of May 1811 on the resumption of cash payments Vansittart had been in the vanguard of those who had argued successfully against the measure.
22   Ibid., 740—2.
23   Ibid., 742—8. Ricardo's letters to McCulloch over this period suggest that this response did much to increase Ricardo's confidence in his role as a parliamentarian. Contrast the letters of 7 April and 22 June, in P. Sraffa, ibid., 21 and 38—9.
24   R. S. Sayers has commented that this stance of Ricardo's was 'a major disaster'. Professor Sayers seeks an explanation for it in A. W. Coats (ed.), op. cit., 37-41. One factor which may be most pertinent in any such explanation is the tendency of Ricardo (shared with many a modern economist) to ignore the

influence of unmeasured variables. Statistical information on the currency was sparse and that which was available determined the range of variables in terms of which Ricardo was prepared to reason formally, *even though he appreciated that other forces (unquantified) were at work.*

25 Lauderdale had just published *Three Letters on the Causes of the Present State of the Exchanges, and Price of Gold Bullion, as printed in 'The Times' under the signature of 'An Old Merchant'* (London: Budd & Calkin, 1819). In the second edition of his *Principles* (1819) Ricardo added a lengthy note to his chapter 'On Currency and Banks' (Chapter 27) in refutation of Lauderdale's argument. See P. Sraffa, op. cit., 1,371.

26 Quoted in P. Sraffa, op. cit., V,17.

27 Hansard, op. cit., 750–7.

28 Ibid., 760–3.

29 Ibid., 763–71. William Pleydell-Bouverie (1779–1869), Viscount Folkestone, and later 3rd Earl of Radnor, was a whig of strong liberal persuasions. He sat in the Commons, 1801–28.

30 Ibid., 780–7. Marryat (1757–1824) represented Horsham, 1808–12, and Sandwich, 1812–24. A merchant with extensive interests in the West Indies trade, he was chairman of Lloyd's and colonial agent for Grenada. His son, Frederick Marryat, was the popular writer of novels of the sea.

31 Three years later in debate (Hansard, n.s. 7 (1822) 938–54) Ricardo informed the House that he had always looked on the bill for resumption of cash payments as an 'experiment'. During 1819 Marryat's attack on Ricardo's methodology was echoed by an anonymous writer in *The British Critic*, XII (December 1819) 561–78.

32 Hansard, 40 (1819) 757–60 and 779.

33 Ibid., 790–6.

34 In his diary J. L. Mallet had noted that at the committee stage Castlereagh and Vansittart had been most reluctant to agree to the plan for resumption. See P. Sraffa, ibid., 365.

35 Hansard, op. cit., 800. F. W. Fetter (op. cit., 95) comments: 'The fears expressed outside Parliament about the distress that might follow from resumption seem to have called forth a bipartisan Parliamentary loyalty. This public attitude toward resumption taken against the background of the political unrest of the time, apparently was an argument, not, as logic might suggest, in favour of postponing resumption until further study could be made, but in favour of unanimous action by Parliament to reassure publc opinion.' To this comment, it can be added that much of the bipartisan loyalty seems to have sprung from the desire of a large proportion of the ordinary members to assert the position and power of the House itself in relation to Cabinet, the Bank, and influential business interests. Postponement of resumption would have been, to many, a defeat for the House as a House.

36 Hansard, op. cit., 1151.

37 Ibid., 1192–3.

38 Ibid., 1193–4.

39 Ibid., 1159–62.

40 Ibid., 1231–2.

41 Ibid., 1225–9.

42 Ibid., 1229–31.

43 On 22 June Ricardo had written to McCulloch: 'I . . . only object to the Bill just passed, because it will impose on the Bank the obligation of buying gold, and preparing for coin payments, in 1821, although such payments may never be necessary.' P. Sraffa, op. cit., VIII, 39. Ricardo was still hopeful that his bullion scheme would commend itself as the better alternative in practice.

44   One of the witnesses before the Commons committee, Thomas Smith, an accountant, had advocated this course. Smith had published *An essay on the theory of money and exchange* (1807; 2nd ed. 1811) and appears to have been the author of *An address to the Right Hon. Robert Peel, late chairman of the Committee on the currency* (1819).
45   P. Sraffa, ibid., 31.

CHAPTER 6

1   For detail, consult D. Read, *Peterloo: The Massacre and its Background* (Manchester, 1958) and R. Walmsley, *Peterloo, the Case Reopened* (Manchester, 1969).
2   E. Halévy, op. cit., 65. Ricardo wrote to Trower (25 September 1819) that disruption of the meeting was 'unwise and inexpedient', and he added that while such gatherings were regrettable, they were justified as a lesser evil than a complete absence of free assembly (P. Sraffa, op. cit., VIII,80).
3   Ricardo and other members of liberal disposition voted against these measures. Ricardo wrote (ibid., 146): 'I consider them as serious infringements on our liberties, and deprecate them because I expect that they will not allay the causes of discontent, but increase them.'
4   Hansard, 41 (1819–20), especially cols 421–5.
5   Corroboration of this point came in a later debate in the Commons (ibid., 921–8). The Lord Advocate, William Rae, found that this circumstance occurred in the Scottish weaving industry. However, Rae distinguished between weavers, who worked at home, and spinners, who did not. Technological and institutional constraints ensured that the spinners 'could not produce a greater quantity of thread during the hours of labour; nor employ a greater number of hands at one time than another.'
6   Ibid., 448–58. William Wyndham Grenville, Baron Grenville (1759–1834) for many years had been a convinced exponent of the *laissez-faire* doctrine. Hence in 1815 he was one of the leading opponents of the corn law bill. After graduation from Oxford in 1780 he studied law, entered the Commons in 1782 and was elevated to the peerage in 1790. He occupied a variety of parliamentary posts, including Speaker of the Commons, Secretary of State for the Home Department, Vice-President of the Board of Trade, President of the Board of Control and Secretary of State for Foreign Affairs. In 1806 he led the short-lived Ministry of All the Talents. Illness forced his retirement from political activity in 1823.
7   Ibid., 914.
8   The 'unproductive' character of investment related to military activities was a common theme in the economic literature of the day. One of the more able dissenters from this view, about this time, was Sir Samuel Egerton Brydges (1762–1837), M.P. for Maidstone, 1812–18. See, e.g., his *Arguments in favour of the practicability of relieving the able-bodied poor* (London, 1817), esp. p. 19, and *The Population and Riches of Nations* (London, 1819). esp. pp. 195–6. Conscious of the role of effective demand, he was a critic of Say and Ricardo. His most interesting work in this latter respect is *What Are Riches?* (Geneva, 1821). In parliament he was a defender of the principle of poor laws. See J. R. Poynter, *Society and Pauperism* (1969), *passim*.
9   Ricardo wrote to Grenville criticising some aspects of this speech, but the letter has not been found. However, from Grenville's reply it seems likely that Ricardo may have objected to the un-Malthusian notion of a necessary tendency for capital to grow at a faster rate than population. He may also have

criticised Grenville's linking capital shortage and war. In Grenville's letter the peer refers to Ricardo as 'my master in this science', i.e. in political economy. See P. Sraffa, ibid., 150—1. When Ricardo died Grenville wrote to Liverpool: 'Radical as he was I consider Ricardo's death a great loss both to the country and to Government. The extreme caution of his mind and conduct contrasted very strikingly with the extravagance of his political opinions.' Quoted in W. R. Brock, op. cit., 188.

10 Hansard, op. cit., 890—900. The Hon. Henry Grey Bennet (1777—1836), a whig, was the second son of the 4th Earl of Tankerville. He was a Cambridge graduate and represented Shrewsbury, 1806—7 and 1811—26.

11 Ibid., 902—10.

12 Ibid., 928—33.

13 In 1816, the first year of peace, the government had repealed a number of wartime taxes, the most notable being the ten per cent income tax. No further relief was forthcoming in 1817 or 1818, and in the current year rates of commodity taxation were actually increased on some commodity items (tea, sugar, coffee, pepper, tobacco, spirits, wine and malt).

14 Ibid., 900—2.

15 Ibid., 914—16.

16 Ibid., 921—8. James Archibald Stuart-Wortley (1776—1845), later 1st Baron Wharncliffe, was a moderate tory and a member for the important constituency of Yorkshire. His family owned extensive estates. He pursued a successful career in the army, 1790—1801, after which he entered the Commons, 1802—26. Wortley was an advocate of a variety of Ricardian policies including reduction of government expenditure, greater freedom of trade, and abolition of the corn laws.

17 Ibid., 933—5.

18 Ibid., 937. Smith (1767—1842) was a banker whose ideas were strongly influenced by those of Robert Owen, at this time. He was in the Commons 1802—34.

19 Smith's allusion was taken up by Ricardo in a speech a week later.

20 Ibid., 1189—94. De Crespigny (1765—1829), a Cambridge graduate, represented Southampton 1818—26.

21 Ibid., 1195—1200. Henry Peter Brougham (1778—1868) was a Scottish barrister and a graduate of the University of Edinburgh. He was particularly active in the educational reform and law reform movements as well as the party politics of his era. Although an intimate of both Bentham and James Mill, he was never a Benthamite. Neither was he an Owenite, despite a lifelong friendship with Robert Owen. He wrote prolifically and contributed many articles to the *Edinburgh Review* from 1802 onward. Those articles of interest to economists include highly critical reviews of Lauderdale's *Enquiry* (July 1804 and July 1805); a discussion of income taxation (February 1816); and a review of Bentham on usury (December 1816). On the phase of Brougham's career relating to the present book consult Chester W. New, *The Life of Henry Brougham to 1830* (Oxford: Clarendon Press, 1961). He wrote a lengthy autobiography and has been the subject of several biographical studies.

22 Hansard, op. cit., 1206—9. Ricardo believed that productive effort must suffer in a community which denied the principle of the pursuit of individual gain. See, e.g., his letters to Trower (8 July 1819) and to Place (9 September 1821).

23 The alternative version reads: 'He never could think that machinery could do mischief to any country, either in its immediate or its permanent effect.' Quoted in P. Sraffa, op. cit., V,31. As noted in Chapter 1, Ricardo did alter his views on machinery. Professor Hollander suggests that this alteration occurred between 25 January and 12 March 1821. See S. Hollander, 'The Development

of Ricardo's Position on Machinery,' *History of Political Economy,* 3,1 (Spring 1971) 105—35.

24 This was Ricardo's first direct attack in parliament on the corn laws. Since 1815 the sale of imported corn was absolutely forbidden, except when domestic market prices exceeded certain limits. The limit price for wheat, for example, was eighty shillings per quarter. Since February of the current year the price of wheat had been below the limit.

25 Ricardo had touched on the desirability of this course in his *Principles,* Chapter 17: 'Taxes on Other Commodities than Raw Produce'. There he had employed a most treacherous analogy: 'That which is wise in an individual, is wise also in a nation.' See P. Sraffa, op. cit., I, 247—8.

26 Hansard, op. cit., 1210—1.

27 Quoted in P. Sraffa, op. cit., VIII,152. See also ibid, 147; *Cobbett's Weekly Political Register,* 20 May 1820, 708; and Henry Lord Brougham, *Historical Sketches of Statesmen who Flourished in the Time of George III, Second Series* (London: Knight, 1839) 188—91.

28 E. Cannan, op. cit., 423. Cannan adds, 'That Ricardo could propose it seriously may perhaps be looked upon as confirming the common view that he was an unpractical theorist.' This aspect of Ricardo's thought is examined in detail in C. S. Shoup, op. cit., 160—5. Professor Shoup adds (p. 254): 'A disturbing emotional overtone marks some of Ricardo's analytical passages, notably those concerned with the total weight of taxation and with his proposal for a capital levy to retire the public debt.' The emotional element in this area of Ricardo's reasoning is attested by his willingness to indulge, and positively admire, the obsession of Joseph Hume with trifling economies in government expenditure.

29 This agricultural technique involved an increase of the labour-capital ratio and it may be some measure of Ricardo's concern at this time with the machinery-unemployment nexus that he was willing to have it given some consideration. Also relevant is the fact that Ricardo (rather against his will) had been pressed to serve, earlier in the year, on a non-parliamentary committee to investigate Owen's scheme. On this latter see P. Sraffa, op. cit., V, 467—8, and VIII, 45—6. The relationship of Ricardo's views on machinery to the spade husbandry question is considered in S. Hollander, op. cit.

30 Hansard, op. cit., 1217—21. John (afterwards Sir John) Maxwell (1791—1865) was a member of a Southern Scottish landed family. He represented Renfrewshire, 1818—30, and Lanarkshire, 1832—37. During 1819 he published *A letter to the honest reformers of Scotland; with remarks on the poor rates, corn law, religious establishments, right of property, equality of ranks and revolution* (Glasgow, 1819). The introduction to this pamphlet is signed 'a Renfrewshire reformer'. Maxwell's view that emigration was a meaningful response to social problems was one coming to be shared by a number of writers on political economy. See, e.g., Robert Torrens, 'Paper on the Means of Reducing the Poor Rates', *The Pamphleteer,* 20 (September 1817); David Buchanan, 'Emigration', *Supplement to Encyclopaedia Britannica,* V (1819); and Richard Whately, 'Emigration to Canada', *Quarterly Review,* 23 (July 1820). However James Mill had reservations concerning the wisdom of the policy. See his article 'Colony', in *Encyclopaedia Britannica Supplement to the Fourth, Fifth and Sixth Editions,* 3 (1818).

31 Hansard, op. cit., 1221—4.

32 Ibid., 1225—6.

33 Ibid., 1394—5.

34 Ibid., 1397.

35 Ibid., 1569—71.

36 Ibid., 1576—8.

37   Ricardo's emphasis on this factor in 1819 may be contrasted with his criticism of McCulloch in 1821 for overrating the self same danger. See his letter to McCulloch (March 1821) in P. Sraffa, ibid., 357.
38   C.f. Ricardo's letter to James Brown (13 October 1819) in which he argues that sudden removal of import restrictions would 'rather aggravate than relieve the distress under which we are now labouring.' The remedy for that distress, Ricardo confessed 'is not very apparent to me.' P. Sraffa, ibid, 103.
39   Hansard, ibid., 1578–9. Finlay (1773–1842) was a major figure in the business and political circles of Glasgow. His main commercial interest was in cotton. In 1812 he became the Lord Provost of Glasgow and he represented the city in the Commons 1812–18. He was member for Malmesbury 1818–20. His economic thought was strongly influenced by Adam Smith's emphasis on the desirability of maximum freedom of trade but, as this speech indicates, he was not an advocate of the doctrine in its unqualified form. On Finlay, see S. G. Checkland, op. cit., Chapter 16. See also, *James Finlay and Co. Ltd, 1750–1950* (Glasgow, 1951).
40   Hansard, op. cit., 1579–81. Designation of Ricardo as 'an oracle' was to prove most unfortunate for the public image of Ricardianism, in that the journalist William Cobbett was to take up Brougham's phrase in his subsequent campaign of ridicule of Ricardian principles. See P. Sraffa, op. cit., V, 40–1.
41   Hansard, ibid., 1582.
42   For a contrasting and sympathetic judgement of Liverpool's administration at this time consult W. R. Brock, op. cit., 114–18.

CHAPTER 7

1   Consult John Stanhope, *The Cato Street Conspiracy* (London: Cape, 1962).
2   The text of the petition was printed in Hansard, n.s. I (1820) cols 179–182. It had been written by Thomas Tooke and had received an imprimatur from Lord Liverpool before its submission. Consult Thomas Tooke and William Newmarch, *A History of Prices*, VI (London, 1857) 331–44.
3   Hansard, op. cit., 163–179.
4   Ibid., 182–5.
5   Ibid., 187–91.
6   Ibid., 191–3.
7   Ibid., 193–4.
8   Ibid., 195–7.
9   Since Ricardo derived his figure of 4 per cent from a comparison of the then market and mint prices of gold, this reply did not meet Baring's point concerning the inadequacy of gold prices as criteria.
10   Ibid., 424–9.
11   In 1793 Finlay had been a leading opponent of that Company's privileged position in the cotton trade.
12   Ibid., 429–31.
13   Cf. Sir Ivor Jennings, *Party Politics*, 3 (Cambridge University Press, 1962) 348: '. . . the conflict over free trade was not a conflict of theories or *a priori* assumptions. Politicians are practical men who absorb their theories through their pores. Essentially the conflict was one of vested interests.' The alarm of the shipping industry, especially on the issue of alterations in timber duties, was soon expressed in the Commons by means of petitions presented by General Isaac Gascoyne (1770–1841), the conservative representative for Liverpool, and by Thomas Wilson and Joseph Marryat on behalf of London-based

interests. Marryat spoke at length in defence of retaining traditional trade restrictions. See Hansard, ibid., 844—62.

14   Ibid., 546—65. At this time the whig leaders may have hoped that the issue of freer trade would prove an embarrassment to the government just as, in 1819, they had hoped the question of resumption of cash payments would prove to be.

15   This explanation has more in common with that of Grenville in 1819 than with Lansdowne's own analysis in that year (see Chapter 6).

16   Ibid., 565—94.

17   Most parliamentarians seem to have recoiled from the proposition that conflict was an omnipresent and inevitable feature of the relationships of landowner, worker and capitalist. Some writers on political economy also found the conflict thesis objectionable, and set out to refute Ricardo's treatment of wages and profits as mutually opposed factor payments. Notable critiques of this aspect of Ricardian thought appeared in *Blackwoods*, V, XXVI (May 1819) 171—3, and in *The British Critic*, XII (December 1819) 561—78. The writer of the latter article depicted Ricardo's handling of the wage-profit relationship as a prime example of what modern historians of economic thought have come to call 'the Ricardian Vice': 'Assuming these facts as a first principle, in all cases, and taking for granted as usual, that money never changes in value, and that the proportion between the supply and the demand of any given commodity never alters, (which is as if the astronomer were to assume as the basis of his calculations, that all the planets stand still, and that they all stand still to all eternity,) he assigns a specific sum to be divided between the master and the workmen, as the unalterable price of the goods which they produce; from adaptation of hypothetical conditions, it naturally follows, that, if the workmen get more the master-manufacturer must receive less, there being only a certain sum to divide between them.'

18   American imports from Great Britain fell from $42 million in 1818 to $14 million in 1820. For detail and discussion, consult Murray N. Rothbard, *The Panic of 1819* (N.Y.: Columbia University Press, 1962).

19   See, e.g., Hansard, 23 (1812) 1249.

20   The term 'fictitious capital' was used quite frequently at this time but, like the related concept 'over-trading', it was rarely used with any precision. At root, it probably meant the ability to contract debts without the backing of realisable physical assets.

21   Here Liverpool was merely reiterating established tory doctrine. R. J. White writes (op. cit., 59): 'It is hardly too much to say that the Younger Pitt had made the political economy of Adam Smith the official doctrine of the Tory Party, and in this, as in so much else, Lord Liverpool and his colleagues were faithful disciples of their master.'

22   Hansard, 1 (1820) 594—6.

23   See also [Earl of Lauderdale], *Sinking Fund, or, the system which recommends the repeal of five millions of taxes . . .* (London, 1822). During the previous month (April) the problem of effective demand was given its greatest prominence in the literature of political economy when Malthus' *Principles of Political Economy* was published. Ricardo found Malthus' views highly objectionable (see his letters of 2 May 1820 and 4 September 1820, in P. Sraffa, op. cit., VIII, 181 and 226—30). However Malthus gained immediate support from the political economy reviewer (possibly John Craig) of *The British Critic* (see XIV (August 1820) 117—30; (September 1820) 275—93; and (December 1820) 647—61). Another to stress the role of effective demand at this time was Simon Gray, *Remarks on the Production of Wealth* (Pamphleteer, XVII, XXXIV, London 1820).

24 House of Lords, *First Report (Relative to the Timber Trade) from the Select Committee of the House of Lords, appointed to inquire into the means of extending and securing the Foreign Trade of the Country* . . . (11 July 1820). Among the witnesses called were Edward Ellice (because of his Canadian experience) and Thomas Tooke who, as a merchant engaged mainly in trade with Russia, had a strong personal interest in increasing the volume of trade with that region of Europe. See *Minutes of Evidence*, 25–33 and 51–55. Both were in favour of a reduction of duties.

25 House of Commons, *Report from the Select Committee appointed to Consider of the Means of Maintaining and Improving the Foreign Trade of the Country* (18 July 1820) 10.

26 Ibid., 11. The relevant legislation was introduced in 1823 (see Chapter 15).

27 Hansard 2 (1820) 545–8. This statement by the Vice-President of the Board of Trade may be contrasted with that of Robinson, the President of the same body, on the navigation laws earlier in the year. See 'The Merchants' Petition' above.

28 Hansard, n.s. 1 (1820) 802–3. On the continuing controversy concerning protection of the Irish linen industry see, R. D. Collison Black, *Economic Thought and the Irish Question, 1817–1870* (Cambridge University Press, 1960) 145–7.

29 Hansard, op. cit., 803.

30 Ibid.

31 Ibid. 1005.

32 Ibid., 1005–6.

33 Ibid., 1106–8.

34 For a discussion of this crisis and its implications for the future of the Irish banking system, see R. D. Collison Black, op. cit., 149–51.

CHAPTER 8

1 Hansard, n.s. 1 (1820) 522.

2 Ibid., 535.

3 Ibid., 635–9. Holme-Sumner (1760–1838) was the member for Surrey. He had been first elected to the House in 1787 and, with two interruptions, remained a member until 1826.

4 Ibid., 641–51.

5 'Agricultural investment and activity were high during the French Revolutionary and Napoleonic wars . . . The edge of cultivation was pushed beyond even the obliterating limits of the Second World War's reclamation campaign, so that abandoned Napoleonic ploughing rig survives far up on the chalk downs and Dartmoor and out on the New Forest heaths.' A. L. Jones, *The Development of English Agriculture, 1815–1873* (London: Macmillan, 1973) 10.

6 Hansard, ibid., 661–5. Thomas (later Sir Thomas) Frankland Lewis (1780–1855) was in parliament 1812–34 and 1847–55. He had been largely responsible for the drafting of the 1817 report of the Commons committee on the poor laws, a report which has been described as 'the boldest and most dogmatic summary of the abolitionist case published in this period'. (J. R. Poynter, op. cit., 245). In 1834 Lewis was appointed first Chairman of the Poor Law Commission.

7 Another contemporary exponent of this view was Nassau William Senior, a protégé of Lansdowne. See his 'Report-on the State of Agriculture', *Quarterly Review*, XXV, L (July 1821) 467–8. Ricardo had written *(Principles*, Chapter 5): 'The natural price of all commodities, excepting raw produce and

labour, has a tendency to fall, in the progress of wealth and population; for though, on one hand, they are enhanced in real value, from the rise in the natural price of the raw material of which they made, this is more than counterbalanced by the improvements in machinery, by the better division and distribution of labour, and by the increasing skill, both in science and art, of the producers.' P. Sraffa, op. cit., 1,92—2.

8   Hansard. op. cit., 651—61.

9   Ibid., 671—6.

10   While most of Ricardo's contemporaries saw the war boom as a once-ever event, Ricardo seems to have developed a clear grasp of the fact that the event had helped create the preconditions for take-off into sustained economic growth, with the export manufacturing sector as the leading edge of the expansionary movement. Only the remnants of past errors of the legislature stood in the way of that expansion. It is paradoxical that in times to come some scholars would interpret Ricardo as the proponent of a stagnation thesis. Cf. G. S. L. Tucker, *Progress and Profits in British Economic Thought* (Cambridge, 1960) 162.

11   Ricardo had made this point earlier in his *An Essay on the Influence of a Low Price of Corn on the Profits of Stock* (1815). See P. Sraffa, op. cit., IV, 27—9.

12   For a consideration of the assumptions underlying this argument see Edmund Silberner, *The Problem of War in Nineteenth Century Economic Thought* (Princeton University Press, 1946) 21—4.

13   Cf. C. S. Shoup, op. cit., 176—7. On the Ricardians and comparative advantage see the recent paper by W. O. Thweatt, in *History of Political Economy*, 8, 2 (1976) 207—34.

14   Hansard, op. cit., 676—7. John Bennett (1773—1852) was in the Commons 1819—52.

15   Ibid., 677—81. Huskisson (1770—1830) is most noted for his work of liberalisation of trading and commercial regulations as President of the Board of Trade from 1823. A close associate of George Canning, he first entered the Commons in 1796. Thereafter he occupied a variety of posts including Secretary to the Treasury, Commissioner for Woods and Forests, and Treasurer of the Navy. He came to be widely regarded as an authority on economic policy and was a major influence in that sphere throughout Liverpool's administration. Consult C. R. Fay, *Huskisson and His Age* (London: Longmans, 1951) and Alexander Brady, *William Huskisson and Liberal Reform* (London: Oxford University Press, 1928).

16   Hansard, op. cit., 683—9.

17   Brougham, who had been instrumental in arranging Ricardo's purchase of a seat in parliament, was almost certainly expressing a view which was gaining ground daily both inside and outside the House. Four months before J. L. Mallet had written (14 January 1820): 'It is this very quality of the man's [Ricardo's] mind; his entire disregard of experience and practice, which makes me doubtful of his opinions on political economy.' (Quoted in P. Straffa, op. cit., VIII, 152.) Towards the end of this year similar sentiments were evident in the anonymous review article 'Ricardo on Political Economy', *Monthly Review*, XCIII (December 1820) 416—30.

18   Ricardo had earlier acknowledged the second of these points in his *Principles* (Chapter 18: 'Poor Rates'). See P. Sraffa, op. cit., 1,260.

19   Three years earlier in the House (13 March 1817) Brougham had declared in favour of free trade as an ultimate goal, but had found the Corn Law of 1815 justified under prevailing conditions.

20   Ricardo wrote to McCulloch (13 June 1820): 'Mr. Brougham very much misrepresented what I said and he himself advanced principles which were

wholly untenable, but the House was much too partial to one view of the subject to allow me to enter into a refutation of them.' P. Sraffa, op. cit., VIII, 196—7. Ricardo also complained that his own speech had been 'in many respects imperfectly reported' in the press.

21 Hansard, op. cit., 719—20. Sir Robert John Wilmot-Horton (1784—1841) is best remembered as a most active advocate of emigration and schemes for colonisation. The only son of a baronet, he graduated from Oxford and entered the Commons in 1818. He became Secretary of State for War and the Colonies in 1821 and was Governor of Ceylon 1831—7. He published a number of pamphlets on economic issues, lectured on political economy at Mechanics' Institutes and was a member of the Political Economy Club, 1829—31.

22 Ibid., 722—30.

23 Ibid., 395—417. Stanhope (1781—1855) was a member of a brilliant and flamboyant family, the best-known of whom are his father Charles, the third earl, and his sister, Lady Hester Lucy Stanhope. Philip Henry pursued a number of scholarly interests and was elected a Fellow of the Royal Society in 1807. He entered the Commons in 1806 and sat until 1816 when he succeeded his father in the Lords. His greatest contemporary notoriety derived from his adoption in 1832 of Kaspar Hauser, the wild boy of Bavaria. Stanhope's publications on economic issues include *A Letter . . . on the Corn Laws* (London 1826); *A Letter on the proposed alteration of the Corn Laws* (London 1827); *A Letter to the owners and occupiers of sheep farms* (London, 1828); and *To the Labouring Classes of Great Britain and Ireland* (London 1850). Consult Aubrey Newman, *The Stanhopes of Chevening* (London: Macmillan, 1969).

24 For a survey of this and other 'make-work schemes' that were suggested about this time, see J. R. Poynter, op. cit., 254—7.

25 During this year a similar view was put forward most cogently by John Barton, *An Inquiry into the Causes of the Progressive Depreciation of Agricultural Labour . . .* (London, 1820) esp. 37—9. Stanhope's and Barton's arguments look forward to those of William Forster Lloyd in his outstanding series of Drummond lectures at Oxford in the 1830s.

26 Hansard, op. cit., 417—22. Stanhope published this speech in pamphlet form later in the year and in 1821 added a *Proposed Address to His Majesty on the Present Distress of the Country* (London: Simpkin & Marshall, 1821).

27 Hansard, n.s. 2 (1820) 116—21.

28 Ibid., 121—2. Concerning Liverpool's administration, R. J. White has observed (op. cit., 112): 'Their favourite adjective when referring to the labouring poor, was not "revolutionary" but "deluded". They were intent less upon exaggerating the disturbed and dangerous state of the country . . . than upon correcting the false impression that there was any necessary connexion between political opinions and social distress.'

29 Hansard, ibid., 122.

30 Ricardo's belief in 'the sacredness of property', his adoption of a 'stock' rather than a 'flow' conception of the nature of property, and his assumption of a labour theory of acquisition of property rights are key factors conditioning the scope and content of his economic analysis. He seems to have shared these attitudes with other thinkers within the Benthamite circle. As Gunnar Myrdal comments, the Benthamites 'were radical in all respects, except in their views on property . . . Their reform interest extended to almost every social sphere. Property alone was sacrosanct.' G. Myrdal, *The Political Element in the Development of Economic Theory* (London, 1953) 118.

31 P. Sraffa, op. cit., 197.

32 Hansard, n.s. 1 (1820) 171—2

208   *Notes*

33   Earl Grey wrote to Lord Holland (23 April 1820): 'In general I should recommend it to you to abstain from pressing any particular measure. The great advantage of our present situation is that it relieves from all responsibility for the measures, which the times require . . . observe the good old opposition maxim of proposing nothing.' Quoted in A. Mitchell, op. cit., 141.

CHAPTER 9

1   On the revival in Manchester, see Arthur Redford, *Manchester Merchants and Foreign Trade, 1794–1858* (1934; Manchester University Press, 1973) 74–6.
2   Also founded in London during this year was the Co-operative and Economical Society, which published a magazine, the *Economist*. It took its inspiration from the ideas of Robert Owen.
3   See John Craig, *Remarks on some fundamental doctrines of political economy* . . . (Edinburgh, 1821); Piercy Ravenstone, *A few doubts as to the correctness of some opinions generally entertained on the subjects of population and political economy* (London, 1821); Anon, 'Mill's Elements of Political Economy', *The British Critic*, XVII (February 1822) 130–47; and Anon, 'Mill's Elements of Political Economy', *Monthly Review*, XCVIII (May 1822) 13–25.
4   Hansard, n.s. 4 (1821) 350–4. The text of this petition, which urged repeal of the currency act of 1819, has been attributed to Thomas Attwood of Birmingham, a banker and an outstanding critic of deflationary monetary policy. Attwood is a most significant figure in the economic thought of this period and his significance was later enhanced when he entered the Commons as an independent member for Birmingham in 1833. For discussion of Attwood's ideas and influence consult Thomas Attwood, *Selected Economic Writings* (intro. by F. W. Fetter) (London School of Economics, 1964); S. G. Checkland, 'The Birmingham Economists, 1815–1850', *Economic History Review* (2nd series) I, 1 (1948) 1–19; A. Briggs, 'Thomas Attwood and the Economic Background of the Birmingham Political Union', *Cambridge Historical Journal* (1948); R. G. Link, *English Theories of Economic Fluctuations 1815–1848* (N.Y.: Columbia University Press, 1959); B. A. Corry, *Money, Saving and Investment in English Economics, 1800–1850* (London: Macmillan, 1962); and G. D. H. Cole, *Chartist Portraits* (N.Y.: Macmillan, 1965) 102–32.
5   Hansard, op. cit., 356–60.
6   Ibid., 526–9.
7   Ibid., 530.
8   Ibid., 530–5.
9   The distinction between 'bees' and 'drones' was prominent in the thought of the reformer Robert Owen.
10   Although such a policy may have been welcomed by the Birmingham ironmasters and many other entrepreneurs, it was against the perceived interests of Manchester businessmen. As Asa Briggs writes, ' . . . one group of industrialists strongly backed Peel. The leaders of the cotton industry, who looked to greatly increased international trade, strongly favoured a gold standard. "We want a regulating medium," the treasurer of the Manchester Chamber of Commerce remarked in 1821, "and there is nothing like gold for that purpose." ' A. Briggs, *The Age of Improvement* (London: Longman, 1959), 204–5. On the divergence between monetary views in Manchester and Birmingham, see A. Redford, op. cit., 158–9.
11   Hansard, ibid., 535–9. Alternative versions of some passages of this speech, as reported in the *Courier*, are given in P. Sraffa, op. cit., V, 72–7.
12   Assuming a rigid version of the quantity theory of money (see Chapter 1)

prices should have fallen in strict proportion if a diminution of the money supply accompanying the act of 1819 was largely to blame for those falls.

13 Ricardo repeated this statement in his pamphlet *On Protection to Agriculture* (1822); see P. Sraffa, op. cit., IV, 240. In 1819 (see Chapter 2) Ricardo had told the House that the bulk of commodity taxation falls on employers of labour. For a discussion of the apparent dichotomy in this aspect of Ricardo's thought, see C. S. Shoup, op. cit., Ch. 4, esp. 74–7.

14 In his *Principles* Ricardo wrote: 'It is not, then, by the payment of the interest on the national debt, that a country is distressed, nor is it by the exoneration from payment that it can be relieved.' (P. Sraffa, op. cit., 1,246). Ricardo had engaged in considerable correspondence on this issue with J. R. McCulloch, who had contemplated the desirability of a reduction of interest (see letters, 9 June, 19 November, 4 December 1816; 6 December 1818; 3 January 1819).

15 Hansard, op. cit., 539.

16 Ibid., 539–41.

17 Ibid., 541–2.

18 In the eyes of businessmen Baring seems to have got the better of this particular exchange. Trower wrote to Ricardo (16 February 1821): 'Mr. Baring's opinions, however, (and deservedly too upon most commercial points) have great weight with men of business, on account of his extensive practical experience. The observations I have heard made upon what passed the other night (8 February) have been to this effect. That Mr. Baring's speech was *practical*, yours *theoretical*.' P. Sraffa, op. cit., VIII, 347.

19 Hansard, op. cit., 572–3. John (later Sir John) Gladstone (1764–1851) was a wealthy Liverpool shipowner, trader and planter. He was a patron of the young George Canning, and father of William Ewart Gladstone. A full-length study is S. G. Checkland, *The Gladstones: A Family Biography, 1764–1851* (Cambridge University Press, 1971). Chapters 13 and 16, in particular, deal with Gladstone's views on economic and social policy.

20 The problem of effective demand was considered in a number of publications on political economy during this year. These included: Edward Solly, *Considerations on Political Economy* (London, 1821), esp. 65–9; Sir Egerton Brydges, *What are Riches?* (Geneva, 1821) *passim*; Anon., *An Essay on the Political Economy of Nations* (London, 1821), esp. Chapters 2 and 3; and James Syme, *The Principles of Political Economy applied to the financial state of Great Britain* (London, 1821) esp. Chapter 3, Sect. 9. See also articles in *The British Critic*, XV (May 1821) 451–63; *Monthly Review*, XCV (May 1821) 60–76; and *New Monthly Magazine*, I (1821) 90–7, and II (1821) 366–76.

21 Hansard, op. cit., 824–9. This committee presented a report on 11 April. The report was concerned with the China and East Indies trades and found, not surprisingly, that little could be done for the cause of freer trade in those regions without the consent of the East India Company whose monopoly under charter was not due to expire until 1834. However, the committee urged that British merchants in general should be permitted to trade with China where such trade did not interfere with the East India Company's monopoly of the British market, especially its monopoly in regard to tea. Later reports by a committee of the Commons advocated the same liberalisation. See House of Lords, *Report relative to trade with the East Indies and China* (7 May 1821), and House of Commons, *Second and Third Reports from the Select Committee appointed to consider . . . the foreign trade of the country* (18 May 1821 and 10 July 1821). Edward Ellice and John Gladstone were among those who gave evidence before the Lords' committee. (*Minutes of Evidence*, 92–100 and 195–203).

22 Hansard, ibid., 829–33.

23   Ibid., 833–4. Erskine (1750–1823) after a most successful legal career had been Lord Chancellor in the brief Grenville administration of 1806. Although notable for his liberal views, he never achieved the political prominence his successes as a lawyer had promised. He published *A Letter to the Proprietors of Land on Agricultural Prosperity* (1823).

24   Hansard, ibid., 835–6. Charles Grey, the second Earl Grey (1764–1845) had first entered parliament for Northumberland in 1786. After the death of Fox in 1806 he was the acknowledged leader of the whigs in the Commons. In 1808 he transferred to the Lords and, after more than two decades in opposition became Prime Minister, 1830–4.

25   Hansard, op. cit., 1139–44. Gooch (1767–1851) represented Suffolk 1806–30. Knatchbull (1781–1849) was an independent tory and sat from 1819 to 1845. In 1834 and again in 1841 Peel appointed him Paymaster of the Forces.

26   As Sir Ivor Jennings has observed (op. cit., 347), arguments for agricultural protection were often based on the view that 'in the English manor, where there was a proper hierarchy of rights and duties, every man was happy in performing the duties of his station. This was natural because it was based on the soil and on the order of society which it had pleased God to establish. There was nothing natural about industry based upon the "spirit of trade", the anxiety of the gambler to make profit.'

27   Hansard, ibid., 1147–50. Curwen was an advocate of an income or a property tax. This type of taxation had been imposed during the war, but had been repealed in 1816. The contemporary taxation problem seems to have been one of administration as well as incidence. L. S. Presnell (op. cit., 552–3) has concluded: 'The history of tax collection forms one more chapter in the responsibility of government for the various difficulties, social and economic, which accompanied the Industrial Revolution. The developments that followed Waterloo give an unexpected reinforcement to the contemporary opinion, expressed most notably by Malthus . . . that public finance was a principal agent in the post-war distress. In particular, it is clear that the widespread bank failures were closely connected with the abrupt shrinkage of government deposits . . . For a quarter of a century after the Napoleonic wars, British governments refused to reintroduce the income-tax, and thereby deprived themselves of an invaluable fiscal aid. There were various arguments adduced for and against the resumption of the tax, but it is likely enough that the memory of the jobbery associated with the war-time collection proved a powerful deterrent.' See also A. Hope-Jones, *Income Tax in the Napoleonic Wars* (Cambridge, 1939); A. Farnsworth, *Addington, Author of the Modern Income Tax* (London, 1951); F. Shehab, *Progressive Taxation* (Oxford, 1953).

28   Hansard, ibid., 1152–5.

29   Ibid., 1155. Peter Denis Browne (1794–1872) was M.P. for Rye, 1818–26.

30   Ibid., 1150. Whitmore (1787–1858) was a director of the East India Company and represented Bridgnorth, 1820–32, and Wolverhampton, 1832–4. In 1822 Ricardo wrote to Trower: 'I have gained an important and powerful ally, in the Committee (on Agriculture), by the nomination of Mr. Whitmore, who is a zealous advocate for the correct doctrines.' (P. Sraffa, op. cit., IX, 176–7.) Ricardo invited Whitmore to a meeting of the Political Economy Club in March 1822 and Whitmore was elected a member in 1824.

31   Hansard, ibid., 1155–61. An alternative account of this speech as given in the *British Press* is reprinted in P. Sraffa, op. cit., V, 81–6.

32   For Ricardo's own published statement concerning a countervailing duty see P. Sraffa, op. cit., IV, 243–4. Ricardo also proposed a payment by way of a drawback on exportation of corn. This plan is discussed in W. D. Grampp, *The Manchester School of Economics* (Stanford University Press, 1960) 17–19.

33   In the concluding chapter (Chapter 32: 'Mr. Malthus's Opinions on Rent') of the third edition of his *Principles* (1821), Ricardo wrote: 'That the stockholder is benefited by a great fall in the value of corn, cannot be doubted; but if no one else be injured, that is no reason why corn should be made dear: for the gains of the stockholder are national gains, and increase, as all other gains do, the real wealth and power of the country. If they are unjustly benefited, let the degree in which they are so, be accurately ascertained, and then it is for the legislature to devise a remedy; but no policy can be more unwise than to shut ourselves out from the great advantages arising from cheap corn, and abundant productions, merely because the stockholder would have an undue proportion of the increase.' See P. Sraffa, op. cit., 1,425.

34   This assertion and the reasoning underlying it were challenged most ably in P. Ravenstone, op. cit., esp. pp. 407—8. Ravenstone rejected Ricardo's notion of a necessary progression over time to production on poorer soils as population expanded. The writer concluded (p. 408): 'The better management of its industry always enables the best-peopled country to produce its corn at the cheapest rate.'

35   Subsequent events justified this optimism. S. G. Checkland writes in *The Rise of Industrial Society in England, 1815—1885* (London: Longmans, 1964) 11: 'Real growth in wealth took place between 1821 and 1836. Indeed it has been suggested that the industrial revolution in Britain, far from tapering off in the twenties and thirties, was then at its height, in the sense of invoking and applying new capital. Men of business showed vigour and daring in the promotion of trade and industry. Real wages in many trades began to rise again.'

36   For comments by Ricardo and others concerning the proceedings of the Committee, see P. Sraffa, op. cit., V, xxiv-xxv, and VII, 368—71 and 373—5. Also of interest is William Smart, *Economic Annals of the Nineteenth Century*, 2 vols (London, 1910—15; republished, N.Y., 1964) II, 6—18.

37   Among the better known witnesses were Thomas Tooke and Thomas Attwood. The latter linked agricultural distress to the currency act of 1819. (See *Minutes of Evidence* 243—76.)

38   Quoted in W. Smart, ibid., 16.

CHAPTER 10

1   Hansard, n.s. 4 (1821) 1315—7.
2   The Bank had increased its bullion reserves from £3.9 million in 1819 to £6.6 million in 1820. Its reserve ratio i.e., the percentage of bullion in terms of the sum of its note circulation plus deposits, increased from 12.3 to 23.4 over the same period. This may have been done partly to demonstrate that the Directors were genuinely concerned with the 'soundness' of the currency, and partly as a direct response to Cabinet pressure. The Bank continued on this course until 1823 when the reserve ratio reached 51.7 per cent.
3   Ibid., 1317—28.
4   The development of commodity price indices as measures was also foreshadowed in Henry James, *Essays on Money, Exchanges, and Political Economy* (1820). James suggests (p. 203) that the purchasing power of money ought to be maintained at a level dictated by the price of wheat and the wages of farm labour.
5   As F. W. Fetter comments (op. cit., 102), here Baring displays 'an ethical and social-justice approach that was quite different from Ricardo's clinical approach'. To this it can be added that Baring seems far more aware of the significance of the distinction between the functions of entrepreneur and rentier than Ricardo is. The Ricardians (like many subsequent thinkers)

generally settled for the vaguer notion of 'the capitalist', which lack of precision was accompanied by the use of the term 'accumulation' so as to blur the important distinctions to be made between the process of saving and that of investing.

6   Before the Lords Committee on resumption in 1819 Baring had stated (*Minutes of Evidence*, 128—9): '. . . in many instances it may perhaps be doubted, whether with a view to strict justice it may not be unfair to increase the value of the money in which those engagements were made. If the depreciation had gone much further than it did, and had lasted longer, I should have thought the ends of justice better answered by legally sanctioning the depreciation, than by returning to the old standard of value.'

7   Tithes were calculated in terms of the gross rather than the net product of agriculture. Another to question the validity of the quantity theory at this time was Ephraim Gompertz in his *A Theoretic Discourse on the Nature and Property of Money* (London: Richardson, 1820). He argued (p. 43) that an increased money supply could lead to reductions in commodity prices by lowering the rate of interest.

8   Hansard, op. cit., 1328—32. Unfortunately this speech was reported in extremely poor fashion. This is indicated by Ricardo's complaint in a letter to McCulloch (P. Sraffa, op. cit., VIII, 358—9) and, even more convincingly, by the Hansard text itself.

9   On 8 February Ricardo had said (Hansard, op. cit., 538): '. . . the Bank being a timid body, seldom clinging to the true principles of circulation, had taken alarm, and had made great and unnecessary purchases of gold, although they found, by experience, that no person applied to them for any.' This was almost certainly the 'accident' to which Ricardo alluded in his present speech. However as Edward Ellice was soon to point out this was no 'accident'. The Bank's behaviour had been entirely predictable.

10   Ibid., 1332—3.

11   Ibid., 1333—7.

12   In February it had been suggested that notes were at a premium in terms of coin in Ireland, and it was rumoured that the Bank of Ireland was refusing to accept deposits in coin. In response to a query from Pascoe Grenfell (2 February 1821), the matter was discussed in the Commons on 28 March. Ricardo attributed the problems of the Irish monetary system mainly to the bank failures of the previous year. He also denied the possibility of notes being more valuable than coins. See P. Sraffa, op. cit., V, 70 and 98—100.

13   Hansard, n.s. 5 (1821) 91—7.

14   This speech called forth a swift, critical reaction from J. R. McCulloch, writing in the *Scotsman* (14 April 1821). He characterised Baring as 'the great patron of the scheme for degrading the standard of the currency.'

15   Hansard, op. cit., 97—130. Mathias Attwood (1779—1851) was the elder brother of the better-known Thomas Attwood. Like his brother he was a banker and was head of the London associate of Thomas' Birmingham company, Spooner and Attwood. The Attwoods had made a fortune in iron and steel and commenced banking operations in Birmingham in 1791. The London office was opened in 1801. Mathias first entered parliament as the Tory candidate for Fowey in 1819. Thereafter he was M.P. for Callington, 1820—30, Boroughbridge, 1830—2, and Whitehaven, 1832—47. Before joining the Commons he published his views on economic policy in an anonymous pamphlet, *Observations Concerning the Distress of the Country* (London, 1817).

16   A similar analysis was put forward in this same year by John Craig, op. cit., 190—204.

17 From the context, the plan referred to was presumably that of Ricardo for abolition of the national debt.
18 Hansard, op. cit., 134—7. Monck (1769—1834) was M.P. for Reading, 1820—30. An earlier statement of his on monetary issues was J. B. Monck, *A Letter to the Right Hon. Spencer Perceval, on the present state of our currency; with hints for its gradual improvement* (London, 1812).
19 Hansard, op. cit., 139—40.
20 Ibid., 140—4.
21 Ibid., 144—5. Irving (1767—1845) was a banker who also had business interests in the West Indies. He was M.P. for Bramber, 1806—32, and Antrim, 1837—45.
22 Ibid., 137—9. Sir John Clapham has observed: 'In the first quarter of 1819, when Peel's Committee was at work, the general price level was 46 per cent above the level of 1790 and wheat was at nearly 80s. In the third quarter of 1821 ... the price level was only 16 per cent above 1790 and wheat was just under 53s. Ricardo had talked about a 4 or 5 per cent price fall following gradual resumption. The far greater fall that had come while resumption was being discussed, and then rather hurriedly consummated, cannot be attributed to it, except, at most, in small part. But the fall was connected in men's minds with resumption, connected with "this wretched Act of Peel's".' J. Clapham, *The Bank of England, A History*, II (1944; Cambridge University Press, 1970), 74.
23 This statement underlines the radical contrast which Ricardo perceived between agriculture and manufacturing. The former was subject to the technical law of diminishing returns, but the latter was not. In addition the demand for rural produce was not extensible, although there was no necessary limit to expansion of the market for maufactured products in general, even with a given size of population.
24 F. W. Fetter writes (op. cit., 101): '... the most significant feature of the debate, and far more important than the technical arguments, was the shift in opinion from two years before. Some who joined Baring in 1821 had been, like him, critics of the inflationary policy of the war years ... Ricardo made two speeches opposing Baring's motion, but he was on the defensive. As on many other occasions, he practically ignored the problems of price adjustment, seemed concerned only with the income transfer effects of changing prices, and in substance denied that inflation or deflation could alter total production.'
25 Hansard, op. cit., 496—500.
26 Ibid., 500—4.
27 Ibid., 505.
28 Ricardo wrote McCulloch (3 January 1822) that the bank directors 'were absolutely forced to come to the legislature for permission last year, to pay in specie, as they had accumulated a large quantity of coin. After they had been foolish enough to do so, it became a matter of indifference whether parliament agreed to their request or refused it — indeed it was more desirable to comply with it:—the evil had already been done by the purchase and accumulation of gold, and no further mischief could arise from the substitution of the coins (in circulation) for the paper which they were desirous of withdrawing.' P. Sraffa, op. cit., IX, 141.
29 Sir John Craig, *The Mint: A History of the London Mint from A.D. 287 to 1948* (Cambridge University Press, 1953) 289.
30 R. G. Hawtrey writes: 'But whereas 5 per cent had been an unduly low rate during the Napoleonic Wars, now under conditions of deflation that had since supervened it had become an unduly high rate. The Government was faithfully carrying out the recommendation of the Resumption Committee of 1819 to repay the Bank's advances, and the resulting gap in the Bank's assets could only

be filled by discounts or by gold. But the Bank's discount rate of 5 per cent was so far above the market rate that no bills were offered for discount, and the note issue could only be maintained in so far as gold could be attracted.' R. G. Hawtrey, *A Century of Bank Rate* (1938; N.Y.: Kelly, 1962) 13–14.

CHAPTER 11

1   The sinking fund was a measure introduced by William Pitt, who became Prime Minister in 1784. It had been anticipated to some extent by Robert Walpole in 1716. Pitt's scheme involved the allocation of budget surpluses to a Board of Commissioners for the Reduction of the National Debt. These employed the surpluses to purchase public stock from its holders and thereafter collect the interest due. That interest was then used to buy further stock, year by year. Thus while the interest payment on the national debt was not reduced, the volume of debt in private hands was diminished. The system was continued during the Napoleonic war period despite the government's need to budget for annual deficits, and there was progressive modification of its operation. By the 1820s the workings of the fund had become interwoven with other aspects of the machinery of government finance. This situation gave rise to considerable controversy in the pamphlet literature of the day, and Ricardo himself contributed an essay on the 'Funding System' in 1820 (reprinted in P. Sraffa, op. cit., IV). An excellent official history of the fund is *National Debt: Report by the Secretary and Comptroller General of the Proceedings of the Commissioners for the Reduction of the National Debt from 1786 to 31st March 1890* (London: H.M.S.O., 1891).

2   Hansard, n.s. 4 (1821) 1384–5. Charles Callis Western (1767–1844) was M.P. for Maldon, 1790–1812, and Essex, 1812–32. He owned extensive estates in Essex, and his interests included prison reform, antiquities and agricultural science. Western published in these fields as well as that of economic policy. In 1833 he was gazetted Baron Western of Rivenhall.

3   Ibid., 1386–93.

4   Ibid., 1395–6.

5   Ibid., 1396–9.

6   The House continued in the same mood the following day (ibid., 1401–9) when on the initiative of Joseph Hume the government was obliged to set up a committee to examine the administrative arrangements for the collection of certain forms of taxation. This led to reforms which were a definite step in the direction of modern Civil Service organisation concerning revenue gathering. Consult L. S. Pressnell, op. cit., 549. Another fruit of Hume's campaign was the important Treasury Minute of 10 August 1821 which urged economy throughout all government departments. For detail, see H. Roseveare, *The Treasury, 1600–1870* (London: Allen & Unwin, 1973) 67–8 and 161–3, and H. Roseveare, *The Treasury: the Evolution of a British Institution* (London: Penguin Press, 1969) 160–1.

7   Hansard, n.s. V (1821) 47.

8   Ricardo had also attacked the fund during the debate on Maberly's motion concerning the window tax (6 March) and he continued the attack in the budget debate (1 June). A major factor in his thinking on this issue was a desire to reduce the risk of war. He wrote to Trower (25 March 1822): 'While ministers have this fund virtually at their disposal they will on the slightest occasion be disposed for war. To keep them peaceable you must keep them poor.' See. P. Sraffa, op. cit., V, 79–80 and 101–2; and IX, 180. For a

discussion of Ricardo's attitude on this question consult E. Silberner, op. cit., 33 ff.

9 Hansard, op. cit., 47—8.

10 Baring could speak on such an issue with far greater authority than Ricardo. Ralph Hidy points out that 'Under Alexander Baring's leadership the House of Baring attained the zenith of its reputation in Continental high finance . . . His forte was in marketing governmental securities, whether they were those of the United Kingdom, the United States, or other countries.' R. W. Hidy, op. cit., 47—8.

11 Wallace (1768—1844), an Oxford associate of Liverpool and Canning, first entered parliament for Grampound in 1790. He became Vice-president of the Board of Trade in 1818 and is sometimes credited with a major share of the responsibility for initiating the first practical steps towards a more liberal commercial policy for England. In this he may have played a more active role than Frederick Robinson, the President of the Board of Trade. (On this consult W. R. Brock, op. cit., 190—1, and W. D. Jones, op. cit., 65—6.) In the Cabinet reshuffle of 1823 Wallace was passed over in favour of Huskisson as the new President. In the opinion of W. D. Jones (ibid., 97), 'His supersession at this time probably was a mistake, for it gave the office to an individual inexperienced in the tariff manipulations, and one who lacked background knowledge of the Anglo-American trade negotiations.' Wallace resigned from the Board, became Master of the Mint in place of Pole and was gazetted Baron Wallace in 1828.

12 House of Commons, *First Report from the Select Committee appointed to consider of the means of improving and maintaining the foreign trade of the country* (9 March 1821), 9. Among those who appeared before this Committee were Thomas Tooke and Edward Solly (*Minutes of Evidence*, 56—65 and 127—30).

13 Hansard, op. cit., 55—7.

14 Shipowners expected to suffer because of the reduction in cross-Atlantic trade. Further, as S. G. Checkland observes (op. cit., 332—3), discrimination against Baltic timber 'served to protect the shipowners, for those with old and sometimes almost worn-out ships were often saved from the competition of new ones because of the high cost of construction.' An overriding consideration was the high degree of unutilised capacity in the shipping industry at the time.

15 Hansard, op. cit., 57—8.

16 Ibid., 58—63.

17 Ibid., 884.

18 House of Lords, *Second Report (Relative to the silk and wine trade) from the Select Committee of the House of Lords appointed to inquire into the means of extending and securing the foreign trade of the country* (28 June 1821).

19 This assurance was given the above committee by William Hale, a representative of the employers. See *Minutes of Evidence*, 17—22.

20 Hansard, n.s. 4 (1821) 1332. In 1818 Ricardo had given evidence in favour of repeal before a select parliamentary committee. His evidence is reproduced in P. Sraffa, op. cit., V, 337—47.

21 Arthur Onslow (1759—1833) was M.P. for Guildford, 1812—30. He was a Serjeant at Law, which was the premier rank among barristers and enabled him to have exclusive audience in the Court of Common Pleas.

22 Hansard, n.s. 5 (1821) 176—8.

23 Ibid., Gordon (1787—1864) was M.P. for Wareham, 1812—18, Cricklade, 1818—37, and Windsor, 1837—41. He was Financial Secretary of the Treasury, 1839—41.

24 Ibid., 178—9.
25 Given the nature of Ricardo's business dealings as a stock jobber (see P. Sraffa, op. cit., X, 67—74) it seems highly probable that much of his early fortune was derived from usury. The ways in which stock jobbers could evade the usury laws are described in L. S. Pressnell, op. cit., 428—30. See also Ricardo's evidence to the parliamentary committee on the usury laws (cited above) and W. T. C. King, *History of the London Discount Market* (1936; London: Cass, 1972) 14—5.
26 Hansard, op. cit., 179.
27 Ibid., 573—82. Like Serjeant Onslow, Scarlett (1769—1844) was a barrister of some distinction. He entered the Commons for Peterborough in 1819 and remained a member until 1834. In that year he was created Lord Abinger, with the post of Lord Chief Baron of the Exchequer. See P. Scarlett, *Memoir of James, First Lord Abinger* (1877).
28 The Elizabethan Settlement Laws were undoubtedly a serious check on geographical mobility of labour, but they were key factors in the operation of the entire welfare system. As S. G. Checkland observes (op. cit., 335): '... there was no other way of making provision for the poor without abandoning the principle upon which the sytem had rested since Elizabethan times, namely parish taxation.'
29 Hansard, ibid., 582—4. Calcraft (1765—1831) was first elected to the Commons for Wareham in 1786. In 1806 he was appointed a Clerk of the Ordinance and eventually rose to the position of Paymaster-general in the administration of the Duke of Wellington. Initially a whig, he supported the tories from 1822 until 1831 when he voted for Reform. Shortly afterwards he committed suicide.
30 Ibid., 584—6.
31 Ibid., 586—7. Taylor (1757—1834) was an Oxford graduate and a prominent London whig member of the Commons from 1784 to his death. One of his oddities was his concern with legislation to improve the environment and he was responsible for the London Metropolitan Paving Act of 1817. In June 1819 he had moved successfully for a committee to investigate 'how far it may be practicable to compel persons using Steam Engines to erect them in a manner less prejudicial to public health and public comfort' (Hansard, 39 (1819) 976).
32 Ibid. Ricardo's attitude to the poor laws, including certain divergences from Malthus' views concerning them, is well surveyed in J. R. Poynter, op. cit., 239—45.
33 Hansard, n.s. 5 (1821) 987—8.
34 Ibid., 994—6.
35 Ibid., 996—8.
36 Ibid., 1228—30.
37 Ibid., 1478—80 and 1483. J. R. Poynter comments (op. cit., 296): 'The bill was a blunt legislative instrument indeed, and a poorly drafted one to come from so eminent a lawyer. The Government greeted it coldly, as did Sturges Bourne ... [it] divided the abolitionists and aroused the ire of most humanitarians, ...'
38 Hansard, ibid., 1480—2.
39 Two very able critiques of Malthus in the literature of political economy during this year were P. Ravenstone, op. cit., esp. 174—86, and Samuel Read, *General statement of an argument on the subject of population, in answer to Mr. Malthus's theory* (Edinburgh, 1821). See also the anonymous 'On the theories of Godwin and Malthus', *New Monthly Magazine*, I (1821) 195—205. A notable neo-Malthusian propaganda tract which appeared shortly after was,

Francis Place, *Illustrations and Proofs of the Principle of Population* (London, 1822).

CHAPTER 12

1   W. R. Brock writes (op. cit., 150–1): 'In the early nineteenth-century world the Grenvilles retained the ideas and methods of the eighteenth-century connection; they had a certain uniformity of political creed, but this creed was of sufficient flexibility to allow them, in normal times, to work with either political party . . . ' In Brock's opinion, ' . . . by crossing the floor of the House this small group passed an emphatic vote of confidence in the Government, and their crossing signified that the Government's difficulties from the King and from doubtful supporters, were at an end.' On the Grenvilles see also A. Mitchell, op. cit., 19–20.

2   Ricardo complained to James Mill (11 December 1821): 'In the country I find much error prevailing on the subject of the currency, every ill which befalls the country is by some ascribed to Peel's bill, and Peel's bill is as invariably ascribed to me.' P. Sraffa, op. cit., IX, 122. On the same day Ricardo wrote to Trower raising doubts concerning Peel's ability to cope with his new Cabinet post. Trower replied: 'I agree with You in thinking, Peel is too much elevated.' (Ibid., 124 and 146.)

3   Hansard, n.s. 6 (1822) 259.

4   Ibid., 253.

5   Ibid., 350–86. Castlereagh had become Marquis of Londonderry on the death of his father in April 1821.

6   Sir John Clapham (op. cit., 86) comments that this measure was undertaken 'with the treble object of helping the Treasury to help Ireland, where there was partial famine, by distress grants and public works; of assisting the conversion of the "Navy fives", by providing funds to pay off dissident stockholders; and of forwarding reflation by increased issues from the Bank. The Bank had agreed to the loan in March (1822) . . . '

7   Hansard, op. cit., 423–44.

8   On 20 June 1822 the Bank reduced the rate from five to four per cent. For an assessment of the impact of this and other reflationary moves, consult L. S. Pressnell, op. cit., 477–81.

9   Hudson Gurney wrote in his diary this same day (11 February): 'Attwood explained to me what they really mean by borrowing the 4 millions of the Bank. If the agriculturists do not take it – which they think they will not – they will buy stocks – and the Bk. notes coming into the market – will glut the bankers – raise the funds – and move prices generally.' Quoted in F. W. Fetter, op. cit., 78–9.

10   Hansard, op. cit., 491–8.

11   Hansard, op. cit., 681–717.

12   On 25 February Vansittart moved for the conversion of each £100 of the Navy five per cents to £105 of a new four per cent stock. Ricardo spoke in favour of the measure which was ultimately agreed to. Concerning the 'Navy Fives', see L. S. Pressnell, op. cit., 424–7.

13   According to Sir John Clapham (op. cit., 85): 'There is no record at the Bank of a rejected government request to reduce (the rate of interest) early in 1822. But the Governor may have rejected one.'

14   Hansard, op. cit., 270–2.

15   The manner in which Ricardo's reasoning was becoming an increasingly useful tool for the tories and an embarrassment for the whigs is well portrayed in the

comments of J. L. Mallet (20 February 1822) on this speech: 'The Ministers immediately perceived the great advantage they were likely to derive from Ricardo's support, and from his opinions as to the influence of taxation on prices; they cheered him throughout; and Lord Londonderry came up to him after the debate to express his concurrence in his view of the subject. The opposition were annoyed and angry in the same proportion; particularly when they saw that several persons who would have voted with them, they say as many as 30, walked away, partly influenced by Ricardo's opinion, and partly by Brougham's unprincipled attempt to catch the country gentlemen.' Quoted in P. Sraffa, op. cit., V, 127–8.

16   Hansard, op. cit., 479–86. Professor Shoup (op. cit., 246) finds that the portions of this speech dealing with taxation contain some of Ricardo's most able parliamentary pronouncements on the subject. However he continues (p. 247) that these do not add materially to the tax analysis of the *Principles of Political Economy and Taxation*: 'Ricardian tax doctrine was set down, in all its essentials, in October and November of 1816.'

17   Ricardo returned to this theme during a debate on Curwen's motion for higher duties on imports of tallow and abolition of the duties on candles (20 March 1822). At this time Ricardo was also concerned with the inadequacies of official accounting procedures. Together with Joseph Hume he was a member of the Select Committee on Public Accounts (1822) which reformed the manner of presentation of such accounts to parliament.

18   Joseph Hume described it as a 'wild scheme' and contended that agriculture should be left to find 'its natural level.' Hansard, op. cit., 445. Despite these criticisms, Ricardo remained an admirer of Huskisson. Ricardo wrote Trower (5 March 1822): 'Huskisson must have great influence in the situation which he fills, and he cannot fail to direct it usefully and scientifically.' P. Sraffa, op. cit., IX, 176. Since 1814 Huskisson had been a close adviser of Liverpool.

19   This speech seems to have drawn a good response from members. *Hansard* reports 'general cheering', and Ricardo wrote to McCulloch (19 February 1822) that 'the House listened to me with some attention.' P. Sraffa, op. cit., IX, 164.

20   Ibid. 994–5.

21   Austin Mitchell observes (op. cit., 163): 'It was the performance of the whigs which was disappointing. Tierney thought the motion too strong and did not vote, twenty-one whigs were shut out, according to Creevey, and Mackintosh considered that nearly forty others were influenced by Ricardo, who, though he voted for the motion, damned it with faint praise and professions of financial orthodoxy. The total of 108 votes against 212 was a severe disappointment.' Later in the session the whigs were more successful with motions aimed at forcing economies in government expenditure.

22   Hansard, op. cit., 247–59.

23   Ricardo wrote McCulloch (19 February 1822): 'Nothing could be worse than the lectures on Political Economy lately given to the House by Brougham – he is not even perfect in Adam Smith's work, and really appears not to have paid any attention to the works which have been published in our day.' Ricardo wrote to Trower in the same vein. P. Sraffa, op. cit., 164 and 167.

24   Hansard, op. cit., 718–30. By this time Lansdowne had become the effective whig leader in that House, although Earl Grey retained the nominal leadership.

25   Ricardian policy was rejected in the same terms in *The Monthly Review*, XCVIII (August 1822) 376–8. See also John Galt, 'Hints to the Country Gentlemen – Letter II', *Blackwoods*, XII, LXX (November 1822) 624–35. The same issue of the latter (525–30) offered a satire (probably by J. Gibson Lockhart) entitled 'Political Economy: Elements of Save-all- ism'.

26 Hansard, op. cit., 734–5.
27 By contrast the Grenvilles showed their Ricardian colours in this debate when the next speaker, the Duke of Buckingham, (ibid., 735–41) urged the abandonment of the poorer lands now in cultivation and the implementation of poor law reform as solutions to current difficulties.
28 Ibid., 498–506.
29 Ibid., 918–19.
30 Ibid., 472–9. See also the subsequent speech by Western (ibid., 1404–5). 'The operations of the legislature as to the money', said Western, 'had been almost the sole cause of the evil.' He predicted a convulsion of society unless the act of 1819 was reconsidered.
31 Ibid., 993–5. Pearse (1760–1836) was M.P. for Devizes, 1818–32. See also the speeches of Pearse, Manning and others in ibid., 1402–6.
32 Ibid., 995.
33 Ibid., 995–6.
34 Ibid., 996–7.

CHAPTER 13

1 House of Commons, *Report from the Select Committee Appointed to Inquire into the Allegations of the several Petitions Presented to the House in the last and present Sessions of Parliament, complaining of the distressed state of the Agriculture of the United Kingdom* (1 April 1822) 6–7. The report also recommended that foreign grain at present stored in England could be released for conversion into flour for export. In addition imported grain in store when the domestic price rose above 70s. could be released for domestic sale on payment of a futher duty of 5s. Authorship of this report was generally attributed to Henry Bankes (1757–1834), the member for Corfe Castle. Huskisson, who had written much of the 1821 report, did not attend the meetings of the second body. His absence was deliberate, in Ricardo's opinion, since ' . . . he cannot approve, and will not oppose, the plan recommended by the Government.' P. Sraffa, op. cit., IX, 177.
2 Hansard, n.s. 6 (1822) 1445–9.
3 There seems to be an assumption here that while the population of Britain would go on expanding there would not be the same or more rapid expansion in nations which were potential exporters of corn to England, or that in those countries corn production would increase at a greater rate than population.
4 Ibid., 1449–54.
5 Hansard, n.s. 7 (1822) 150–98.
6 The reference here is to Ricardo's *On Protection to Agriculture* (London, 1822). Not all the writers on political economy shared Londonderry's enthusiasm and there were some notable replies, including two pamphlets from Sir John Sinclair (1754–1835), the former M.P. from Scotland who had become President of the Board of Agriculture in 1793. Other critical pamphlets were published by Samuel Turner and Thomas Wentworth Buller. Two periodical articles of interest in this respect appeared in *The British Critic* (XVII, May 1822, 449–68) and *The Monthly Review* (XCVIII, August 1822, 370–85).
7 The right was due to expire in 1825 and it would seem that country banks had already begun to contract their issues in anticipation of the event. Parliament gave its assent to the extension on 16 July and according to Professor Fetter (op. cit., 107) country bank circulation thereafter increased substantially until

the crisis of 1825. As L. S. Presnell (op. cit., 551—2) points out, this extension may have helped magnify the impact of the panic of 1825 by delaying reform of the banking system.

8   On these negotiations and their failure to produce any definite outcome, see J. Clapham, op. cit., 87—8. An able contemporary advocate of the type of change envisaged by the government was Thomas Joplin. He published *An Essay on the General Principles and Present Practice of Banking* (Newcastle, 1822).

9   Hansard, op. cit., 206—10.

10   Ibid., 199—202.

11   On 31 May when Pascoe Grenfell introduced a petition against renewal of the Bank of England charter, Ricardo stated: '... he was satisfied that every farthing made by the Bank ought to belong to the public. Even if a paper currency were wanted, ministers could accomplish the object more advantageously for the public without, than with the assistance of the Bank of England.'

12   In a letter to McCulloch the previous year Ricardo had indicated the difference between his own and Huskisson's position as follows: '... he would uphold agriculture permanently up to its present height — I would reduce it gradually to the level at which it would have been if the trade had been free, for I should call the trade free if wheat was subject to a permanent duty of 8/- p.^{r} q.^{r} to countervail the peculiar taxes to which Land is subject.' P. Sraffa, ibid., 8.

13   The relevant passage is given in P. Sraffa, op. cit., V, 157—8.

14   In 1815 Ricardo had written that '... the interest of the landlord is *always* [my italics] opposed to the interest of every other class in the community.' P. Sraffa, op. cit., IV, 21. However by this time (1822), Ricardo may have begun to perceive that his simplistic conflict thesis was unreal. As A. L. Jones points out (op. cit., 16): 'Many landowners substantially helped their tenants ride out the stormy years after Waterloo by hefty but irregular remissions of rent, and by taking over the burden of farm repairs which they had tended to throw onto the tenantry during the prosperous years of war.'

15   Cf. the remarks of Professor Collison Black (op. cit., 243) on Irish landlords and the economists.

16   Hansard, n.s. 7, 359—60.

17   Ibid, 364.

18   Ibid, 364—5. Since the end of the war farmers had found increasing difficulty in obtaining short-term loans from country banks. See L. S. Pressnell, op. cit., 347—9. This may help explain the desire for government action.

19   Having directly opposed a motion by his leader in the House, Huskisson offered to resign his post as Commissioner of Woods and Forests. The resignation was not accepted.

20   Hansard, ibid., 371—92. Attwood also continued his assault on Ricardian monetary theory and policy and this is taken up in Chapter 14.

21   Attwood was correct here. Modern research on the technology of agriculture in the Napoleonic period highlights the stark unreality of Ricardo's basic model. See, e.g., A. L. Jones, op. cit., 15—16.

22   Commenting on this passage in 1894 Edwin Cannan (op. cit., 260) wrote that it 'puts forward an objection to Ricardo's theory which those who take their history of economic theory exclusively from J. S. Mill imagine to have been discovered by H. C. Carey.' The substance of Attwood's argument had been enunciated during the previous year in P. Ravenstone, op. cit., 417—8. It should be noted here that Ricardo did not completely ignore 'improvements of agriculture'. See, e.g., P. Sraffa, op. cit., VI, 94—5 and 194.

23   Hansard, op. cit., 392—6.

24   Fellow parliamentarians could also be forgiven on this score. For example, ten days later (17 May), Ricardo had recourse to a differing qualities of soil

argument in opposing protection of cultivators in the West Indies (ibid., 691). No mention was made of the point on which the intensive margin argument turned, i.e., different degrees of capitalisation.

25 Edwin Cannan wrote later (op. cit., 260–1) that this answer by Ricardo was 'feeble in the extreme'. Cannan continued: 'These remarks are almost pointless, since Attwood obviously intended to argue not only that there was "in the progress of society" no diminution in the productiveness land (produce per acre), but also that there was no diminution in the productiveness of labour (produce per man).'

26 One contemporary work to deal explicitly with Ricardo's intensive margin argument was Thomas Hopkins, *Economical Enquiries relative to the laws which regulate rent, profit, wages, and the value of money* (London, 1822) 21–3. Notable press criticism of Ricardo's performance in these debates came from David Buchanan in the *Caledonian Mercury* (13 and 25 May, 20 and 22 June and 6 July). Later, Buchanan wrote *Inquiry into the taxation and commercial policy of Great Britain* (Edinburgh, 1844) which is highly critical of Ricardo on value and distribution (see, especially, 322–39). Earlier Buchanan had produced a critical edition of Smith's *Wealth of Nations* in which he anticipates the development of the concept of quasi-rent (see *Observations*, 39–41) and denies the Ricardian view that money wages are governed by the price of food (ibid., 59–60). McCulloch replied to Buchanan's critique of 1822 in the *Scotsman* (8 and 27 June).

27 Hansard, op. cit., 396–402.

28 Ibid., 402–14. Lethbridge (1778–1849) represented Somerset, 1806–12 and 1820–30. Burdett (1770–1844) was a prominent member of the Westminster rump. In the Commons 1796–1844 he represented Westminster for thirty years during that period. See M. W. Patterson, *Sir Francis Burdett and his Times, 1770–1844* (London: Macmillan, 1931).

29 Hansard, ibid., 417–21.

30 Ibid., 424–6. William Elliott-Lockhart (1764–1832) was a Scottish M. P. and landowner. He represented Selkirkshire, 1806–30.

31 The problem of factor mobility and its relative neglect by political economists was noted during this year in Anon, *Observations on the Causes and Cure of the Present Distressed State of Agriculture* (Chester, 1822), especially 63–4. See also *The Monthly Review* XCVII (August 1822), 370 and XCIX (November 1822) 266–7.

32 Hansard, op. cit., 426–30.

33 Ibid., 449–52.

34 Hansard, op. cit., 455–61.

35 William Whitmore published *A Letter on the Present State and Future Prospects of Agriculture* (London, 1822).

36 Henry Vane, Lord Barnard (1788–1864), was later second Duke of Cleveland. William Lamb (1779–1848) became Prime Minister in 1834, as Viscount Melbourne. The latter's biographer notes that about this time Melbourne had been reading the political economists and was a convert to *laissez-faire*. David Cecil, *Melbourne* (1954, London: Pan, 1969) 236.

37 Ricardo's supporters included the bankers William Joseph Denison (1770–1849), John Maberly (1780–1845), William Thompson (1792–1854) and William Haldimand (1784–1862). These last two were directors of the Bank of England, and Thompson became Lord Mayor of London and Chairman of Lloyds. Maberly had a wide range of business interests including contracting for the army and the operation of a linen works in Scotland. Three manufacturers voted with Ricardo: Philips, William Evans (1788–1856) and John Bonham-Carter (1788–1838), a brewer of Portsmouth. Whitmore was a

director of the East India Company, as was George Smith (1765—1836). Other merchants in Ricardo's minority were Joseph Birch (1755—1833), a Liverpool corn dealer, William Wrixon-Becher (1780—1850), and Stewart Marjoribanks (1774—1863), who had interests in the India trade. Charles Rumbold (1788—1857) was a nabob, like Hume.

38   Hansard, op. cit., 533—45. In this he was supported by Edward Ellice (ibid., 553—7).
39   Ibid., 548—52.
40   Ibid., 530—3.
41   Ibid., 547—8. A week later (20 May) Ricardo wrote to Trower: 'I have not one good supporter. There are some who understand the subject but they are on the ministerial bench, and dare not always speak as they think.' P. Sraffa, op. cit., IX, 198.
42   Ibid., 558—60.
43   Ibid., 1556—8. See also his *Sketch of a Petition to the Commons House of Parliament submitted to the consideration of all who feel for the welfare of the country* (Edinburgh, 1822).

CHAPTER 14

1   Hansard, n.s. 7, 877—96. See also Western's *Address to the Landowners of the United Empire* (London, 1822): *Second Address to the Landowners of the United Empire* (London, 1822); and *Supplement to the address to the landowners of the United Empire* (London, 1822).
2   Because he was concerned to stress the stimulus arising from the suspension of cash payments, Western did not indicate why the period had been so advantageous for the application of industry. Hence he failed to bring out the role that increased effective demand may have played in the process he was describing. By contrast that role was highlighted during this year in an outstanding work from John Cazenove, *Considerations on the Accumulation of Capital and its Effects on Exchangeable Value* (London, 1822). Cazenove was a member of the Political Economy Club and according to the excerpts from Mallet's diary reproduced in the *Centenary Volume of the Political Economy Club* (1921) 212, he was a leading critic of the Ricardians in debate at Club gatherings. His treatise is notable for its rejection of Say's Law of Markets and for an attempt to define the conditions for equilibrium growth of the economy by reference to the relationship of the actual rate of profit and a 'natural' rate.
3   Hansard, op. cit., 933—4.
4   Ibid., 934—6.
5   Ibid., 938—54. Edwin Cannan (op. cit., 255) found this 'the most interesting' of Ricardo's speeches on the currency. It was published as a pamphlet later in the year.
6   Here Ricardo appears to have forgotten that it was on this very ground that Joseph Marryat anathemised Ricardian methodology in the House during 1819. Hansard, 39 (1819) 780—7.
7   For a similar criticism in the current literature see Thomas Paget, *A Letter addressed to David Ricardo, Esq. M.P. on the True Principle of Estimating the Extent of the Late Depreciation in the Currency* (London 1822). Ricardo complained to Malthus (16 December 1822) that he had been misinterpreted by Paget. P. Sraffa, op. cit., IX, 249—50.

8 This acknowledgement was in his speech on the Birmingham petition, 8 February 1821. *Hansard*, n.s. 4 (1821) 536.

9 Less than two weeks before (31 May) Ricardo had stated that he now believed government ministers and not the Bank should control the issue of paper currency. Hansard, n.s. 7 (1822) 761.

10 In the third edition of his *Principles* Ricardo added a section 'On an invariable measure of value' to his opening chapter 'On Value'. Here he states: '*To facilitate, then, the object of this enquiry*, although I fully allow that money made of gold is subject to most of the variations of other things, I shall suppose it to be invariable . . . ' [my italics]. See P. Sraffa, op. cit., I, 46.

11 McCulloch obediently took the same line in his article 'Pernicious Effects of Degrading the Standard of Value', *Edinburgh Review*, 35 (July 1822) art. xi.

12 Hansard, op. cit., 965—1009.

13 This is presumably a reference to the decision in 1819 to vote £50,000 in aid of a scheme for emigration to South Africa (see Hansard, 40 (1819) 1549—51). On that occasion Vansittart recommended the measure as a good means of employing 'the surplus population'. Joseph Hume thought the government should go further and have parishes subscribe funds in aid of the work. With this assistance, Hume added 'if men under such circumstances were unwilling to emigrate, it might even be advisable to transport them without their consent.'

14 Sir John Clapham writes (op. cit., 71—2): 'Adopting, perhaps without completely understanding it, what was in effect Ricardian finance, the House (in 1819) approved a motion of Peel's for the repayment of no less than £10,000,000 of short term debt . . . This deflationary policy, if applied, would supplement, almost brutally, the working of those forces — cessation of foreign loans, better harvest, and the rest — which already were tending to rectify the price of gold and the exchange position. Neither price nor position was desperate: causes other than over-issue might have produced both . . . The Bank's public securities fell by millions each half-year: by February 1821 they were at £16,000,000, down by nearly £10,000,000 from the level of eighteen months earlier.' Ricardo did not approve of this (see Ch. 5).

15 For evidence concerning the contraction of country note issues and accompanying bank failures, 1819—22, see L. S. Pressnell, op. cit., 474—7.

16 This was almost certainly a reference to the French loan which was under way at this juncture. On that loan and its impact, see Clapham, ibid., 67—70.

17 Outside parliament, the wage-profit opposition emphasised in Ricardian theory was denied in Edward Rogers, *An Essay on some general principles of Political Economy, on Taxes upon Raw Produce, and on the commutation of tithes* (London, 1822) 19—28; John Wright, *Remarks on the erroneous opinions which led to the new corn law* (London, 1823), 12—3; Anon, 'Mill's Elements of Political Economy', *The British Critic*, XVII (February 1822) 140—2; Anon, 'Ricardo on Protection to Agriculture', op. cit. (May 1822) 462; and Anon, 'Mill's Elements of Political Economy', *The Monthly Review*, XCVII (May 1822) 19.

18 Hansard, op. cit., 1009—17. As Walter Bagehot later observed (op. cit., 261): 'The word which exactly fits his [Peel's] oratory is — specious. He hardly ever said anything which struck you in a moment to be true; he never uttered a sentence which for a moment anybody could deny to be plausible.'

19 There is no doubt that manufacturing had undergone revival after some seven years of depression. By pre-depression standards money wages and profits were low but output and employment had expanded in such centres as Manchester, Leeds, Glasgow, Bolton and Rochdale. Again, at £4.4 million contributions to the poor rates were their lowest for seven years.

20   It is difficult to judge between Peel and Attwood on this issue. Consult, e.g., R. M. Hartwell, 'The Rising Standard of Living in England, 1800–1850', in E. C. Black (ed.), *European Political History, 1800–1850* (Harper & Row, 1967).

21   Hansard, n.s. 7, 954–64.

22   This problem had been recognised by John Wheatley who proposed that long-term contracts should include a clause which permitted the debt owing to be adjusted in terms of changes in an index of commodity prices. The same idea was put forward by Joseph Lowe. See John Wheatley, *An essay on the theory of money and principles of commerce*, 2 vols (London, 1807–22) and Joseph Lowe, *The present state of England in regard to agriculture, trade and finance with a comparison of the prospects of England and France* (London, 1822; 2nd ed. 1823).

23   Hansard, op. cit., 1017–26.

24   McCulloch did not appreciate this speech at all and he wrote to Ricardo (22 June 1822): 'It is not easy to fathom Brougham – I should think he must have gone far to destroy all reliability on his knowledge of the principles of economic science.' P. Sraffa, op. cit., IX, 207.

25   Hansard, op. cit., 1596–606.

26   Ibid., 1606–10. A much longer version of this speech, as written by Ricardo himself, is reproduced in P. Sraffa, op. cit., V, 231–45. Ricardo's analysis of the distress here may be compared with that by the Prime Minister in the Lords six days later (16 July). Liverpool still claimed that the basic problem was the continuing cultivation of the poor quality soils which had been brought into production during the war. Hansard, op. cit., 1663–4.

27   The organisation of agriculture in Ireland was quite different from that of England. In Ireland many small farmers 'employed no labour outside their own families, but those who did usually did not pay their labourers money wages. Instead they gave their labourers a cabin and a plot of ground on which to grow potatoes, and allowed them to work out the rent in labour . . . It provided the farmer with labour without need for working capital, and the labourer with the security of subsistence at least for himself and his family – so long as the potato crop was good.' R. D. Collison Black, op. cit., 7–8.

28   Hansard, op. cit., 1611–33.

29   Attwood took considerable satisfaction in pointing out that in his pamphlet *A second letter to the Right Hon. Robert Peel M.P. for the University of Oxford, on the causes of the increase of pauperism and on the poor laws* (Oxford and London, 1819) Edward Copleston had concluded that pauperism had decreased between 1802 and 1814.

30   Modern scholarship concerning the incidence of poor rates payments and the impact of the poor laws vindicates Attwood's position on these issues. See especially, M. Blaug, 'The Myth of the Old Poor Law and the Making of the New', *Journal of Economic History*, XXIII (June 1963) 151–84, and D. A. Baugh, 'The Cost of Poor Relief in South-East England, 1790–1834', *The Economic History Review*, XXVIII (February 1975) 50–68.

31   In the latter months of 1821 and again early in 1822 there was serious violence in the south and west of Ireland. Civil liberties were revoked. By mid-year starvation and disease were widespread and public subscriptions for relief were raised in England. A popular explanation of the famine, in England, was the failure of the potato crop.

32   In 1815 Malthus published *The grounds of an opinion on the policy of restricting the importation of foreign corn*, and *An inquiry into the nature and progress of rent*.

33   Parliament reacted to the Irish situation during this session on 24 May when it

passed an act for the employment of the poor. This was supplemented (26 July) by an act permitting public funds to be used to create employment in road construction and other public works. Such government intervention was supported even by members who accepted Ricardian theory as generally valid.

34 Ibid., 1633. Two recent discussions which consider the relative roles of parliament and the potato in the problems of Ireland are Nicholas Mansergh, *The Irish Question, 1840—1921* (London: Allen & Unwin, 1968), see esp. 288—97; and Angus MacIntyre, *The Liberator* (London: Hamish Hamilton, 1965) 202—5.

35 Hansard, ibid. Professor Fetter has noted: 'Ireland had suffered a series of bank failures in 1820, and the Bank of Ireland, for reasons that are not clear, had contributed to the monetary stringency by restricting its credits.' F. W. Fetter, *The Irish Pound, 1797—1826* (London: Allen & Unwin, 1955) 58.

36 R. D. Collison Black, op. cit., 243.

CHAPTER 15

1 'The beginning of 1823 saw a campaign of county meetings as large as any hitherto mounted . . . Distress, the main source of pressure for economy and reform, began to lift after the first months of 1823, and even the sharp set-back of 1825—6 hardly revived it as a political force. Apart from a few meetings on the corn laws, assessed taxes, and catholic emancipation, county meetings did not reappear until 1830.' A. Mitchell, op. cit., 180—1.

2 Henry Brougham, his whig opponent, observed: 'This is really a considerable event in point of size. Put all their other men together in one scale and poor Castlereagh in the other, single he plainly weighed them down.' Quoted in C. New, op. cit., 265.

3 Inasmuch as Canning had contributed, the following remarks by Walter Bagehot are applicable: 'The peculiar irritation which Mr. Canning excited through life was at least in part owing to the natural wrath with which you hear the changing talk of the practised talker running away about all the universe; never saying anything which indicates real knowledge, never saying anything which at the very moment can be shown to be a blunder; ever on the surface, and ever ingratiating itself with the superficial.' W. Bagehot, op. cit., 268—9.

4 Concerning Canning, Ricardo had written Trower (11 December 1821): 'Will things be arranged finally without some provision being made for Canning? He is a formidable opponent, but I suppose he cannot under any circumstances fairly come over to our side.' P. Sraffa, op. cit., IX, 124.

5 The fact that Huskisson was passed over for the Chancellorship was attributed by J. L. Mallet to doubts about his youthful political affiliations and to opposition in the City stemming from Huskisson's bullion pamphlet of 1810. See ibid., 270. The same suspicions continued to dog Huskisson for the remainder of his career. See, e.g., the tory *Birmingham Argus* (March 1830) as quoted in A. Briggs, op. cit., 221.

6 On events at the Mint under Wellesley-Pole see Sir John Craig, op. cit., Chapter 16. For discussion of the factors at work in the Cabinet reshuffle consult W. D. Jones, op. cit., 91—7, and W. R. Brock, op. cit., 156—69.

7 McCulloch visited London for six weeks during May and June of 1823 and returned in April 1824 to deliver the Ricardo Memorial lecture series.

8 On Coleridge see W. F. Kennedy, *Humanist Versus Economist: The Economic Thought of Samuel Taylor Coleridge* (Berkeley: University of California Press, 1958) and J. A. Colmer, *Coleridge: Critic of Society* (Oxford: Clarendon, 1959). On Maurice, see K. S. Inglis, *Churches and the Working Classes in*

Victorian England (London: Routledge, 1963) and Stephen Mayor, *The Churches and the Labour Movement* (London: Independent, 1967).

9   Hansard, n.s. 8 (1823) 194—219.

10   W. D. Jones (op. cit., 100) designates this as 'Robinson's hour — probably the finest in his career'. W. R. Brock (op. cit., 173) observes: '. . . Liverpool and Vansittart had already agreed upon the scheme of finance which was to win much praise for Robinson in his first two years as Chancellor.'

11   Hansard, op. cit., 219—21. See also Ricardo's tribute to Thomas Wallace in the House on 12 February.

12   This was somewhat hyperbolic in the light of Ricardo's comments to Trower concerning Robinson just three weeks before (30 January 1823). See P. Sraffa, op. cit., 269.

13   This terse statement, which almost certainly meant little to most of the assembled Commons, is illumined by Ricardo's analysis in his 1820 essay on the funding system (see P. Sraffa, op. cit., IV, especially 177—8). Put briefly, his position was that while government expenditure out of taxation revenue merely went to support 'unproductive labour', redemption of the debt through taxation would lead to either an increase of available capital or redistribution of capital. Some remarks by Professor Shoup (op. cit., 50—1) are particularly helpful on this point. On the principles underlying, and actual operation of, the sinking fund, see A. W. Acworth, *Financial Reconstruction in England, 1815—1822* (London; King, 1925) Chapter 4.

14   Hansard, op. cit., 221—4.

15   Ibid., 229—32.

16   Ibid., 314—9.

17   Under existing legislation Vansittart had been one of the commissioners. These included: the Speaker of the House; the Chancellor of the Exchequer; the Master of the Rolls; the Accountant-General of the Court of Chancery; the Governor and the Deputy Governor of the Bank of England; and the Chief Baron of the Exchequer. In his *Principles* (Chapter 27) Ricardo had put forward the commission system of management of the sinking fund as a model for management of the note issue. See P. Sraffa, op. cit., I, 362—3.

18   Ibid., 319—24. By this time Baring seems to have realised that on this question Ricardo had lost his customary balance. The loss of balance has been noted by C. S. Shoup, op. cit., 254.

19   Hansard, op. cit., 330—5.

20   Ibid., 505—7.

21   For statistics relating to the debt, 1816—23, see A. C. Acworth, op. cit., 137—40. From 1818 to 1823 the payment of debt charges each year accounted for over £30 millions of government expenditure. Total annual expenditure by the government was slightly less than £60 million. The remaining half of this £60 million was mainly devoted to military expenditure so that only £10 million per annum was allocated to 'Civil Government'.

22   Hansard, op. cit., 507—9.

23   Ibid., 535.

24   Ibid., 536—8. Sir Henry Parnell (1776—1842), later the first Baron Congleton, had been a member of the Bullion Committee of 1810. He was an avid supporter of Peel's bill of 1819 and, like Joseph Hume, was predisposed to be obsessive about the need for the utmost economy in government expenditure. He was opposed to the corn laws, and published on this question. His most influential work was *On Financial Reform* (London: 1830, 4th ed. (enlarged) 1832). Parnell was an Irish Landowner and first entered the Commons in 1802 for Queen's County (where his estates were located) and, later in the same year, for Portarlington. In 1831 he became Secretary at War but was dismissed

in 1832. Under Melbourne he was appointed Paymaster-General in 1835. He held this position until he hanged himself in 1842. For the last twenty years of his life he was an active member of the Political Economy Club.

25 Hansard, ibid., 579—80.
26 Ibid., 579—89.
27 Ibid.
28 The debate is not recorded in Hansard, but Ricardo's speech is given in P. Sraffa, op. cit., V, 197—8.
29 See W. Smart, op. cit., 2, 106.
30 For example, on 13 March 1822 a petition was presented to the Commons from the House of Assembly of Lower Canada protesting at the devastating effects of the alteration of timber duties in 1821.
31 Hansard, op. cit., 337—40. It was coincidental, of course, that Whitmore was a director of the East India Company. J. R. McCulloch argued for equalisation in the *Edinburgh Review* (February 1823) Art. X.
32 Hansard, ibid., 264—9.
33 Ibid., 269—73.
34 See also T. Vaux, *Relative taxation; or, observations on the impolicy of taxing malt, hops, beer, soap, candles,and leather . . . with reasons for substituting a tax on property* (London, 1823).
35 Ibid., 273—5.
36 Ibid., 277—80.
37 Ibid., 280—2.
38 Ibid., 282—7.
39 The duty on East Indies sugar was ten to fifteen shillings higher than that imposed on the West Indian product.
40 Hansard, n.s. 9 (1823) 451—6. Charles Rose Ellis (1771—1845), the first Baron Seaford, was in the Commons 1793—1826. The Scottish M.P., William Robert Keith Douglas (1783—1859) represented Dumfries 1812—32. Douglas had been a foundation member of the Political Economy Club in 1821, but he resigned the following year.
41 Ibid., 457—9.
42 This view was challenged during the year by Thomas Malthus in a review of Tooke's pioneering *Thoughts and details of the high and low prices of the thirty years from 1793 to 1822.* Malthus claimed that Tooke's work offered conclusive proof that demand and supply were both relevant determinants in the long as well as the short run. *Quarterly Review*, XXIX (April 1823), especially 218.
43 Hansard, op. cit., 459—61. There was a considerable flurry of pamphlet literature on this issue and Marryat published *A reply to the arguments contained in various publications recommending an equalization of the duties on East and West India sugar* (London, 1823).
44 Hansard, n.s. 8 (1823) 642—6.
45 Ibid., 666—7. On parliament's treatment of the Irish linen industry see R. D. Collison Black, op. cit., 145—7. The Scottish linen industry was not so fortunate. On 9 May Huskisson moved for a committee to consider repeal of statutes which 'impose regulations injurious' to Scottish linen manufacturers (Hansard, 9 (1823) 150—1). The motion was successful and the statutes were repealed, although there is no further record of debate in Hansard. However, in the course of debate on another issue on 22 May, Stuart-Wortley indicated the consternation which the move aroused: 'Many persons in Scotland connected with the linen manufacture were, he understood, dissatisfied with that measure. It was supposed, that an intention existed to throw the monopoly of that trade into the hands of the great capitalists.' (Ibid., 437—8.)

46   Hansard, n.s. 8 (1823) 1131—2.
47   Hansard, n.s. 5 (1821) 1292.
48   Hansard, n.s. 9 (1823) 795—9.
49   Ibid., 800—1.
50   Ibid., 801—2.
51   Ibid., 802.
52   Marryat may have now perceived that it was desirable to set up a common European front against American shipping policy. Huskisson's proposed legislative change permitted the King in Council not only to reduce duties but also to impose them if another nation discriminated against goods carried in British ships. This latter power was exercised against America in 1824 and the two countries continued to retaliate by way of duties until 1830. See W. Smart, ibid., 160. Given this outcome it may not have been entirely coincidental that the measure was finally passed by the Commons on 4 July.
53   Hansard, op. cit., 1434—9. Grant (1778—1866), later the first Baron Glenelg, was M.P. for Inverness Burghs, 1811—18, and Inverness-shire, 1818—35. He eventually succeeded Huskisson as President of the Board of Trade and had been Commissioner of the Treasury, 1813—19, and Chief Secretary for Ireland, 1819—23. Robertson (d. 1856) was a London-based merchant who represented Grampound 1818—26.
54   By this time, the Navigation Acts 'had become so complex that only the expert knew what they contained; and they were out of date because the American colonies were now the United States of America, most of the Spanish colonies were independent countries, the Royal Navy no longer fought with merchant ships, the British mercantile marine was the largest in the world, and the Dutch were no longer serious competitors.' I. Jennings, op. cit., 352. This new legislation paved the way for the later establishment of treaties for reciprocity in trade with a number of European states and eventually with America. The Navigation Laws were not finally repealed until 1849 and even then, various regulations concerning the British coastal trade were retained until 1854.
55   Of men like Huskisson and Robinson, one historian writes (A. Briggs, op. cit., 206) that they 'were clear about the need for official action and exceptionally lucid in their exposition of "abstract topics" in the House of Commons. They were indeed the political personalities who provided a link between the Age of Pitt and the Age of Gladstone ... Placed in power, he [Huskisson] contrived, with the help of new-style civil servants like James Deacon Hume to raise the Board of Trade "to a consequence before unknown" and in better times than the immediate post-war period to frame a comprehensive economic policy.' J. D. Hume was a member of the Political Economy Club, 1834—41.

CHAPTER 16

1   Hansard, n.s. 8 (1823) col. 366.
2   Ibid.
3   Hansard, n.s. 9, 546—7. Edward John Littleton (1791—1863), later the first Baron Hatherton, was M.P. for Staffordshire 1812—32, and for South Staffordshire 1832—5.
4   Ibid., 547—8.
5   Ibid., 548—9.
6   Ibid., 550.
7   Joseph Hume obtained leave to bring in a bill for repeal of the Combination Laws in May 1824 and the measure was slipped quietly through parliament with little awareness of the event either inside or outside the legislature.

8   Hansard, n.s. 8 (1823) 1292.
9   Hansard, n.s. 9 (1823), 598—9.
10   Ibid., 599—600.
11   Ibid., 600.
12   Ibid. The work referred to was 'A Letter to the Luddites', which was first
    published in *Cobbett's Weekly Political Register*, 30 November 1816. It
    proclaimed the beneficial results deriving from the use of machinery.
13   Hansard, op. cit., 601—2.
14   Ricardo had indicated his change of opinion on this issue in 1821 when he
    added a chapter 'On Machinery' (Chapter 31) to the third edition of his
    Principles.
15   In this same year Byron expressed his perception of this doctrine, as follows:

> But Rapp is the reverse of zealous matrons,
>   Who favour *malgré* Malthus, generation —
> Professors of that genial art, and patrons
>   Of all the modest part of propagation;
> Which after all at such a desperate rate runs,
>   That half its produce tends to emigration,
> That sad result of passions and potatoes —
>   Two weeds which pose our economic Catos.
>
> Had Adeline read Malthus? I can't tell;
>   I wish she had: his book's the eleventh commandment,
> Which says, 'Thou shalt not marry,' unless *well*:
>   This he (as far as I can understand) meant.
> 'Tis not my purpose on his views to dwell,
>   Nor canvass what 'so eminent a hand' meant;
> But certes it conducts to lives ascetic,
>   Or turning marriage into arithmetic.

> *Don Juan*, Canto XV, 37 and 38 (1823)

16   Hansard, ibid.
17   The role of effective demand was stressed also by William Blake in his
    *Observations on the Effects produced by the Expenditure of Government
    during the Restriction of Cash Payments* (London, 1823), see especially
    54—76. Ricardo read and discussed this pamphlet with its author before its
    publication. The two agreed to differ. See P. Sraffa, op. cit., IX, 275—6.
18   Hansard, n.s. 8 (1823) 551—2.
19   Ibid., 663.
20   Ibid., 663—4.
21   Ibid., 664—5.
22   Ibid., 665—6.
23   Ibid., 1126.
24   Ibid.
25   It is possible that Ricardo was prepared to press this matter so far because of
    the connection between a strong merchant marine and preparedness for war.
    Another of his ventures into the politically unpopular and intellectually
    dubious — abolition of the national debt and the sinking fund — was certainly
    motivated to a large degree by his desire to curb the government's potential for
    belligerence.
26   This move may have been motivated by the belief that, with improvement in
    their position with regard to the importation of raw silk from India, the
    manufacturers could be better able to challenge the French product. To achieve

this they needed to be free of the restrictions of the Act. The petitioners complained that because the magistrates had set the same rate for machine-made and hand-made products, the introduction of machinery was being obstructed. As a result, production costs were unnecessarily inflated and business was being transferred elsewhere. One week before the presentation of the petition (2 May), Liverpool's 'economic cabinet' had been called to meet at the Board of Trade at Huskisson's request to consider three policy measures, one of which was repeal of the Spitalfields Act. W. R. Brock, op. cit., 192–3. The Cabinet as a whole was divided on this issue. Concerning the petition and subsequent events, see J. L. Hammond and B. Hammond, *The Skilled Labourer, 1760–1832* (London, 1919) 216 ff.

27   Hansard, n.s. 9, 149. In a speech on 21 June 1822, Ricardo had touched briefly on the desirability of repeal of this Act.

28   Ibid., 150.

29   Ibid., 217–18.

30   Ibid., 377–8.

31   Ibid., 378.

32   Ibid., 378–9. Thomas Fowell Buxton (1786–1845) had been active in social work in the Spitalfields area for some years. An outstanding graduate of Trinity College Dublin, in 1808, he chose a commercial career with the Spitalfields brewery firm of Truman, Hanbury & Co. At the same time he began the study of political economy but became increasingly involved in practical reform through such organisations as the Bible Society, the Society for the Reformation of Prison Discipline and the Anti-Slavery Society. He represented Weymouth from 1818 to 1837 and was knighted in 1840. Buxton was an intimate of the Gurneys of Norwich and the reformer Elizabeth Fry (neé Gurney) was his sister-in-law. See Charles Buxton (ed.), *Memoirs of Sir Thomas Fowell Buxton Bart.* (1872), and R. H. Mottram, *Buxton the Liberator* (London: Hutchinson, n.d.).

33   Hansard, op. cit., 380–1.

34   Ibid., 382–4.

35   Ibid., 384. Buxton's informant was possibly William Hale who had given evidence to the Lords committee on foreign trade in 1821 (see Chapter 11). Hale published *An appeal to the public, in defence of the Spitalfields Act ...* (London, 1822). See also Anon, *Remarks upon Mr. Hale's Appeal to the public, in defence of the Spitalfields Act* (London, 1822); Anon, *Observations on the ruinous tendency of the Spitalfields Act ... To which is added a Reply to Mr. Hale's Appeal to the public in defence of the Act* (London, 1822); and 'Verax' (pseud.), *Review of the statements in Mr. Hale's Appeal to the public on the Spitalfields Act* (London, 1822).

36   Hansard, ibid., 382.

37   Ibid., 379–80.

38   Ibid., 810–13.

39   Ibid., 813–14.

40   Ibid., 816.

41   By 1823 Ricardo had become so self-confident and overtly intransigent in the House it is little wonder that opponents might have felt obliged to seek 'a substitute for an argument'. Here, for example, he plainly implies that he would deny members an enquiry because his own convictions are unshakeable.

42   Ibid., 814.

43   Ibid., 815–16. Bright (1784–1869) was a Cambridge graduate and West Indies merchant who represented Bristol, 1820–30.

44   Ibid., 817–18.

45   Ibid., 831.

46   Ibid., 831–2.
47   Ibid., 832–3. The committee was appointed the following year.
48   Ibid., 985–6.
49   Ibid., 986–8. Edward Law, Earl of Ellenborough (1790–1871) had entered the Commons in 1813 and the Lords in 1818. After 1828 he occupied a number of significant positions including that of Lord Privy Seal, President of the Board of Control for the Affairs of India, Governor-General of India and First Lord of the Admiralty. His first wife was Castlereagh's sister and Ellenborough was a declared opponent of Canning. In particular he disliked Canning's protégé Huskisson, which helps account for his attitude on the Spitalfields issue. His uncle, George Henry Law (1761–1845), the Bishop of Chester, was active in promoting the factory legislation of 1819 (see Chapter 2).
50   Ibid., 1529–30.
51   Ibid., 1530–2. Dudley Ryder, Earl of Harrowby and Viscount Sandon (1762–1847), was President of the Council in Liverpool's administration. He spoke with considerable authority on economic issues, having occupied, among other important posts, the vice-presidency of the Board of Trade from 1791 to 1801. In 1819 he had been the chairman of the Lords committee on the resumption of cash payments.
52   This same effect had been noted by the Marquis of Lansdowne and by William Rae in 1819 (see Chapter 6).
53   Ibid., 1532.
54   Ibid., 1532–3.
55   Ibid., 1533–4.
56   Ibid., 1540–1.
57   For a later, general statement of Huskisson's economic views see his *Essays On Political Economy* (1830; reprinted with introduction by G. S. L. Tucker, Canberra, 1976).
58   Ibid., 1542–3. Ricardo wrote Trower (24 July): 'Huskisson behaved very well after I left London in refusing to have anything to do with the Lords' amended bill respecting the magistrates' interference with wages in Spitalfields – the bill was quite spoiled, there was nothing left in it worth retaining.' P. Sraffa, op. cit., IX, 318.

CHAPTER 17

1   There seems little doubt that the government's policy had intensified a trend which, in earlier years, the enclosure acts had done so much to promote, namely, the demise of the small landowner. See Arthur Johnson, *The Disappearance of the Small Landowner* (1909: Oxford University Press, 1963) 122. Government (and Ricardian) policy also favoured those agriculturalists who had access to capital without the need to mortgage estates. See A. L. Jones, op. cit., 14. Professor Jones' analysis brings out the point that the 'rural interest' (like the 'commercial interest') was a far from homogeneous group politically or socially. On enclosures and accompanying trends, see P. Deane and W. A. Cole, *British Economic Growth, 1688–1959* (Cambridge, 1967).
2   Wodehouse (1784–1855), an Oxford graduate, was the Tory M.P. for Norfolk, 1817–30, and East Norfolk, 1835–55.
3   Hansard, n.s. 8, cols 12–22.
4   Ibid., 117–18.
5   Ibid., 120–1.
6   Ibid., 121–3.
7   Ibid., 255–8.
8   Ricardo's reasoning was based explicitly on the calculations of Robert Mushet

who had published *A Series of Tables, exhibiting the Gain and Loss to the Fundholder, arising from the Fluctuations in the Value of the Currency, from 1800 to 1821* (2nd ed., London, 1821). Since 1811 Mushet had held the melting house contract and was second clerk to the Master at the Mint. He was a foundation member of the Political Economy Club.

9   The pamphlet referred to is Samuel Turner, *Considerations upon the Agriculture, Commerce, and Manufactures of the British Empire* (London, 1822). The above argument had been put forward by Mathias Attwood in the debates on Western's motions on the currency in 1822 and by this he had sought to show that government policy was reponsible for distress. It should be noted also that in 1819 Ricardo had been opposed to repayment of the Bank's advances to the government (see Chapter 5).

10   Hansard, op. cit., 259.

11   Thornton's speech is reported in Hansard, 19 (1811) 895 ff.

12   Hansard, n.s. 8 (1823) 263–4.

13   Ibid., 260–2.

14   Ibid., 262–3.

15   Ibid., 258–9.

16   Ibid., 264. This same figure, ten per cent, had been the estimate given in evidence to the 1821 committee on agricultural distress by Thomas Tooke. See *Minutes of Evidence* 295–6.

17   Hansard, ibid.

18   Hansard, n.s. 9 (1823), 833–49. In March of this year Western had published a reply to criticisms of his position during the previous session. See *Observations on the speech of the Right Hon. W. Huskisson, in the House of Commons, Tuesday 11th June, 1822, on Mr. Western's motion concerning the resumption of cash payments* (London, 1823).

19   This passage may be found in the Sraffa edition of Ricardo's works in IV, 227–8.

20   Hansard, op. cit., 902–13.

21   See Henry James, *Essays on money, exchanges, and political economy*, 2 vols (London, 1820). The quality of James' work has been underlined by Professor Fetter, op. cit., 75.

22   Hansard, op. cit., 922–34.

23   Ibid., 939–45.

24   It would seem that Huskisson had come round to see merit in Baring's viewpoint on the currency. In January of this year Ricardo had written Trower: 'There has been a talk, I believe nothing more, amongst ministers about restoring the two standards, but I am assured all thoughts of it are relinquished. – Lord Liverpool is very decidedly against it. I am sorry to hear that Huskisson is not much disinclined to it ... Lord Lansdowne I have been informed is inclined to the two standards – Baring, I suspect is the ringleader in this conspiracy.' P. Sraffa, op. cit., IX, 270. At the meeting of the Political Economy Club in February, Robert Mushet proposed discussion of the question of the introduction of a bimetallic system.

25   Hansard, op. cit., 849–59. A letter to James Mill (P. Sraffa, ibid., 265) indicates that Ricardo had been preparing for this confrontation for some time. He had gone back over Western's speeches and had made notes on Western's *Second Address to the Landowners of the United Empire*. These notes are reproduced in P. Sraffa, op. cit., V, 522–8.

26   By this time Ricardo was quite convinced that the Bank should be deprived of the power of issuing paper money. Accordingly when the session was over he wrote his last pamphlet, *Plan for the establishment of a National Bank*. Under this plan control of the note issue would be vested in Commissioners

responsible to parliament. The wider significance of this change of stance was to be perceived by one of Ricardo's radical associates, J. C. Hobhouse. Thus, in justifying governmental intervention in 1826, he stated (Hansard, n.s. 14, col 885): 'Advocate as he (Ricardo) was for free trade, he deemed it necessary for the government to interfere with the dealings of the traders in paper-money, and to secure for the community a guarantee against loss.' Cf. R. E. Zegger, *John Cam Hobhouse, a Political Life, 1819—1852* (Columbia: University of Missouri Press, 1973) 91—2. R. S. Sayers has traced the germ of this idea of Ricardo's to correspondence with J. B. Say in 1814. See A. W. Coats (ed.), op. cit., 50—2.

27   Hansard, op. cit., 896—901.

28   Ibid., 945—61. Earlier this same year, Attwood had published anonymously the pamphlet, *A Letter to Lord Archibald Hamilton, on the alterations in the Value of Money; and containing an Examination of Some Opinions recently published on that Subject* (London, 1823).

29   Attwood refrained from quoting or was not aware of a recent publication of Malthus' which gave scant comfort to the proponents of equitable adjustment of contracts. In his *The Measure of Value Stated and Illustrated* (London, 1823), Malthus wrote (80—1): 'But whatever may have been the pressure on the owners of land since the peace, they cannot have the slightest pleas for an attempt to indemnify themselves at the expense of the public creditor. In the turns of the wheel of fortune all parties should have fair play, no class of persons can be justified in endeavouring to lift themselves by using unfair and dishonourable methods to pull others down.' A passage like this should give cause to pause to historians who portray Malthus as an inveterate supporter of 'the landed interest'. To label Malthus in this fashion is as an unhelpful a practice as the labelling of Ricardo as the spokesman of a so-called 'middle class'.

30   Hansard, op. cit., 934—9.

31   This speech is not mentioned in either Hansard or Sraffa's edition of Ricardo's works. However it is outlined in R. D. Collison Black, op. cit., 207.

32   *Report from Select Committee on Employment of the Poor in Ireland* (1823). There was no time to debate this report in 1823 and it appears to have been ignored in the next session.

33   Ricardo was far from happy with this solution. He was prepared to admit, however, that the behaviour of the Irish quite defeated him. See P. Sraffa, op. cit., IX, 313—14.

34   Ibid., 316—18.

35   In his thinking on this matter Ricardo was influenced considerably by the contrasting behaviour of ministers and commissioners in the administration of the Sinking Fund (see Chapter 15).

36   Quoted in D. P. O'Brien, *J. R. McCulloch: A Study in Classical Economics* (London: Allen & Unwin, 1970) 48. Hudson Gurney and William Huskisson were two who, according to Mill, exemplified the prevailing attitude.

37   On some aspects of later developments, see F. W. Fetter, 'The Influence of Economists in Parliament on British Legislation from Ricardo to John Stuart Mill', *Journal of Political Economy*, 83, 5 (1975) 1051—64.

Index of Persons

Page numbers in italics indicate locations of biographical information concerning individual members of parliament. 'M.P.' designates membership of the House of Commons during the period 1819 – 23.

Subject Index

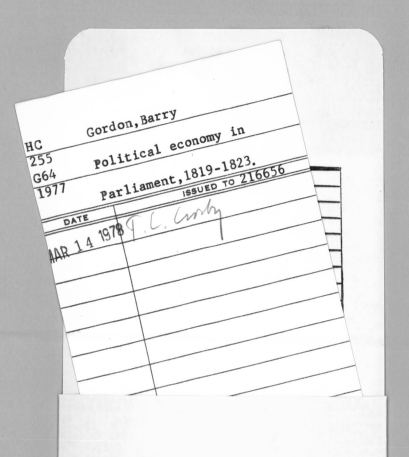